W9-BRT-232

$$\frac{34=}{407/204}$$
D

Ritual Criticism

Studies in Comparative Religion
Frederick M. Denny, Editor

The Holy Book in Comparative Perspective
Edited by Frederick M. Denny and Rodney L. Taylor

Dr. Strangegod: On the Symbolic Meaning of Nuclear Weapons
By Ira Chernus

Native American Religious Action: A Performance Approach to Religion
By Sam Gill

The Confucian Way of Contemplation: Okada Takehiko and the Tradition of Quiet-Sitting
By Rodney L. Taylor

Human Rights and the Conflict of Cultures: Western and Islamic Perspectives on Religious Liberty
By David Little, John Kelsay, and Abdulaziz A. Sachedina

The Munshidin of Egypt: Their World and Their Song
By Earle H. Waugh

The Buddhist Revival in Sri Lanka: Religious Tradition, Reinterpretation and Response
By George D. Bond

A History of the Jews of Arabia: From Ancient Times to Their Eclipse Under Islam
By Gordon Darnell Newby

Arjuna in the Mahabharata: Where Krishna Is, There Is Victory
By Ruth Cecily Katz

Ritual Criticism

Case Studies in Its Practice, Essays on Its Theory

Ronald L. Grimes

University of South Carolina Press

Copyright © University of South Carolina 1990

Published in Columbia, South Carolina, by the
University of South Carolina Press

First Edition

Manufactured in the United States of America

Library of Congress Cataloging-in-Publication Data

Grimes, Ronald L., 1943–
    Ritual criticism : case studies in its practice, essays on its
theory / Ronald L. Grimes. — 1st ed.
        p.   cm. — (Studies in comparative religion)
    Includes bibliographical references.
    ISBN 0-87249-692-9
    1. Rites and ceremonies.   2. Rites and ceremonies—Study and
teaching.   3. Rites and ceremonies—North America—Case studies.
4. North America—Religious life and customs.   I. Title.
II. Series: Studies in comparative religion (Columbia, S.C.)
BL600.G76   1990
291.3'8—dc20   90-30970
                                                                                CIP

Let us never cease from thinking—what is this "civilization" in which we find ourselves? What are these ceremonies and why should we take part in them?

—Virginia Woolf
(1936:62–63)

The dancer has his ear in his toes.

—Friedrich Nietzsche
(1956:224)

They ain't quit doing it as long as I'm doing it.

—Haze Motes
in Flannery O'Connor
(1962:122)

CONTENTS

viii   Contents

ILLUSTRATIONS

EDITOR'S PREFACE

Although ritual processes are not limited to religious systems, they mostly pertain to religion, at least in some sense. Studies of ritual have focused on a standard range of types, such as rites of passage, seasonal observances, communal worship, sacrifice, the placating of spirits before the hunt, avoiding pollution, naming; and on familiar contexts, like sanctuaries, sacred itineraries, holy geographies, urban ceremonial centers, and pilgrimage. But there have also been fascinating studies of the rituals of social relations, such as the interaction ritual of Erving Goffman; of performance and play, as in the work of Victor Turner and Richard Schechner; and ritualization in animals as well as humans, as treated in ethological studies.

Ronald L. Grimes has been in the forefront of ritual studies in North America for some years now. His interests in ritual have extended from religious to secular types and contexts. He has both published important new research and led in the formation of constructive and critical discourse on ritual. All the while, he has been empirically grounded and not theoretically detached, so that whenever he generalizes we can be fairly certain that he does so with a strong sense of specific cases.

Ritual Criticism: Case Studies in Its Practice, Essays on Its Theory is the first study of its kind, so far as I am aware. It is an ambitious and even risky undertaking that raises more questions than it answers. But that is desirable in pioneering ventures that have yet to enjoy and be strengthened by public debate and testing. Any meaningful and persistent cultural activity—for example art, music, literature—requires criticism as a complementary mode of discourse. Ritual is no exception, although conscious criticism of it may strike some, scholars no less than custodians of cultural and spiritual values, as inappropriate, perhaps irreverent, and even wrongheaded. But, as Grimes states in his Introduction, "ritual and criticism require one another. . . . The difficulty is how to make visible what is often invisible: the critical dimensions of ritual. To accomplish such an aim successfully is to deny the persistent tendency in our society to isolate the inspired body from the inquiring mind, as if these were not only separable but enemies."

In *Ritual Criticism*, Grimes shows us a wide variety of rites and suggests ways by which participant observation can help us assess them. There is no grand theorizing involved, nor an attempt to define a universal model for ritual criticism. This exploration is, rather, a series of related case studies and essays in how such different but humanly related cultural and social activities as religious liturgies, theatrical productions, field excavations and museum displays, workshop/classroom experiments, and North American hospital ritual can be better understood and more satisfactorily related to the complexities of our pluralistic culture. All of this is fresh and appealing, but Grimes goes further by also looking at the phenomenon of "infelicitous" performances, ritual "failures," and thus moves beyond the safe terrain of descriptive/analytical to evaluative discourse, grounded, as his subject is, in real life.

Frederick Mathewson Denny
General Editor

ACKNOWLEDGMENTS

This book was written with the financial support of a grant from the National Endowment for the Humanities through the School of American Research in Santa Fe, New Mexico, which provided the rich geography and congenial scholarly atmosphere necessary for its completion. The Wilfrid Laurier University Research Office also provided funds for some of the fieldwork that forms the basis of the case studies.

I am especially indebted to Tom Driver and Ruel Tyson, who bored deeply into the entire manuscript, took me to task, encouraged me, and posed many telling questions.

My thanks go to the research staff and scholars in residence at the School of American Research during 1988–89. They were provocative and exceedingly tolerant of my struggles to turn the shifting sands of a manuscript into the solidity of a book.

Others who read parts of it or responded to oral presentations and provided much needed critique and support include Kathleen Ashley, Fred Clothey, Jenny DeBouzek, Madeline Duntley, James Lopresti, Tom Peterson, Susan Scott, Donna Seamone, Mark Searle, and Tom Sinclair-Faulkner, along with members of the Ritual Studies Group of the American Academy of Religion and faculty in the departments of Religion and Culture, Philosophy, and Anthropology of Wilfrid Laurier University.

Ritual Criticism

INTRODUCTION

Whoever first exclaimed that religion is not thought but danced echoed a scholarly as well as a popular attitude. In this view religion and thinking are incommensurate. Such a stereotype implies that dancing—symbolic of all embodied, ritualized aspects of religion—is what people do when they turn off their brains and that thinking is what they do when they turn off their bodies. But religions are little nourished by disembodied reflection, and it is a mistake to assume that dancing one's religion precludes thinking about it.

Because of this pervasive split between dancing and thinking, the notion of ritual criticism may seem to be what philosophers call a "category mistake," a self-contradiction compounded of two mutually canceling ideas. Upon hearing the phrase "ritual criticism," a common response is for the person to look baffled and utter a puzzled "What?" Ritual and criticism do not initially strike us as bedfellows. They seem like some mismatched couple doomed for divorce because they did not belong together in the first place. Where ritual transpires, one does not ordinarily expect to find criticism, and where criticism occurs, one does not usually look for ritual. A typical strategy that reinforces this dualism is to consign the one to sacred precincts and condemn the other to the academy.

The aim of this book is to demonstrate the complementarity of ritual and criticism. We shall explore case studies in which ritual and criticism require one another. Then we shall reflect on ways this mutuality alters conceptions of both ritual and criticism. The difficulty is how to make visible what is often invisible: the critical dimensions of ritual. To accomplish such an aim successfully is to deny the persistent tendency in our society to isolate the inspired body from the inquiring mind, as if these were not only separable but enemies.

There are several reasons one might find it worthwhile to engage in ritual criticism: to enable the revision and construction of more effective rites; to negotiate among conflicting alternatives in a highly pluralistic culture; to protect oneself from exploitation by ritual means; to ground aesthetic, moral, and religious judgments in the tangible stuff of ceremony

1

and celebration. Anyone who has struggled to plan an effective wedding or birthday party, been unable to decide between private devotion or public worship, or been lured into (or kept away from) public demonstrations against his or her own better judgment has reason to be interested in the problem of assessing rites.

This volume is centered on several cases studies from urban, North American social contexts. Out of these the idea and practice of ritual criticism was born. What is presented here is not a model, much less *the* model for doing ritual criticism. The case studies and essays are not the outcome of a single, unified method. Rather, they are explorations, tacks taken toward different kinds of ritually significant activity. The goal is not to formulate a universal set of criteria by which one can judge other people's rites, nor is it to propose a theory or apply a method. Rather, it is to explore styles of participant observation that can inform assessments of rites.

The rites studied are as varied as the strategies utilized. This diversity is deliberate; its purpose is to illustrate the ways criticism shifts as types of ritual vary. One rite is a traditional liturgy; another is invented rather than traditional; a third is a hybrid genre, ritual drama; and in a fourth instance the ritualization is so tacit that some might deny it is ritual at all. Such a diversity among the events studied takes us into territory traditionally the purview of other disciplines beyond my own, religious studies. The domains of drama, literature, education, psychology, medicine, archaeology, anthropology, philosophy, and theology are traversed in this effort to understand ritual, an unusually "impure" genre of human activity. Ritual implicates, but does not belong to, these and other disciplines.

The case studies that form the heart of the book are unlike those of long-term anthropological fieldwork in several respects. Most are based on short-term events rather than enduring social structures. My role in them typically lasted for days, weeks, or months rather than years. And my task was assessment and interpretation rather than objective description or dispassionate explanation. Some of the cases involved controversies in which I functioned as consultant or mediator; one involved me as initiator and supervisor. In all of the case studies I was either a participant, an observer, or both.

Insofar as the case studies required observation, participation, and documentation, they resemble anthropological field study. But insofar as they called for overt judgments and involve discussions about the adequacy, authenticity, and effectiveness of enactments and performances, they resemble liturgiological and aesthetic criticism. In several instances one of the conditions of my observation was that I be willing to participate as well as respond. Seldom was I given the luxury of detachment, scientific or otherwise.

Ritual criticism is neither ethnography nor literary criticism; it is not an established practice. In none of the instances of field consultation did anyone either use the term "ritual criticism," specify a single, clear aim, or define the process. My role had to be invented in the act of performing it. But it is probably not entirely new: from time immemorial ritual specialists have likely asked participants and others what they thought about the rites they participated in or observed.

In these studies and essays my identities are obviously multiple: scholar, critic, fieldworker, teacher, maker of rites. This plurality of interests creates considerable torque in the presentation, but I hope I have resisted the temptation to eliminate or unfairly subordinate any one of these roles, because I consider them equally valuable.

In North American contexts one is sometimes invited under the rubric of "critic" or "respondent" when the unspoken expectation is that one function as publicity agent or chronicler. Since I had not sought many of the occasions studied here, I was not initially very self-conscious about defining what I was doing or about resisting hidden agendas. Neither were hosts; often they were motivated by curiosity: What would "a ritual studies person" observe and say? The actual process was sometimes unnerving to them. Even educated, literate audiences become self-conscious when someone actively observes them, especially when it becomes known that the whole event, not just the officially designated enactments, is being watched and interpreted. Ritual criticism involves documenting and assessing those who perform. For this reason it evokes considerable self-consciousness.

The case studies move in the direction of a theory, but they do not culminate in a formal one. The relation between cases and theory is complex. Typically, cases provide the particulars from which the generalizations that constitute theory are derived. In the sciences the logic that warrants movement from case to theory is inductive. Most of the movements made in these cases are inductive; a few are not.

In my view the case/theory relation, as well the inductive/deductive connection, is radically dialectical. By this I mean that, not only is the case the mother of theory, but the theory is the mother of the case.[1] One is not first, the other second. The relation is circular and simultaneous. If I were to chronicle my case studies, "facts" would sometimes precede, sometimes follow, theories.

This collection of cases does not culminate in a theory, if by "theory" one means a generalized, unified statement, subject to verification, about the causes, covariances, or other consistent relations that obtain between two items or processes observed. Rather, the cases eventuate in essays, "attempts" (to call upon the etymology of the word) to reflect at an order of generalization higher than that of the particular case. The resulting generalizations are not inferences, effects, inductions, or formal theories; they are positions. I conclude having taken a stance rather than proved a hypothesis. Like most essays, these have an ethical and autobiographical quality not characteristic of proofs and scientific arguments.

Certainly the cases inform the essays, though, for the most part, indirectly. Many of the contexts that provide the data for the chapters of *Ritual Criticism* are typified by syncretism, the eclectic mixing and matching of ritual elements from diverse traditions. And many involve attempts to engage in ritual invention and experimentation. The largely contemporary, North American, experimental ethos of some of the cases shapes the generalizations that are derived from them. Such is the nature of all case studies: the question of their applicability to other historical periods and geographical areas must be left to other scholars and subsequent discussions.

The first chapter orients readers to some of the basics of ritual studies. It illustrates briefly what ritual criticism is, formally defines both ritual and criticism, and then locates ritual criticism in its practical and cultural contexts.

The next four chapters are case studies spanning a very diverse group of consultations on the pragmatics of ritual enactment. The situations include liturgical revisions in a major religious denomination; field excavations, the display of sacred artifacts, and the use of ritualized performances in a museum; celebration in a cycle of medieval plays in a modern urban university; inventing and borrowing rites in experimental workshops and classrooms.

Chapter 6 is a transition chapter. Though it utilizes data from working in hospitals and observing both medical personnel and patients, it is really a prescriptive and evaluative essay on illness as a ritualized process rooted in human embodiment.

The remaining chapters are essays on theoretical matters rather than case studies based directly on fieldwork. Their aim is the criticism of theory rather than the criticism of practice. They illustrate the reciprocal interaction between formal theory and the practical work of constructing and interpreting rites.

Chapter 7 criticizes the overextension of language-based theories and metaphors (for example, cultures as "texts," lives as "stories," and rites as "communication") by utilizing performance-based theories and metaphors.

Chapter 8 puts Victor Turner's theory of social drama in conversation with a dramatic text, T. S. Eliot's *Murder in the Cathedral*.

Chapter 9 employs J. L. Austin's theory of performative utterances to develop a vocabulary for conceptualizing the varieties of ritual failure.

The last chapter sets ritual criticism in its academic context and then criticizes an example of ritual criticism.

1

THE PRACTICAL AND CULTURAL

CONTEXTS OF RITUAL CRITICISM*

If the practice precedes the theory of it and if the explication of methods presupposes a history of application, then field work should precede theories of culture, including the relation between religious action and other cultural forms; and practical criticism should precede theoretical criticism.

—Ruel Tyson (1975:12)

In August 1982 performers from all over the world gathered in Peterborough, Ontario, for the second Indigenous People's Theatre Celebration. The gathering was extremely diverse. Among the participants were a traditional dance-drama group from the New Mexico Pueblos, a Danish Inuit professional theater company, an Australian aboriginal theater group, and two folk drama groups from India.

In addition to performances, workshops, and discussions there were formal critique sessions. Criticism took place on two levels: formally between performers and critics, and informally among performers themselves. The designated critics were two non-Native professors. Their roles were as predictable and perhaps just as stylized as those of the actors. They played typical professorial roles—judge, critic, devil's advocate. As one might expect, between Native performers and non-Native critics there were conflicting cultural presuppositions, and thus conflicting critical assumptions.

A source of considerable controversy was that formal critiques were offered by two non-Native professors. Ross Kidd (1984:109,119), who reported the event for the *Canadian Journal of Native Studies*, noted that the professors were hard on Native performers who depended on mainstream, Western theater techniques; they criticized those who took their examples from White directors. They preferred instead the more tradition-

---

*Part of this chapter is based on a paper called "On Ritual Criticism," presented in 1986 to the Ritual Studies Group of the American Academy of Religion.

al, "authentic" techniques. Native performers took considerable issue with this criterion. They argued that such a preference implied an erroneous assumption that indigenous cultures are static. They resented this attempt to restrict them to traditional forms.

Among performers criticism was not explicitly formalized into a specific role but was implicit in the act of trading ideas and techniques. Nevertheless, divergence was also evident among performers; they used varying criteria for making judgments. A source of controversy during the festival was a split between performers who saw their work as cultural and those who saw it as political. "Culturalists" emphasized form and technique, while "the engaged" emphasized social content and political relevance. Several definitions of the situation emerged. Some viewed it as ritual or communal celebration; some thought of it as informal education. Some held that it was a way of preserving culture; others, a way of transforming it. Each genre of performance implied a different basis for criticism.

The Indigenous Peoples' Theatre Celebration is an example of an event—partly theatrical, partly ritualistic, partly educational, partly political—that overtly included criticism. Ongoing, overt, formal criticism is a normal part of Western artistic and academic culture, but in traditionally religious cultures it seldom takes this form. So criticism can create trouble when the circumstances change and the situations become more sharply cross-cultural.

This brief example condenses the main topic that concerns us here: criticism in the ambience of changing and borderline ritual contexts. It is an easier example than some of those that follow, because in it assessment at first seems to take a familiar shape, that of Western theater criticism. But as the example unfolds, the theatrical model begins to seem inappropriate, because neither the actors nor the critics share a common definition of the situation. There is no consensus regarding the genre of the action in which they are engaged.

When response is modeled after mainline Western theater, critics and performers constitute two different groups. Critics exist either to help inform the spectating, ticket-buying public (not the case in this example) or they try to help improve the skills of actors. In this instance the critics not only played a fixed role but were of another ethnic group and socioeconomic class, thus conflict was virtually assured. The fact that some of the performances were understood by participants to be ritual rather than theater deepened the difficulty of exercising judgments, because ritual traditions are considered by many to be exempt from criticism, particularly if it is of the overt and formalized variety.

DEFINITIONS OF RITUAL

This brief illustration forces us to raise larger, more general issues such as the definition of ritual and the nature of criticism. Ritual studies is a relatively new discipline in the field of religious studies. The scope of ritology[2] reaches from ritualization among animals through ordinary interaction ritual to highly differentiated religious liturgy. It includes all types of ritual: celebrations, political ceremonies, funerals, weddings, initiations, and so on. Although ritual studies may include textual analysis, it pays primary attention to performance, enactment, and other forms of overt gestural activity. Thus its nearest academic kin are symbolic anthropology, liturgiology, kinesics, and performance studies. And it has a fundamental commitment to field study and participant-observation. When working with ancient ritual texts, these methods are not possible. Nevertheless, they ought to inform readings of texts, because in all but the most bookish traditions, ritual texts exist to serve ritual enactments, not the other way around.

Ritual criticism is an important phase in the study of ritual. The practice of ritual criticism depends on the basic humanistic premise that rites, though they may be revealed by the gods, are also constructed by human beings and therefore imperfect and subject to political manipulation. However sacred, rites are not beyond the ken of mortals. Therefore, they are subject to ongoing assessment. They can be judged wanting. They can be improved upon. They can fail.

Beyond this fundamental premise ritual criticism does not presuppose any specific theory or definition of ritual, though one's actual practice of it may imply preferences. Some preliminary reflection on the nature of ritual itself can help pave the way to an understanding of the criticism of it.

First, we need a terminological division of labor among "rite," "ritual," "ritualizing," and "ritualization." The suggestions that follow are prescriptive rather than descriptive, the aim being to divide up the terminological labor rather than treat the terms as synonyms.

As I use it, the term "rite" (from the noun *ritus*) denotes specific enactments located in concrete times and places. Usually, they can be named: Bar Mitzvah (the rite of becoming a man in Judaism), Baptism (the rite of becoming a Christian in some denominations). They are the actions enacted by "ritualists" and observed and studied by "ritologists." The term "rite" as used here refers to a set of actions widely recognized by members of a culture. Rites are differentiated (compartmentalized, segregated) from ordinary behavior. Typically, they are classified as "other" than ordinary experience and assigned a place discrete from such activities. A rite is often part of some larger whole, a ritual system or ritual tradition that includes other rites as well.

"Ritual" (from the Latin adjective *ritualis*) refers here to the general idea of which a rite is a specific instance. As such, ritual does not "exist," even though it is what we must try to define; ritual is an idea scholars formulate. Strictly speaking then, one would not refer to "a" ritual or to "rituals" but to "ritual" and to "a rite" or "rites." Ritual is what one defines in formal definitions and characterizations; rites are what people enact.

The word "ritualizing" refers to the activity of deliberately cultivating rites. Elsewhere I have said, "Ritualizing transpires as animated persons enact formative gestures in the face of receptivity during crucial times in founded places" (Grimes 1982a:55). Some readers have mistaken this earlier formulation for a definition of ritual. However, the "-izing" ending was a deliberate attempt to suggest a process, a quality of nascence or emergence. Ritualizing is the act of cultivating or inventing rites. Ritualizing is not often socially supported. Rather, it happens in the margins, on the thresholds; therefore it is alternately stigmatized and eulogized.

In performance theory it is common to distinguish social drama from stage drama; the latter is a transformation of the former. Likewise, there is need in ritual studies for a concept to designate the basic, ordinary stuff out of which special rites emerge. Before a rite becomes a rite, it is not literally something or somewhere else. But imagining a process whereby a rite is born out of processes less formed or formal helps us see the connections between ordinary life and ritual life. This is the reason for my usage of the term "ritualization," which is borrowed from ethologists but modified so it does not refer only to the aggressive and mating behavior of animals.

"Ritualization," then, refers to activity that is not culturally framed as ritual but which someone, often an observer, interprets as if it were potential ritual. One might think of it as infra-, quasi-, or pre-ritualistic. Ritualization is to a rite as a forest is to a house. Nothing makes a forest appear to be lumber except a carpenter's eye. (In a bird's eye the tree is already home.) Whereas the notion of ritualization invokes metaphor—one "sees" such and such an activity "as" ritual—rites of various types are "there." A cultural consensus recognizes them. Ritualization includes processes that fall below the threshold of social recognition as rites. Like social drama, ritualization is deeply embedded in ordinary human interaction. Erving Goffman refers to the stylized routines of everyday life as "interaction ritual" (1967). Both social drama and ritualization go on all the time, but on occasion we focus and concentrate these processes and produce a drama and a rite respectively.

The usefulness of the idea of ritualization is clearer if we consider the following three activities: TV watching, canoeing, and housework. In our society thinking of any of these as ritual is rare. Yet all three have been discussed as if they were ritualistic by reputable religiologists:[3] Gregor Goethals (1981), William James (1981), and Kathryn Rabuzzi (1982) respectively.

Watching TV, Goethals says, is not only *like* ritual; in some circumstances it *is* ritual, for instance, when someone lays a hand on the set to receive the blessing of a TV evangelist, or when a nation participates at a distance in the funeral of an assassinated president. Furthermore, argues Goethals, TV provides icons, images that govern our lives. People watch TV regularly and seasonally. The TV set occupies a privileged, often central, place in the household. TV watching is an example of that form of ritual we call ritualization.

Like Goethals, Katherine Rabuzzi notices implicit ritual transpiring in domestic space. Housework can be mere profane drudgery, but, argues Rabuzzi,

> . . . When woman's housework is viewed as having intrinsic merit for its own sake, then we begin to glimpse beneath the articulated visible masculine edifice of culture a tenacious belief system for which there is cultic ritual but essentially no mythos. And at the heart of this cultic ritual lies the shadowy presence of deity—the goddess Hestia.
>
> When I say Hestia, I do not mean Hestia literally. . . . Hestia is unstoried. In fact, she is not even personified—her name actually means "hearth" (Rabuzzi 1982:94).[4]

In a similar vein William James, using a pattern derived from the archetypal quest in myth (Joseph Campbell's terms), finds in the canoe trip all the marks of a rite of passage (Arnold van Gennep's term) and a paradigm for the basic rhythm of Canadian life.[5]

Since there is no cultural consensus that defines canoeing, housekeeping, and TV watching as ritual, one balks at calling such activities rites. This problem is avoided by the strategy I have suggested, namely, dividing ritual into a "hard," discrete sense (rites), on the one hand, and a "soft," metaphoric sense (ritualization), on the other. Later this tactic will allow us to study mixed genres such as ritual drama and to notice activities that fall on the borderlines of our usual categories.

But what is ritual? We have not yet really specified what it is that the critical attitude will be taking as its object. Someone recently compared the search for an adequate definition of ritual with the search for the holy grail. Rather than embark on a systematic search among the seemingly infinite possibilities, a better strategy for grasping some of the issues at stake is to consider one influential definition. Victor Turner's definition of ritual is a good one with which to illustrate the problem because of his widespread influence in a variety of fields and because of the similarity between his definition and those presupposed in ordinary parlance. He says ritual is " . . . formal behavior prescribed for occasions not given over to technological routine that have reference to beliefs in mystical beings or powers" (Turner and Turner 1978:243).[6] Despite the fruitfulness of Turner's theories for fields far beyond his own and for topics much broader than ritual, his formal definition of ritual is at best conventional and at worst obstructive.[7] It is a host for a brood of problems. Not only does it limit ritual to religious ritual, that is, liturgy, it limits religion to two of its subtypes, theism (implied by the term "mystical beings) or animism (implied by "powers"). Moreover, it implies that ritual is by definition related to belief—a distinctly Western preoccupation, one that ignores instances of disjunction and dissonance between ritual and belief. Ritual's relation to belief is no more automatic than its relation to myth. Because the same rite can migrate across various eras, cultural settings, and cosmologies, one cannot infer beliefs from it. It is not at all uncommon to find people participating in rites they do not believe in. Or if they do believe in them, they do so in some special way—in a "subjunctive" or "as if " mode. In addition, they may believe in one part of a rite but not in some other part.[8] The problem with Turner's making belief a definitional requirement lies in the Western, rationalist assumptions packed into the notion of belief. The assumption that belief is a primary and action a secondary expression of it is peculiar to certain phases of Western thought. Thus it is ethnocentric if built into a definition. One might ask, When a dancer dons a lion mask to become a lion god, is "believing" what is going on?

There is no inherent connection among religion, belief, and ritual. Each culture has its own way of forging or ignoring links among these cultural phenomena. Since there are rites that have nothing to do with religion (e.g., civil ceremonies) and religions that have little to do with mystical beings or powers (e.g., Zen Buddhism), building such qualifiers into a definition is a mistake.

Furthermore, Turner's differentiating ritual from "occasions not given over to technological routine" is only partly successful. The tactic helps us recognize the noninstrumental quality of festivals, celebrations, and other rites permeated by the spirit of play. But it obscures the link between ritual and technology that develops when "technicians of the sacred" (Mircea Eliade's term for shamans) engage in magical rites aimed at specific, empirical results such as making crops grow or healing patients. Surely there is a technology of ritual, and surely modern technology has its ritualistic qualities. And these ought to be illuminated, not obscured, by a definition of ritual.

Ideally, a formal definition is firmly grounded in an anthropologist's fieldwork and serves as a condensation of his or her theories. But such is not the case with Turner's definition of ritual. One can either attribute to him considerable wisdom because he ignored his own definition or fault him for failing to make it consistent with either his theory or his sense of ritual. Since Turner's descriptions and theories of ritual are so rich and nuanced, I read his failure to pay heed to his own definition as an implicit critique of it.

QUALITIES OF RITUAL

Formal definitions are sometimes too dense to be very helpful, and they often isolate one or two characteristics as definitive. A better way to get at the nature of ritual is to identify its "family characteristics," expecting only some of them to show up in specific instances. This approach keeps us from thinking of activities as if they either are or are not ritual. It allows us to specify in what respects and to what extent an action is ritualized. Ritual is not a "what," not a "thing." It is a "how," a quality, and there are "degrees" of it. Any action can be ritualized, though not every action is a rite.

Below is a list of the qualities scholars find in ritual action; they are the indicators that begin to appear when action moves in the direction of ritual. Just as no two family members have *all* the pool of family characteristics, so no ritual action is likely to display all of these. Assuming that some of the terms used in scholars' definitions are either synonymous with, or rough approximations of, others, I have lumped them into clusters denoting the variables, the qualities that appear frequently in the family of activities we label "ritual." Items in parentheses indicate what ritual supposedly is not. For instance, the first item suggests that ritual is enacted, not merely thought about. However, be warned; considerable controversy exists around some of these denied characteristics. I have listed them so as to represent dominant scholarly views, but there are exceptions and minority reports. For example, some theorists argue that ritual can be invented or secular. And some Freudians hold that ritual is maladaptive rather than adaptive.

1.1. Qualities of Ritual

performed, embodied, enacted, gestural (not merely thought or said)

formalized, elevated, stylized, differentiated (not ordinary, unadorned, or undifferentiated)

repetitive, redundant, rhythmic (not singular or once-for-all)

collective, institutionalized, consensual (not personal or private)

patterned, invariant, standardized, sterotyped, ordered, rehearsed (not improvised, idiosyncratic, or spontaneous)

traditional, archaic, primordial (not invented or recent)

valued highly or ultimately, deeply felt, sentiment-laden, meaningful, serious (not trivial or shallow)

condensed, multilayered (not obvious; requiring interpretation)

symbolic, referential (not merely technological or primarily means-end oriented)

perfected, idealized, pure, ideal (not conflictual or subject to criticism and failure)

dramatic, ludic [i.e., playlike] (not primarily discursive or explanatory; not without special framing or boundaries)

paradigmatic (not ineffectual in modeling either other rites or non-ritualized action)

mystical, transcendent, religious, cosmic (not secular or merely empirical)

adaptive, functional (not obsessional, neurotic, dysfunctional)

conscious, deliberate (not unconscious or preconscious)

The advantages of this chart over definitions are that (1) it is fuller than any one of them, and (2) it does not imply that any one (or other minimal number) of qualities is definitive. No single quality is unique to ritual. Since symbolization, for example, appears in nonritual contexts, we cannot define ritual as symbolic action, though symbolization may be important to many rites.[9] Stylization occurs elsewhere—in professional modeling and Japanese Kabuki theater—so we cannot make it definitive. And so on. When these qualities begin to multiply, when an activity becomes dense with them, it becomes increasingly proper to speak of it as ritualized, if not a rite as such.

Providing an exposition of each of these characteristics could consume an entire volume and would go beyond our purposes here. The point is simply to indicate the qualities of actions that are to be the object of criticism and to say briefly how the family-characteristic approach affects criticism. The main implication is that this way avoids premature decisions about genre. We do not begin by asking, Is this ritual or drama or politics? Rather, we ask, To what extent are the actions that compose the genre—whatever it is—stylized, repeated, and so on? Thus we are enabled to explore all kinds of composite, boundary-line, or anomalous activities such as ritual drama, civil ceremony, military parades, and museum openings.

THE NATURE OF CRITICISM

The Greek root of "criticism" means "to judge." The *Oxford English Dictionary* notes that Dryden in 1674 linked the term to Aristotle's *Poetics* and used it to denote the observation of the "excellencies" of a work. When Matthew Arnold used it in 1865, he meant the disinterested endeavor to learn and propagate "the best." And when Dowden used it in 1878, he was referring to the ability to see things as they are, without partiality, without the intrusion of personal likes and dislikes.

Meanings change. The term once referred to positive qualities, then to neutral ones, now to negative ones. No longer a term denoting a search for positive instances or the superior qualities of something, in current popular usage the term "criticism" often carries a radically different connotation: it refers to expressions of personal tastes, particularly those that are negative.

The very phrase "ritual criticism" can raise eyebrows and provoke suspicion. On the one hand, it may sound too negative for liturgical theologians or too reductive for historians of religion. On the other, it may sound too normative for social scientists who study ritual. Many scholars avoid the term "criticism" altogether. They prefer "interpretation," because it sounds less judgmental. They argue that even though criticism among academics is not supposed to connote the making of negative judgments, it nevertheless encourages an insidious judgmentalism. But I am not convinced. Scholars who deny the element of criticism implicit in both the study and the practice of ritual are like Pentecostals who deny they engage in ritual even though their spontaneous actions are stylized and predictable. Covert criticism too easily becomes repressed and then generalized unconsciously. So I prefer to retain the term with all its prickliness precisely because it reminds us of the possibility of intercultural and interreligious conflict. Scholars are not likely to overturn ordinary usage of the term "criticism" by ridding it of its negative overtones. Nor should we try.[10]

Criticism involves discovering, formulating, utilizing, and questioning presuppositions and criteria. It is an exercise of judgment that makes value-commitments and value-conflicts overt. Unlike theory, the aim of which is to explain, criticism aims to assess. And unlike interpretation, which is the effort to understand in general, criticism is an attempt to understand specifically in the service of practice.

Ritual criticism is the interpretation of a rite or ritual system with a view to implicating its practice. Because ritual criticism is itself a practice, it implies a politics and an ethic, as well as an aesthetic or poetics. Because the practice of criticism recontextualizes rites in a way that makes overt their means of negotiating and utilizing power—no matter how that power is conceived, sacralized, or explained[11]—one cannot escape its conflictual nature.

Part of the work of ritual criticism is reflecting on the ways participants and observers decide that one way of doing a rite is more effective or appropriate than some other way. Ritual criticism may include evaluative judgments, but only insofar as it takes into account the circumstances and contexts in which ritual knowledge (see Jennings 1982b) is produced.

Because power is so variously mythologized—as material, as supernatural, as plural, as singular—the rhetoric of criticism need not be restricted to that of the moral imperative: this ought to be changed, that is bad, stop doing things that way. Often critique is embedded in the telling description that calls attention to vested interests, political implications, inherent contradictions, unconscious motives, or dissonant values. Much that passes as description or analysis is actually disguised or unwitting criticism. Among the case studies that follow this chapter, only some of them utilize the rhetoric of prescription, but this does not make them less critical. Chapter 4, for instance, does not even consider the question, How might these performances be improved? But it brings vested interests to light and thus functions critically.

Criticism re-contextualizes. One can re-contextualize rites in any number of ways. Bringing moral or esthetic standards to bear on them are only two such ways. Another is to wrap a rite in a theory that smothers or extols it. Another is to reduce a rite to an assemblage of parts. Another is to perform a counter-rite in an adjacent space. So we cannot presume beforehand to know precisely what form ritual criticism will take. Context is determinative.

Ritual criticism is value-laden, but not merely personal, inasmuch as it is contextualist in its approach and because it sometimes appeals to traditions, principles, or theories for its validation. This contextualism does not mean that in practicing criticism one lapses into mere relativism—the view that one view is as good as another—only that criticism is never absolute and thus should never attempt to gain a privileged position. Judgment-making is always political, always interested, and thus always negotiated. There is no such thing as disinterested criticism, and for this reason we must systematically attend to the conditions of its constitution and practice. Neither disinterested nor purely personal, ritual criticism is essentially dialectical. Thus it should not be centered in a single religious tradition, academic discipline, or role such as "the critic." It can be negative, but it is not only negative; it may also be constructive. At its best it is reflexive, that is, self-critical. Ritual criticism is neither disinterested, as some critics would have us believe, nor purely personal, as popular wisdom has it. Rather, it should be multidisciplinary, cross-cultural, and collective in order to avoid the wholesale imposition of biases and private tastes.

The presence of ritual criticism is scarcely recognized, much less studied. There is a widespread assumption that ritual, because of its imputed sacrality and conservatism, is beyond the pale of critical thought and evaluative response. One regularly encounters the easy assumptions that participants who engage in ritual practices suspend their capacity for assessment and that scholarly observers who watch it only want to explain it, not evaluate it. Nevertheless, ritual criticism goes on informally all the time, and its contexts are various—both popular and scholarly. People walk out of weddings complaining that the solo was too sentimental. They leave funerals bemoaning the length of the homily. Shamans, priests, and rabbis debate the efficacy of this way versus that way of doing things. And councils meet to reform liturgical texts and practices. The contradiction between complaining about and revising rites, on the one hand, and treating them as a sacrosanct preserve, on the other, is blatant and persistent.

In addition to ritualists' criticism *of* their own and other people's rites, there is criticism *by* rites. For instance, Gandhi's *satyagraha* practices were ceremonial assaults. His nonviolent protests were not merely effective political strategies but highly stylized, mythically inspired actions, which gave them a distinctly ritualistic quality. On some occasions Christian liturgy, often noted for its conservative tenor, becomes a means of taking current values to task. Christian theologian Mark Searle (1981:349) makes a "critical liturgy" conceptually central rather than peripheral to Christian tradition. In his view the liturgy does not tranquillize the questioning mind but raises critical social consciousness and cuts across the grain of the status quo.

Ritual criticism is not limited to the religious—to laity, clergy, or theologians. One also finds it among social scientists, even though anthropology has typically eschewed the evaluative task. For example, Clifford Geertz (1973:ch. 6) reports on a Javanese funeral that failed, and he was able to some scholars' satisfaction, to say why it had done so. Whether he was correct or not, the sheer fact of his making such a judgment has not been regarded as ethnocentric, as one might have assumed.

If ritual is not restricted to its most formalized liturgical expressions, then neither is ritual criticism restricted to one of its formal varieties, for example, verbal treatises written by scholarly observers of rites other than their own. It can appear informally or covertly among participants, and it can take nonverbal forms. These ways are as valid as any other. Ritual criticism ought not be an elite domain. A mother trying to figure out the best way to plan a birthday party for her one-year-old daughter is as much a ritual critic as a sociologist hired by a religious denomination to evaluate its liturgy. For this reason I regard ritual criticism as a practice, not a profession. To repeat, *ritual criticism is the interpretation of a rite or ritual system with a view to implicating its practice*. Practice implies imperfection. It implies trial and error. It implies participation and involvement, on the one hand, distancing and perspective, on the other.

THE PRACTICAL CONTEXT OF RITUAL CRITICISM

Ritual criticism is not only theoretical and interpretive, it has an applied dimension that makes it resemble applied anthropology and liturgics. The place of practice we call "the field." Generalizations need to be tested as well as developed in the field. But not all field situations are alike. What is expected of fieldworkers—by themselves as well as their hosts—varies widely. For some, the fields are foreign. For others they are close to home. Though other trends are now emerging, theories of ritual have typically been generated by anthropologists in exotic fields, by historians of religion working on texts imported to their studies from non-Euroamerican contexts, or by theologians whose fields were in their own traditions. The fields in which the following consultations are situated are mostly borderline situations. All these contexts are essential if our understanding of ritual and its criticism is to be adequate.

Assessing rites in the field is tricky business. The motives and methods appropriate to it are often mixed; the results, controversial. Fieldworkers, especially new ones, are usually preoccupied with their motivations and purposes. Thus they often forget that participants, performers, and ritualists have their own purposes for inviting or allowing observers. So consultation, though it aims at mutuality, can be conflictual. The presence of a fieldworker in a tribal household may bring prestige or blame. The attendance of an outsider at sacred functions in esoteric traditions threatens to compromise the integrity of the rites. Participant-observers are sometimes invited and respected, but often they are merely tolerated for reasons that are in tension with their own motives.

The practical contexts of ritual criticism include both emic and etic approaches. "Emic" criticism refers to intracultural or intrareligious judgments. This anthropological notion parallels the theological idea of "dogmatic" theology. Used technically, this latter term does not refer to a stodgy, unyielding attitude but to religious reflection directed to the faithful. When denominational committees sit around tables revising liturgical documents and appealing to scripture and tradition as their warrants for doing so, this is an example of ongoing, emic ritual criticism. The aim is usually to produce a more effective or more authentic rite. Ritual criticism is implicit in the normal course of transmitting, enculturating, and adapting rites. As an example, in chapter 2, we consider a ritually focused self-study by the North American Roman Catholic Church.

There is a second form of emic or dogmatic criticism, one that is less verbal. This is the sort implied by contests between rival sorcerers, rebel ordinations of Episcopalian women as priests, or "guerrilla" masses celebrated on Fifth Avenue during the 1960s in defiance of church authorities. In these instances rites rather than committee discussions are the means of evoking change. In many respects the most effective ritual criticism is the development of an alternative rite. Some of the best examples of criticism in this kind of context are feminist and countercultural. Examples of these are considered in chapter 5.

Not all ritual criticism is of the in-house variety. Some traditions open themselves to other traditions in cross-cultural or interreligious contact. One variant of polite, self-conscious, interreligious dialogue is that which sometimes occurs between Buddhists and Christians or Jews and Christians. Much of this dialogue has been preoccupied with belief rather than practice, but recently there has been more interest in joint practices in which each religion minimizes its distinctive or polemical stance for the sake of side-by-side ceremonial engagement. For example, in the first half of chapter 3 we consider a situation that has forced Native Americans to formulate intertribal rites that minimize tribal differences.

Not all ritualized forms of cooperation are formal or friendly. Ordinary ritualists—in contrast to their intellectual or priestly representatives—are sometimes less interested in subtle theological distinctions and friendly debate. Instead they engage in ritual shopping, with all the bustle and elbow-jousting this implies. In regions less dominated by exclusive religions, ritual criticism can take the form of picking and choosing rites to suit one's own purposes. The result is what we might call ritually mediated culture-contact, which can be quite polemical and not very verbal.

Intercultural performances such as those mentioned at the beginning of this chapter are another kind of context for practical ritual criticism. There are some crass versions and some with considerable integrity. In Haitian bars one can watch tourist Voodoo. In Africa tourists are taken on safaris, where they just "happen" upon a Masai rite that they can photograph and participate in. Rites in such circumstances typically elicit aesthetic rather than religious responses. In Euroamerican societies the domain of the aesthetic is regarded as the proper locus of criticism.

As the distance between participants and quasi-participants grows, ritual criticism becomes increasing "etic," that is, based on an outsider's perspective and values. Etic ethnographies, like apologetic theologies, have to take seriously the cultural differences between insiders and outsiders. Field study is a situation typically characterized by verbal give-and-take between observers and participants. This give-and-take assumes the character of negotiation. On the one hand, the field observer is often an authority of some sort. One the other, he or she is a neophyte, a student ignorant of the proper ritual procedures and their sanctioned meanings.

The situation changes considerably in the shift from field to academic forum, which some think of as the only locus of ritual criticism. Such criticism, which transpires in front of colleagues rather than the original participants, changes in tone and intention. The very currency of academic verbal exchange is critical; this is the idiom that is assumed. In this forum ritual performance seems to serve criticism; not criticism, performance. An illustration of such an academic context for engaging in criticism appears in chapter 4.

The last sort of context in which ritual criticism occurs is probably the least typical, but it is the one that characterizes many of the essays in this book. External evaluative consultation is what occurs when an outsider, sometimes considered an authority, assumes—or is invited to assume—the posture of observer-evaluator. This role arises from a cultural context in which other kinds of criticism—literary and dramatic—already exist. And it presupposes the value of "perspective" and "objectivity," no matter how infrequently these may actually characterize criticism.

THE CULTURAL CONTEXT OF RITUAL CRITICISM

Criticism is not practiced in a vacuum. It has deep cultural roots. For this reason critics long for universality in their judgments but never achieve it.

Why does the notion of ritual criticism emerge now, and in North America? Fundamental to its possibility is a change in ways of imagining ritual itself. In North American religion and art the image of ritual has undergone dramatic shifts during this century. Beginning in the mid–1960s scholars begin to think of ritual as having subversive, creative, and culturally critical capacities. Such an image is exactly what one would expect of the 1960s. Does this fact mean the insights were wrong? I doubt it. Any idea is a child of its time. Until the 1960s the dominant image of ritual had been that it was wed to the status quo. Because we began to imagine, and ultimately define, ritual differently, we began to imagine that ritual creativity was not a contradiction in terms. But the notion of creativity requires its companion, ritual criticism. It should not be surprising that scholars began to find examples of both ritual creativity and ritual criticism to fit new images and theories.

Where did this imaginative impulse come from? Some would attribute it to Victor Turner; others to the 1960s in general. Some would say Turner absorbed it from his students in the 1960s; others would say his students of the 1960s absorbed it from him. The truth is probably that the relations between culture and counterculture are circular, or systematic. However we account for the shift, it is clear that academic culture—which includes the definitions, methods, and theories worked out in institutions of "higher" learning — is permeable by popular culture. Evidence for this claim can be found in the ways in which ideas and technical terms come into and go out of fashion. Presently, ritual is a fashionable idea.

Among scholars ritual is not only an "object" of study. Periodically, it has also become a cause (along with myth and symbol), and in this penchant for causes and fads, academic culture shares a clear link with popular culture. Employed as a hermeneutical principle, the idea of ritual becomes a metaphor, a tool to "think by," a way of conceiving aspects of the human experience, if not the world itself.[12]

In North American society, literature and the arts often bridge the distance between popular and scholarly cultures. Scholarly ideas traverse this bridge to become popularized, and popular currents gain academic respectability. Two examples that have directly influenced the perception of ritual are the Cambridge myth and ritual school and the more recent postmodernism movement.[13]

The so-called Cambridge School of Classical Anthropology (which included James Frazer, Jane Harrison, Francis Cornford, A. B. Cook, and Gilbert Murray) has been dismissed recently as "modern moonshine," but Rainer Friedrich, one of its current interpreters, is more appreciative despite his barbs at "the Great Idol Ritual" (1983:204). In his article, "Drama and Ritual," he arrives at a number of conclusions that are so significant they warrant summarizing.

"Friedrich Nietzsche's *Birth of Tragedy*," Ranier Friedrich argues, "was also the birth of the ritual theory" (1983:161). Obviously, Nietzsche's book is also about Greek drama, so in his writings a link was forged for the Western academic mind among philosophy, theater, religion, and theorizing about ritual. Subsequently, theories of the myth-and-ritual school, which were derived in part from Nietzsche, influenced literary and dramatic theory as well as art. T. S. Eliot's poetry, for example, is shot through with the values and symbols championed by the Cambridge school, which is the reason a play such as *Murder in the Cathedral* so readily enters into dialogue with ritual theory. Friedrich believes the school influenced literature and the arts more than it did classical studies or anthropology, because it sparked the imagination. Yet its research was based on scanty evidence and proponents showed little awareness of the hypothetical nature of their claims. In the hands of Murray and Cornford the myth and ritual theory changed from being a historical one concerned with the origins of ritual to being an a-historical, archetypal one concerned with the essence of ritual. It shifted from looking for remnants of myths and ritual in modern culture to looking for enduring, a-cultural patterns. This general search for universal patterns sometimes took the more specific form of a search for a generic "ur-performance," which Walter Burkert (1966; 1972) identified with sacrifice and E. T. Kirby (1974) with shamanism. In its latter days, says Friedrich, the archetypal hypothesis provoked the de-ritualized theater of Bertolt Brecht and the re-ritualized theater of Antonin Artaud, Jean Genet, and Jerzy Grotowski.

The danger with the myth-and-ritual hypothesis was that it was so seldom used as a hypothesis. It was not really tested. Rather, one sought for examples of it. As Friedrich suggests, "It enters *post festum* through the ritualist's exegesis . . ." (1983:202). Borrowing an image from Hegel, he says the effect of the myth-and-ritual hermeneutic was like "a night in which all cows are black" (203). In sum, the nostalgia for ritual led to its discovery everywhere and thus ironically reinforced its absence in modern, secular culture.

The importance of Friedrich's reconstruction of the history and consequences of the myth and ritual school is that it notices the close links between artistic creativity, scholarly theory, and broad, cultural trends. And it demonstrates how this complex influences both the way ritual is conceived and how it is enacted.

With this systematic interconnectedness in mind, we can now take a brief look at postmodernism, another way of trying to get perspective on the cultural context of ritual and its criticism. Ritual and performance are to postmodernism what myth, symbol, and ritual were to the Cambridge school: celebrated causes. Postmodernism is becoming a widespread concept, especially in cultural history, literary criticism, and theater criticism. The shift into a postmodern age—first named as such by Arnold Toynbee—is being pegged to the heightening of several factors, among the most recurrent of which are reflexivity (Turner 1979a; Hutcheon 1980) and ritual performance[14] (Benamou and Caramello 1977). Reflexivity is not just the self focusing on itself but an experience of that reflection as "other" (see Schechner 1980:13). Performance is not just pretending but a sense that the world itself is an acting out, a play, and that language "does" rather than "means." A less kind way of describing postmodernism would be to say that it is typified by narcissistic theatricalization. But more is at stake than a pejorative can so easily dismiss.

Defining what we are in the process of living out is always precarious business. At best one may try to discern what possibilities are presenting themselves in our time. We seem to be in the middle of a transition of eras from late modern to postmodern.[15] An era is not just a change of century or millennium but an evolution of sensibility, a shift in basic worldview. The breaks between one age and another are seldom sharp, but that does not make them less real.

The term "postmodernism" is clumsy and often lacking in definitional precision. Nevertheless, it indicates a cluster of phenomena that imply the possibility of our entering another historical era. If the term has little chronological worth, it at least has some typological value. The chart on page 24 summarizes some of the essential contrasts being discussed by various proponents and theorists.

The onset of the modern era was marked by several events, among them the invention of the printing press, the Protestant reformations, the discovery of perspective, the voyages of discovery to the West, the rise of nationalism, and the industrial revolution. Modernity is roughly four hundred years old. Richard Palmer (1977:24–25) summarizes the modern era thus: time is linear; spatial extension is the measure of the real; matter is inert; language is an arbitrary convention; persons are autonomous subjects; and truth is an agreement between propositions and facts.

Postmodernism is quite evident in fiction, where it is linked to writers such as John Barth, Gabriel García Màrquez, Jorgé Luis Borges, Kurt Vonnegut, Samuel Beckett, and Italo Calvino. In their works we find no

1.2. A Comparison of the Modern and Postmodern Eras

The Modern Era	The Postmodern Era
Humanistic	Nonhumanistic
Theistic/Atheistic	Polytheistic/Multicentric
Individualistic/Social	Collectivist
Product	Process
Narrative	Ritual
Purpose	Play
Mastery/Logos	Exhaustion/Silence
Synthesis	Antithesis
Centering	Dispersal
Root/Depth	Rhizome/Surface
Genital/Phallic	Polymorphous/Androgynous
Determinacy	Indeterminacy
Transcendence	Immanence
Active/Indicative	Passive/Subjunctive
Presence	Absence
Distance	Participation
Performance	Workshop
Art Object/Finished Work	Process
Performance	Process

single common denominator but a family of characteristics that mark both culture and fiction: the annulment of distance between life and art; writing about writing and reading; emphasizing play and flow; a growing taste for ritual; the crossing of categories; a longing for intimate community; a critique of cause-and-effect reasoning; and a celebration of private and collective (as opposed to hierarchically structured) experience.

Just as postmodernism is not free of modernism, so postmodern ritual is not likely to be free of narrative, one of the marks of modern and classical rites. But ritual in a postmodern culture cannot be a replica of ritual in a premodern or ancient one. A number of theologians, anthropologists, and drama theorists have begun to articulate the demands that postmodern culture makes on religion, on ritual specifically. One of these is the need to limit the role of narrative continuity in ritual performance.[16] Clearly, we need theories adequate to the task of handling the new forms ritual is taking in postmodern culture.

In both performances and novels narrative is being caught up in a whirlwind of ritualization—not ritual in the highly differentiated sense, not religious liturgy or political ceremony. As Richard Schechner (1980:13)

puts it, "When I say that ritual replaces narrative I mean ritual in its ethological sense of repetition, exaggeration (enlarging, diminishing, speed-
ing, slowing, freezing), use of masks and costumes that significantly change
the human silhouette." Accompanying the shift, he argues, is an apprehen-
sion of truth as play and a conjoining of economics to religion rather than
to politics.

Ihab Hassan, whose *The Dismemberment of Orpheus: Toward a Postmodern Literature* (1971:34–36) is one of the most influential works on
postmodernism, isolates several traits that inform the emergent sense of
ritual: an invocation of silences; a will to unmaking; a fusion of high and
low cultures; genuine planetization or violent transhumanization; a gnosti-
cizing of media; a worldview of indeterminacy; and a sense for surfaces. In
his view the religious symbol signifying this complex of processes is the
Holy Ghost.[17]

Hassan believes the transition between modern and postmodern is not
merely sociocultural but epistemic as well. As in the case of romanticism,
it remains to be seen how deeply the sensibility will permeate popular
culture from its rather lofty heights in literature and theater. Hassan thinks
postmodernism does not originate in either literature or theater but, rather,
arises from the "violent transhumanization of the Earth" (which may end in
either planetization or cataclysm) and from the technological extension of
consciousness, "a kind of twentieth-century gnosis" (1980:35). The result
is a fracturing of language and narrative and a corresponding shift toward
playful, disjunctive, fragmentary modes. And, one might add, a disruption
of continuous traditions and communities for the sake of momentary communitas (Victor Turner's term).

Schechner's addition to the discussion of postmodernism is important for
our purposes, because he emphasizes the movement away from narrative
and other linear forms that lend continuity to performance. He summarizes
the differences between the modern and postmodern in this way, "The
modern proposes the analytic, the critical, the narrative, the skeptical, the
contentious—what used to be called the rational, intellectual, and humanist; the postmodern is the religious, the synthetic, the holistic, the ritualized, the uniform" (1980:22). In the place of narrative is projection and
reification leading to a sense of ritual. But postmodern ritualizing is not, he
insists (19), a mere retribalization. Ritual in oral and traditional cultures
derives from myth and oral lore or written texts, but in postmodern culture
ritual performances are detached from these traditional value systems and
ideologies to become religious and cultural entertainment. Some postmod-
ernists believe postmodern consciousness implies a dissolution of genres,

implying that ritual itself, ritual as a distinct type of action, disappears. This claim goes too far—genres are always being made up and dissolving—but there is little doubt that the boundaries between ritual and other sorts of action are bleeding.

In Schechner's view postmodernism spells the end of humanism, the anthrocentric insistence that "Man is the measure of all things." And yet he characterizes postmodern performance as narcissistic. In contemporary discussions of ritual, reflexivity figures significantly (see, e.g., Ruby 1982). Scholars, particularly cultural anthropologists, claim that rites are occasions on which a society performs itself and thus is in a position to examine itself as if it were an object. Reflexivity is cultural self-consciousness. To what extent reflexivity, narcissism, and self-consciousness are characteristics of scholars rather than the literary works and rites they study is debatable (see, e.g., Kapferer 1986:203). Do we postmoderns find reflexivity elsewhere because we ourselves are presently so reflexive? Or does our reflexivity enable us to see what has been previously invisible? If the postmodern theorists are right, the impact of postmodernism leads to a differently understood—if not constituted—self. Not just *what* is experienced but *how* experience occurs is changed.

Schechner suggests that in the postmodern consciousness "rearranging information is the main way of changing experience" (1980:14). This view implies that experience is no longer something that merely happens to us; rather, it is something that can be manipulated. Such a view stands in considerable tension with a postmodern emphasis upon receptivity and passivity. The postmodern self seems at once actively to shape experience and to undergo it. It is at once in the center and at the edge. And it is collective, yet focused on the self. Apparently the postmodern self is neither the collective self ascribed to tribal or traditional culture nor the individualistic self of modern culture. What has broken down is a specific historical form of the self/society dualism.

What about religion in the postmodern era? By "religion" Schechner (1980:14) means,

> . . . the creation of "mysteries" or sanctums, access to which is limited to a special class of people who know the language of the "truth speakers." These "speakers" may be computers or other artificial beings, and their oracles will slowly organize themselves into a priestly caste.

Schechner's view is more cynical than mine; he understands religion only in terms of its worst possibilities—as mystification serving to legitimate economic powers. His view of truth as *maya-lila* (illusory play) and Lonnie Kliever's (1981) "fictive religion" may sound like the same thing, but the implied attitudes are different. Schechner's suspicion of religion is itself a modernist stance. Certainly both modernism (which defined truth as verifiability) and postmodernism (which takes truth to consist of vitality) have their respective risks and demonic possibilities. Postmodern ritualizing runs the risk of becoming religious entertainment, but this is no worse than modern ritual's having risked the identification of ritual with work and success.

The postmodern climate is in many respects more favorable to ritual than the modern one was. Liturgists can expect a growing hunger for ritual, but many liturgies are just now in the process of being modernized, a move that will leave them less, not more, in touch with postmodern culture. It is not enough for liturgists to tune into the postmodern interest in ritual; they must also absorb the capacity for critical deconstruction that is also a part of postmodernism. The craving for ritual may seem to create a favorable market for synagogues and churches, but it may—even more than the modern "crisis of belief"—leave them in the lurch. Longing for ritual is an exceedingly dangerous motive. It is dangerous if it leads to either reactionary rites or the vandalizing of other traditions. Ritual aspirations are notoriously easy prey for political, economic, and media exploitation.

Jackson Lears (1983) has shown how the therapeutic ethos and the yearning for intense, authentic experience are entwined with the historical shift from a producing to a consuming culture. Accordingly, one wonders whether ritual, particularly when it is packaged as experiential and experimental, is merely one more symptom of the shift from salvation toward self-realization that occurred in North America between the 1880s and the present. It is easy to see how Victor Turner's emphasis on ritual process, however theoretically useful it may be, could also serve as a rationalization for a new cult of growth and process. Insofar as ritual becomes a primary means in the search for a reintegrated selfhood, it is also in danger of contributing to the uprooting of symbols from specific, traditional cultures. The performance ethic, as Lears notes (25), underlies advertising. What results should we expect if ritual and advertising come to share a common performance ethic as they sometimes do on the workshop circuit?

Ritual criticism is necessary not merely to keep scholars employed but to keep participants aware of the possibilities of religious imperialism. The postmodern ethos generates a climate that encourages experimentation with the *rites* of others and thus precipitates questions about the *rights* of others: the ritual issue leads to an ethical one.[18]

2

RITUAL CRITICISM OF A

CATHOLIC LITURGICAL EVALUATION*

It [the liturgy] is highly familiar and easily ignored.

Everyone never does everything together.

We kind of have to do this because if we don't, we're not.
                                        —Anonymous participants in Catholic liturgy
                                                (*Liturgical Renewal* IX:158,134,171)

Religiologists are used to dealing with ritual texts. However, the texts familiar to religious studies are usually prescriptive, not descriptive and evaluative like *Liturgical Renewal, 1963–1988: A Study of English Speaking Parishes in the United States* (referred to hereafter as *LR*). This document is a compilation of reports on liturgy as presently practiced in fifteen Roman Catholic parishes. It was designed to be the basis of a colloquium held in 1988 to celebrate the twenty-fifth anniversary of the Constitution on the Sacred Liturgy, the document of the Vatican Council that both reflected and precipitated widespread liturgical reforms in the Roman Catholic Church.

The editors of *Worship*, one of the most respected North American scholarly journals on liturgy, recently wrote,

> As worshiping communities continue to internalize the meaning of the extensive liturgical reforms that have taken place in the last twenty-five years, to evaluate critically the effectiveness of those

---

*Though I have observed and participated in post-Vatican II Roman rites at other times and places (see Grimes 1976 and 1982), in this instance I did none of the participant-observation.

I am indebted to Koichi Shinohara of McMaster University for having so eloquently and insistently reminded me that there is no *absolute* difference between studying texts and observing performances, because reading and writing are performances of sorts, and performances are texts of sorts.

A modified version of this chapter is forthcoming in the proceedings of the conference, at which a summary of my conclusions was presented. Portions of the proceedings used here are reprinted with the permission of James Lopresti, S.J., of the North American Forum on the Catechumenate.

reforms and to search for new rituals that enable worshippers to praise and serve God amidst the rapidly changing cultural patterns in the world, we are convinced that we should continue to concentrate on a theoretic approach to liturgical issues. This does not mean that we shall not be concerned with practical matters. As experience has shown, the doctrinal study of liturgy is often best situated at the level of concrete ritual structures and explicit pastoral problems. Liturgical materials of all kinds are being issued at the present time, many of which would be better left unpublished. There is a great need to provide liturgists with sound criteria for evaluating what appears on the market from both popular and official sources (Editors, *Worship* 1987:80).

In keeping with this aim I shall spend most of my time reflecting critically and theoretically upon *LR*, but first there are some obvious strengths in this study that deserve to be summarized: (1) That it was done at all, that a concerted effort was made to assess one of the hardest cultural forms to evaluate, liturgy, is remarkable. Though the organizers do not call what they are doing "ritual criticism," assessment for the sake of improvement is clearly one of their aims. (2) The scale of the study is considerable; it clearly reflects much commitment, devotion, and energy. What the liturgy centers propose to evaluate is not one performance of one rite, but the key rite in a whole family of rites across a wide geographical and cultural area. (3) The research involved many kinds of people: lay, clergy, less active and more active parishioners, Catholic scholars, non-Catholic scholars, and church staff. (4) It records some actual words of participants and attempts to document actually enacted rites. (5) It attempts to formulate and apply a critical instrument for the study of liturgy. (6) It submits itself to critical scrutiny and ongoing revision.

One can only be staggered by the massive effort represented by *LR*'s 820 pages. Critical self-studies by religious bodies are rare enough; those aimed specifically at ritual, even rarer. Any group that attempts ritual criticism deserves commendation. One must also be impressed that the church would invite outsiders, non-Roman Catholics, to contribute substantially to the evaluation process, because liturgy is that aspect of religion that is usually the most heavily guarded, thus making discussions of it the most in-house. Faced with any ritual account, secular scholars of ritual (whom I refer to as "ritologists" so as not to confuse them with liturgiologists and theologians) must reflect on the document that presents it before proceeding to the ritual as such.

James Lopresti (1988), director of the North American Forum on the

Catechumenate, describes this ecclesiastical self-study as a "purely descriptive work," done by amateurs in social scientific research. One must take his "purely" with a grain of salt, because more than mere data-gathering is going on. A pedagogical motive is also at work. Lopresti says that, even though the liturgy centers that conducted the study were not attempting to prove any hypotheses, their aim was to "stimulate insight." The unspoken but determinative aim may have been even more specific: to continue to renew Roman Catholic liturgy. One of the interviewers says to a participant:

> Well, see, that was why we wanted to do this study. We wanted to give encouragement, to say, "Look, it [the liturgy] is being taken seriously and not in just a couple of parishes but in more and more and more of them"—as a way of stimulating other parishes to say, "Look, you're not alone; there's a lot of other places doing it," and to say where it's being taken seriously. "This is some of the things that we have found are being done commonly or are not being done commonly" (*LR* VII:133).

One purpose of this self-study in ritual is to improve a rite and to consolidate participants. The aims are multiple—to celebrate, to describe, to teach, to evaluate—thus making the critical task complicated. A critic or interpreter has to ask, Which of these motives is primary and which, secondary? The question persists, How critical can one be without botching the celebration?[19]

LR is not a purely descriptive document on the basis of which we scholars, like surgeons, can exercise some evaluative expertise in a germ-free atmosphere. Not only is the document full of faith statements—which one would of course expect—it is full of superlatives. Repeatedly, one encounters people who are putting their best faces forward. Who, after all, wants to be responsible for depicting his or her parish, priest, or liturgy as poor or even mediocre? Lopresti (1988) says of these parishes:

> These are not necessarily the best parishes in the country, whatever that might mean. They offer, however, at least a partial picture of what the liturgy looks like in communities which have taken seriously the task of liturgical renewal. These parishes were chosen because they have approached the liturgy centers for help in their efforts at renewal. They were chosen not so much because they were doing a remarkable job, but because they were determined to do the best they could with the gifts available to them.

The critical task requires distinguishing several layers that stand between a ritologist and the liturgical events being studied:

The instrument—the questions, checklists, and other devices used on site to evoke memories, reflections, and judgments about re-collected rites.

The document—the reports as organized, summarized, prefaced, and edited by staff, editors, and ghost writers at four liturgy centers.[20]

Participants' memories and perceptions—the rites as selectively perceived and partially remembered by those who filled out the forms and wrote the reports as directed by the instrument.

The texts—official liturgical writings and directives that formed the liturgical enactments.

The rites—the liturgical enactments themselves, which, like all per formative genres, are performed in a particular time and place and then, at least socially and humanly considered, are no more (except as "residue" in texts, memories, and documents).

Although pulling apart the layers of this palimpsest may seem to distance us unnecessarily from the living, breathing stuff of liturgy, doing so is essential because the eight critics[21] were asked to begin reflecting on Vatican II liturgical reforms with this multilayered document. These layers themselves do the work of distancing. How can I, a professional "ignorant observer," a mere outsider, hope to understand, much less evaluate, someone else's sacred liturgical rites when I must see them through this series of stained glass windows? The chance of getting a clear view of the rites themselves is remote. But I am determined not be daunted, because I can at least contemplate the windows themselves.

It is essential to describe the document, since readers will not have access to it. *LR* is physically divided into nine sections (referred to herein by Roman numerals) but conceptually organized under three major headings and their subheadings (indicated by Arabic numerals):[22]

2.1. **Outline of** *Liturgical Renewal, 1963–1988*

1. The demographics: location, size, etc., of each parish (I)

2. Liturgical roles, planning, and context
   2.1. Liturgical ministries (II)
   2.2. Liturgical planning process (III)
   2.3. Music, art, and liturgical environment (IV)
   2.4. Evaluation of the program (V)

2.1 Continued

3. The liturgy itself
   3.1. Liturgical structure and enactment
      3.1.1. A *typical* Sunday celebration described by the director of liturgy (VI)
      3.1.2. A *specific* liturgy described by a participant-observer (VII)
   3.2. Recollections of a specific liturgy by a less active and a more active parishioner in response to prompting and/or interviewing by the participant-observer (VIII)
   3.3. Group interview between a researcher [usually the participant-observer] and church staff regarding this same Sunday's liturgy (IX)*

---

*Note: Numerical divisions, both Arabic and Roman (e.g., 2.1, IV, etc.), in this outline appear as citation references in the discussion that follows.

THE DEMOGRAPHICS

From this section one can infer a few demographic parameters of the study. Of the fifteen parishes most are large (1,250+), diocesan territorial, middle class, inner city or suburban, and White, though there are two or three wealthy ones, a couple of poor ones, a rural one, a medium-sized one (750+), a largely Black, a largely Hispanic, a French Acadian, and a largely West Indian one; there are no Native American ones. Three are clustered in New York, four in the D.C./Virginia area.

No claim is made that this is a typical cross-section of American Roman Catholic practice, though one can see that the project designers tried to make the study somewhat representative. We are not told what the factual data are based on; much of it seems impressionistic, the product of rough estimates. I doubt that anyone would want to base a hypothesis concerning the co-variance of liturgical and demographic factors on the data as provided. Constructing one or more profiles of the following types might have been (but was not) the aim of the study:

Catholicism in the United States
kinds of parishes (e.g., urban, Hispanic, etc.)
specific parishes
kinds of liturgies
specific liturgies
specific parishioners or staff members

Because there is no guiding hypothesis, it is extremely difficult to construct a fleshed-out portrait of any one of these.

This first section of the report is not merely factual; it concludes with a question in which respondents—who vary from the parish secretary to the pastor—give examples of the community's vitality. Saying what is vital, valuable, unique, or notable about the parish is called for not only in section 1 but also by two questions in section 2.4. Mixing evaluative with descriptive strategies is evident from the very beginning. Neither a systematic separation nor a systematic integration of descriptive and evaluative modes is maintained. No attempt is made at full or ethnographic description. Because the descriptive summaries focus on "vital" aspects only, and because they "tell" us rather than "show" us, it is exceedingly difficult to form clear images of the fifteen parishes.

LITURGICAL ROLES, PLANNING, AND CONTEXT

The four subsections of this unit consist of responses to short-answer or multiple-choice questions obtained by a written questionnaire. The first three sets are mainly descriptive, the last, evaluative. On the basis of the first, one can ascertain what roles are being played in the liturgics of each parish, for example, priest-presider, deacon, lay communion ministers, gift-bearers, hospitality ministers (ushers), and so forth, and what sorts of training there are for some of these roles. The second set inquires about leadership, the extent of lay participation, and the basics of the planning process. The third set asks for cursory information about musical style and the use of art and architectural space. The last subsection identifies significant changes, the trouble and opposition created by them, the process by which they were introduced, and the values that have emerged from them.

Since I am focusing specifically on the problem of ritual criticism, I shall concentrate on the seven evaluation questions (2.4). The organizers of the study are to be credited for pursuing their assumption that participant criticism was in fact present and worth getting at. But a surprising feature is that they never raise the question of criteria, that is, How does a person or group decide what is liturgically valid or invalid? Even the last section (3.3), a group interview among the liturgical professionals focused on what "works" (their quotation marks) and what "does not work," does not systematically raise the question. Asked to identify the "three most troublesome things about the way the liturgy is done in your worshipping community," parishioners note features such as:

too little understanding of roles, for example, that of hospitality minister
liturgies too long, too noisy, or too many things happening
too little creativity or vibrancy, too staid or formal

too much diversity or too many factions, not enough unity
improper attitude:not warm, vibrant, receptive, joyful
lack of coordination, precision, or timing
lack of spiritual dimension
late arrivals, too little rehearsing
no kneelers or holy-water fonts
bad sound system, too confining a space, too little parking
not enough money
too little lay participation, passivity
insufficiently attuned to seasons and environment
insufficiently attuned to ethnic and/or gender priorities

No one doubts that any of these can constitute real problems, but what kinds of problems are they? And what kinds of criteria do they imply? For the most part they are either practical/technical or aesthetic—at least as stated. Seldom do parishioners address the questions in theological terms; as far as I can tell, the Constitution on the Sacred Liturgy is never mentioned. Perhaps this omission is because clergy and laypeople alike presuppose it, or presuppose that they are adhering to it, so we have to surmise that questions about theological criteria are handled at one level, practical and aesthetic ones at another. Very few of these criticisms are specific to the Roman Rite as such. Except for references to kneelers and holy water, the list could probably obtain at any Protestant church or Jewish synagogue. The questions provided by the research instrument do not help us get at underlying attitudes, values, and criteria. So have we really achieved much that is specifically relevant to post-Vatican II liturgy? Or are these generic (albeit undeniably real) complaints? Although interviewees are asked about musical styles (e.g., folk music, etc.), they are not asked to do critiques in a way that recognizes that different genres or different liturgical intentions might imply different criteria. No doubt, many participants understand the relation of genre to criticism, but the connections remain unexpressed in the reports. A possible conclusion is that much ritual knowledge, and thus much ritual criticism, is tacit: it exists in the doing and is not explicitly articulated.

Sometimes the criteria seem to be beneath the threshold of articulation, not only among parishioners but among the question-askers who, for instance, in the music, art, and environment section (2.3) ask four questions about the baptismal font and none about sculpture, stained-glass windows, or paintings. Is anyone interested in knowing which works of art are contemplated in churches and why? Why are the questions pertaining to music about style, genre, and music education and not about people's actual reception of music? What we learn from the brief answers is so decontextualized as to be almost useless—at least to anyone who wants to understand how liturgical revision takes root or how liturgical criticism transpires.

LR's conception of liturgical context is narrower than that of either ritual studies or the anthropology of ritual, both of which would want to know more about the social, political, geographical, and economic parameters of liturgical enactment. The study inquires into internal processes such as planning, but never treats the planning process as inherently political as well as religious. The masters of ceremonies, homilists, and presiders do not jockey for power or compete for recognition. They do not envy one another or resent authority.

It would be easy for liturgical scholars to write off such a comment by arguing that they did not intend to produce a social scientific work. But one can also put the matter in theological terms. Participants are not depicted as sinful, as human beings with all the usual conflicts and mixed motives that attend human interaction. They are free of desire and passion and thus one-dimensional. One does not have to be ridden with a penchant for debunking or hauling skeletons out of closets to argue that the study of liturgy ought to include the study of socially and physically incarnate human beings; otherwise, the liturgy will seem to float above the lived life of a congregation.

THE LITURGY ITSELF

Section 3 is a major one. Not only is it substantially longer than sections 1 and 2, it contains the descriptive and evaluative heart of the study by focusing on the liturgy itself. In anthropological terms one might say that it contains "the ethnography," the description of an actual ritual "performance." This description is preceded by a template of a typical liturgy.

Liturgy Coordinators' Reports

The liturgy coordinators' reports (3.1.1) are one step removed from being liturgical texts. By "liturgical text" I mean one that prescribes, rather than describes, a rite. For example, the script contained in the Sacramentary, like a script in theater, dictates liturgical action. The liturgy coordinators' reports are certainly not what anthropologists call "indigenous exegesis," that is, a spontaneous, free-ranging reflection on a rite. The reports show clear rhetorical and stylistic signs of having been reworked by an editor and/or summarizer who is not identified, thus complicating the task of interpretation and evaluation. The writing is terse, clear, to the point. Only twice do the reports require more than two pages to describe a typical liturgy. All of them introduce the same liturgical subdivisions: gathering, introductory rites, liturgy of the word, liturgy of the Eucharist, Communion rite, concluding rites. For comparative purposes it is useful to see two examples of descriptions of the concluding rites, one of the least formalized phases of a liturgy:

> Announcements are almost always made at this time. After Mass is pronounced over and the congregation dismissed, the priest and ministers go to the front to greet the people. Many of them gather to socialize, and occasionally, refreshments are served (*LR* VI:1, St. Barbara in Brookfield, IL).[23]

> Announcements are made at the beginning of the liturgy, so there are none at this time. After the Mass is pronounced over, the priest and ministers go to the front to greet the people. Many gather for coffee and take time for visiting with friends (*LR* VI:13, Franciscan Renewal Center in Scottsdale, AZ).

All the other descriptions sound like these. In fact, these differ the most from one another. One might assume that the final phase is the least important so it receives the least detailed, least differentiated description. But if one examines the descriptions of the liturgy of the Eucharist or the Communion rite, which are more central, the same rhetorical uniformity appears. One might conclude the obvious, namely, that the liturgies do not in fact vary much from parish to parish.[24] Add to this the fact that parishioners were asked to describe a typical, not an actual, rite. Granting both points, I nevertheless believe people's unedited descriptions vary more than this. So my conclusion is that the stylistic uniformity of the descriptions is largely the product of the researchers and/or editors, not the local liturgy coordinators to whom the reports are attributed. The net effect makes the fifteen liturgies themselves seem much less varied than they probably were.

What one learns from reading the liturgy coordinators' reports is either how people are taught to *perceive* liturgy or how researchers (not grassroots participants) want to *present* it. The criteria that inform such a perception or presentation are not hard to find. The Constitution on the Sacred Liturgy in effect canonizes a liturgical aesthetic:

> The rites should be distinguished by a noble simplicity; they should be short, clear, and unencumbered by useless repetitions; they should be within the people's power of comprehension, and normally should not require much explanation [Abbott 1966:149, sec. 34].

The process of typification that marks this section of *LR* is familiar in ritual studies generally, so it is not a problem peculiar to liturgiology.

Ritual action is so easily typified because so much of it is repetitive and stylized. In fact, some would define ritual as precisely that kind of action which is deliberately employed as a barrier against change. Liturgical rites, one might say, are those actions that most strenuously attempt typification.[25]

As true as such a view may be, it still is only half the truth. Heraclitus' insight is as true of ritual as it is of revolutions: You cannot step in the same river twice even when you try. One can *choose* to attune one's attention to the uniform aspects of a rite only by a persistent effort at tuning out what is defined as noise. When we typify anything, we tune out local, idiosyncratic variations for the sake of concentrating on invariant structures. In other words, when rites appear static or eternal, it is because someone has an investment in presenting them as such.

The liturgy coordinators' reports are attempts to reconstruct, apart from the variations of season and the specificities of geography, a typical Mass of a particular local congregation. Lay fifteen such reports side by side and what is perceived by my observer's (really, reader's) eye is a liturgical style in which the variations are minor, largely concentrated on details. What does not emerge is a portrait of cultural adaptation, an activity valued by both social scientists and liturgists. Even within English-speaking parishes in the United States there is ethnic and class-based adaptation. But most of the variations presented here are not at the level of cultural adaptation. I suspect that such adaptation is in fact going on but, because of the researchers' formation of the reports, it does not come to the surface. Such invisibility of adaptation is unfortunate because, as Constantine Koser (1966:222,223,225), vicar general of the Order of Friars Minor, notes, the Constitution on the Sacred Liturgy implies more than adaptation of expression; it implies profound modification of content.

What we need instead is an attempt to depict what we might call "the indigenous style" of each parish's worship. Assuming that considerable consistency and uniformity is desirable and in fact operative, we still need to know what is distinctive about the tone, tenor, and ambience of each parish's celebrations. Conveying such qualities is a difficult task, but it is essential if we want to take account of the localization of liturgy and not just its universalization.

Participant-Observers' Reports

I approached the participant-observers' reports (3.1.2) with the most anticipation, because they promised to provide me with what my ethnographically nurtured appetite was most hungry for: the minute particulars of a specific rite as narrated by observers who would question what seemed obvious to participants. Now I would get dates, times, actual enactments, and embodied observers.

The described liturgies occurred in the fall of 1987. According to Lopresti (1988:2) they were selected for inclusion "because they each represented one of the best efforts of the parishes participating in the study." They were not selected because they were typical but because they were exceptional. Clear and explicit judgments have already determined the shape of the data.

There is no such thing as research without presuppositions. My complaint about previous sections of *LR* is not that they are based on religious presuppositions but that such presuppositions remain covert. Here they become overt. Two factors shape the accounts and both are explicit. The first is that the organization of the reports comes from a participant-observation schedule (which we critic-respondents were not given) used by the Notre Dame Study of Catholic Parish Life. The second is the kind of person chosen to do the participant-observation. In Lopresti's words, they were "participants who observed" rather than "observers who participated." Not professional ethnographers, they were selected because they were considered "naturally gifted as observers" (3).

These attempts to document a specific liturgy are disappointing because our naturally gifted observers are so obviously absent from their own reports. As in the preceding section (the liturgy coordinators' reports), a uniform voice and rhetoric—not just an organizing framework—permeates the whole. The observers already know what counts as liturgy, so they systematically ignore the less differentiated ritualization that surrounds it. All the observers attend to the "correct" features of the liturgy, whereas actual observers in actual field situations seldom agree on what is central or obvious. With a broader view of ritual, such as that proposed in chapter 1, observers might have been open to discovering that the most important gestures, as indicated by the degree of their stylization and repetitiveness, transpired in the coffee hour following the liturgy, not in the liturgy itself.

The presentation of these liturgies is dominated by the instrument that forms the observations. The observers know technical terms (e.g., "under both kinds"), but they seldom notice dress, facial expressions, noise, liturgical errors, the temperature, the hue of light, or other features that make one liturgy and one congregation itself and not some other.

If there is any virtue in actual field observation, it arises out of observing how the life of a ritual interfaces with ordinary, nonritualized life. And it arises out of the interaction between the "ignorance" of observers and the "expertise" of participants. The observers in *LR* are for the most part too expert to notice the banal, the ordinary. Perhaps these omissions are not surprising, because such features are typically viewed as nonreligious or nonliturgical features of the Mass.

There are some surprising things in the observers' reports. For instance, they often note the length of homilies but almost never their content. Surely, if we are to understand how the liturgies of Word and of Eucharist interrelate, we need to know the content of the former. For the most part liturgical gestures are not described either, and, if they are, we are told *that* they occurred, not *how* they were executed. We have no sense of their quality and style. Curiously, the observers seem to have been asked to characterize the delivery style of the homilist—a useful idea—but they apparently had a short checklist, because we are told in report after report that the style was "explanatory," "polished," and so forth. One can only be delighted by the observer who had the courage to say that his or her homilist's style was "neither particularly dull nor moving, hortatory nor explanatory, lamenting nor celebrating, simple nor polished" (*LR* VII:22, St. Brigid in Westbury, NY) and then to proceed without another word about the sermon to tell us that the Nicene Creed was recited by all.

Some of the checklists in *Liturgical Renewal* are not hidden; they do not have to be inferred from the reports. Rather, they are appended to the end of the reports. Observers were asked to rate on a scale of 0 to 5 a number of items, some quantitative and some qualitative. For example, they rate the informality of the celebrant. They also rate his dominance of the Mass and his reverence. If one reads these checklists against the prose reports, some confusion appears. Parishioners seem not to know what a "high" degree (i.e., a rating of 5) of informality means. Like the parishioners I am not sure either, since we ordinarily associate high with formality and low with informality. Some of the questions are clearly normative; they seem to prescribe answers rather than call for them. For instance, the category "acting for the people rather than with the people" lets us know what the project designers thought *ought* to be the case: priests ought to act with the people, of course. But if parishioners want to give their priest a good mark, do they give him a "high" mark such as 5 or a low mark such as 1? Quite a few celebrants received "high" ratings on their dominance of the Mass. Since the prose reports were almost never critical, one suspects parishioners sometimes interpreted dominance to mean competence.

Observers were asked to rate the liturgy itself according to its "awareness of horizontal relations (community)" and "awareness of vertical relations (sacred)." Besides having reified the liturgy (it, like persons, has awareness), the categories introduce a theologically and sociologically suspect dualism. Are not certain ways of being in community sacred? And are not sacred things always known in community? Would a one-time participant-observer really be able to perceive and assess a parish's "vertical relations" or a priest's reverence? Only if we think of both as displayed emotions.[26]

Observers seem to have been asked to provide percentages based on impressions. Most of them say what percentage of the congregation goes to Communion, receives from the cup, participates in various parts of the liturgy. One observer (*LR* VII:40, Holy Redeemer in Jenison, MI) judges participation in spoken responses and hymns but then tells us he or she was seated at the back of the church "in a small Eucharistic prayer space." Most participant-observers would have a hard time judging participation from the fervor displayed by worshipers' backs. How much stock should we put in impressions rendered as ratings and percentages when we are not provided with either the physiological or the ideological viewpoints of the observers?

Recall Interviews

One of the most interesting parts of *LR* is the set of recall interviews (3.2). It is the least enamored with standard sociological techniques, and it requires the most from both interviewers and interviewees. For the first time distinct personalities of both researchers and participants begin to emerge. Parishioners—one more active and one less active—were

> invited to recall their "inner experiences" of the liturgy just celebrated. To gain that perspective, the researcher [i.e., a participant-observer] invited the respondents to relive, section by section, the liturgy in which they had just participated [Lopresti 1988:2].

No doubt, theologians will question whether inner experiences are what liturgies are supposed to precipitate, but this theological question aside, the psychology of recollecting ritual is a fascinating topic.

The first recall experience by a less active parishioner is the shortest. Though it is not typical because the interviewer is missing (the rest are in dialogue form), it is forthright, one of the least formed by self-conscious attempts to meet interviewers' expectations, so I shall quote it in full:

> The priest and readers came down the aisle, bowed and kissed the table. I don't remember the color of vestments he was wearing. Then they had two readings and the Gospel was read by the priest while pacing back and forth. I think he had it memorized. The sound system was not very good however. Because it is new, I think no one

knows how to operate it well. I notice that the priest did a lot more movements and gestures than in other Masses. I like the things he says during the sermon, but I can never really remember the content. Then the wine and bread was brought forward by a couple; the priest took it and put it on top of the table. We then all held hands while we prayed the "Our Father." Then he blessed us all and told us to go in peace [*LR* VIII:1, Christ the King in Las Vegas, NE].

Though I cannot say for certain why, I imagine the parishioner to be a woman, so I shall speak of "her." I trust this voice whereas I felt compelled to read between the lines or probe beneath the surface of many others. Perhaps the reason is that here in a paragraph we have the essence of the 305 pages of recollections. What is said by this parishioner is amplified and echoed in many of the others. The most striking feature of the recollections is how little people remember or can reconstruct of what just happened. Like most of us their ritual memories are short. The woman likes what the priest says in his sermon though she can never remember what it is. We laugh; we know the experience well.

But appealing to our common humanity is not enough. This participant's "disremembering" may not be merely laughable, it might indicate, for instance, that ritual memory is kinesthetic rather than verbal or visual. Perhaps this woman's bones remember what her brain has forgotten. What is the significance of worshipers' forgetting the Eucharistic Prayer, a difficulty some interviewers notice?

This participant notices the priest's gestures; there are a lot more of them. One wonders whether he had just taken a summer homiletics course. Other participants were likewise surprisingly attentive to postural and gesture qualities.[27] Remembering style more clearly than content is a recurrent pattern in these recollections of liturgy. As a parishioner from St. Barbara (in Brookfield, IL) puts it, "I remember the gentleman that did the reading. I don't remember the contents" (*LR* VIII:294). Our first participant attends to the qualities of her liturgist's movements, but she does not comment on their symbolism. She does not make the "proper" theological response. But does this indicate that she does not understand or that the movements are meaningless? I doubt it. Perhaps their meaning is "orectic," to use Victor Turner's (1967:29) term, not ideological; therefore, they drop below the threshold of verbal articulation.

Our exemplary, less active participant knows she should know the color of the vestments. Probably she knows she should know what those colors symbolize, but she continues without apology to report on the occurrence of the readings. She notices the priest's style: he paces. She draws a possible conclusion: perhaps he has memorized the passage [that summer homiletics course again?]. Her observations are terse and precise, though theologically unformed.

From her account we learn something basic about the phenomenology (as opposed to the theology) of liturgical consciousness. It is not linear, which makes havoc of the interviewers' intentions insofar as they are preoccupied with order. Some of them insist on asking examlike questions to see if participants can remember which phase came first and which, second. Although our participant clearly narrates the beginning, middle, and end of the Mass, and thus has a sense of chronological order, her attention takes side trips and goes in loops and coils. She apprehends spatially as well as temporally. For instance, she notices that the sound system is not so good and thinks she knows why. *In her experience* the homily does not follow the readings. Rather, awareness of the bad sound follows awareness of the readings and precedes awareness of the sermon. The order of the liturgy and the order of consciousness are not totally congruent, and if we are serious about the study of ritual, we cannot afford to overlook this incongruence.

I have chosen a minute example, but it illustrates an important principle: that "the" meaning of "the" liturgy is a fiction, because meaning is always meaning-to-somebody. And people do not appropriate only liturgy while they are participating in it. They notice other things as well. Rites are radically embodied—socially, psychologically, physiologically—and any method or theological presupposition that overrides this fact is in my estimation simply wrong. It misconstrues the nature of both rites and human beings.

I have tried to show how this "woman's" recollection is more precise than purely theological criteria would allow. Her account is also generalized. And such abstraction is typical of the recollections of other people. Even when interviewers ask for specific recollections, they often get typified responses.[28] The phrasing by an interviewee from Holy Rosary (St. Amant, LA) illustrates the point: "I always like the way we . . . ," the parishioner says (*LR* VIII:22). What is recollected and described is not the specific liturgy just enacted, but liturgy in general, a person's cumulative experience of many liturgies, the way it is always done. What always happens tends to displace what did happen. Like myth, ritual recollections overlook the punctual for the sake of what endures. At least this is how the American Catholic memory represented by this sample seems to operate. In some cultures people discuss rites with a great deal of precision and a high investment. In fact, the recollection and discussion of a rite can supersede the performance of it. For instance, North American weddings sometimes undergo this kind of treatment.

The researchers use a number of metaphors to elicit recall. Interviewers call for a "picturing" of the actions and words of the Mass, a "walking" through the ritual, a "getting into" the experience. Some of them appear to think the meaning of a liturgy consists of the thoughts people have while doing it. They seem to believe that theologically informed, chronologically accurate, thought-filled participation is best. They expect liturgies to "touch off" something, preferably something one can verbalize or some specific feeling, say, peacefulness. But a woman from Bellarmine (in Cincinnati, OH) protests: "I find it hard to hear it [the liturgy] recalled" (*LR* VIII:280). The liturgy is for doing, not recollecting, she implies.

Interviewers frequently try to elicit what we might call a "narrative of feeling." The results are typically not very informative because the responses are vague; the lexicon of emotions is small. A parishioner from Holy Trinity in Washington, DC, reports "the feeling of confusion," "a good feeling," and "a feeling of participation" (*LR* VIII:242). A few participants offer precise, self-conscious reflections. For instance, a parishioner at Holy Redeemer (in Jenison, MI) notes:

> I find myself . . . , maybe because I heard it for so long . . . I say it [the Eucharistic Prayer] with him [the priest]. That's the time during the liturgy when I really become disconnected from everybody around me a lot. I'm concentrating there and I don't see the people around me a lot [*LR* VIII:15].

Theologically, this worshiper should be most in contact with others, because this is the ritual beginning of divine incarnation, the descent into flesh and society. But psychologically, she knows she is not in contact. Hers is a bit of astute self-observation not typical of the interviews. It raises an important question: What if a given liturgical act has one meaning psychologically and another theologically? The parishioner's reflection reminds us that we cannot assume ritual symbols are harmonious and concordant; they are frequently discordant. And methods for studying ritual that tune out or systematically ignore dissonances are inadequate.

Even though the interviewers clearly have their own values and agendas, the dialogue format in this section preserves some of these dissonances. For instance, some of the interviewers implicitly define participation as active and overt, but some of the participants, not quite yielding to interviewers' expectations, describe themselves as just sitting and listening (*LR* VIII:30) or letting words and music flow over them (*LR* VIII:26). They do not "do" or "act." They resist the Westernized expectation that identifies participation with overt activity.

This section of *LR* may have as its basic intention to assess what we in ritual studies call the "paradigmatic" function of ritual, its capacity to form values and guide activity outside the context of the rite itself. Yet the research design calls for questions dependent on memory rather than anticipation. People were not asked what they would do after the liturgy but what they did during it. We need to know both. And we should not assume that what people say they did or will do is the same as what they in fact did or will do. This view is not meant to be a cynical one, only one that recognizes that human consistency is an achievement, not a presupposition. If we want to know how full and regular participation in liturgy affects a human life, we must study both the "how" of liturgical gestures and the relation of such liturgical style to nonliturgical behavior. One parishioner from the Church of the Incarnation (in Charlottesville, VA) is grateful to have been taught ". . . how we carry the book, how we hold it" (*LR* VIII:137). If we want to grasp the paradigmatic force of liturgy, we need to know if this person handles his or her teapot with the same recollected attentiveness. The question is not whether a parishioner remembers the liturgy while pouring tea but whether he or she pours mindfully.

Another way to assess the paradigmatic richness of a rite is to investigate its links with other rites. For example, funerals and weddings often evoke participants' narration of other funerals and weddings. Liturgies, on the other hand, seldom seem to evoke other liturgies. If this hypothesis is true, what should we make of it?

Some of the interviewers know what the proper kind of liturgical attention is; others are searching for what it in fact is. One participant is on the verge of confessing he or she is not sure what a proper liturgical attitude is:

> I think the congregation tends to do it [enter the Eucharistic dialogue] automatically, not think about. You know, we sing these words every Sunday or every day, so you just say it and not even think about it. And I don't know what could be done to bring it more into focus (*LR* VIII:289, St. Barbara in Brookfield, IL).

Is focus the proper mode of consciousness for liturgy? Is thinking? There are ritual traditions in Hinduism, for instance, in which excessive focus would be a problem, not a virtue—in which diffuse awareness rather than focalized attention is called for. What is the proper Catholic Christian attitude? Reverence? Perhaps. But how do we recognize reverence? When it appears as thoughtful focus? Or when it appears as diffuse awareness?

Liturgies not only convey doctrines and values, they cultivate attitudes and mold ways of being conscious. And these are very poorly studied and understood, not just in *LR* but generally. Participants recognize that there is a normative liturgical atmosphere or mood but the norms are largely unconscious, so participants wonder what constitutes a holy attitude.

> A: I noticed one lady poking another as she came down, with a big smile. People say "hello" to one another as they come back from communion. I don't know whether they're supposed to, but people do that, people who have been sitting other places as they go by friends, who are back in their seats, often giving greetings. That's often going on. I'm not sure it's as spiritual as it's supposed to be, but that's the way it works here.
>
> Q: And do you think that's appropriate?
>
> A: I think it . . . . I don't think it detracts from the spiritual end of it. Perhaps it's part of the celebration, part of the communal aspect of Mass [*LR* VIII:231, Sacred Heart in Richmond, VA].

Group Interviews

The last subsection of *LR* (3.3) contains the group interviews. These are transcripts or summaries of discussions among the participant-observer, liturgy coordinator, presider, and music director. Most of the discussions follow a questionnaire that requires explicit evaluation of the major phases of a specific liturgy. Whereas the recall interviews with laypeople elicited largely associative or mnemonic responses, these ask for assessment. Though in this section there is still a tendency to put best faces forward, there is also a fair amount of critical candor, perhaps because participants experience the interviews more as talking shop than as taking an exam, as was sometimes the case in the previous section. However sacred the Eucharistic Prayer, for example, may be, it is not sacrosanct in these interviews. Leaders regularly criticize it or at least worry about its effect on the people: what was magical in the Middle Ages is boring in postmodern times. The section reveals a willingness to be critical of one's own tradition. For instance, one ritual leader says:

> . . . Some of the Gospels are lousy—I prefer the Acts . . . . If I don't find anything in the Gospel and the first reading, then I don't hesitate to go to the epistle and take something out of that and use that [*LR* IX:278, St. Brigid, Westbury, NY].

If we who study ritual ever allow ourselves to believe that ritual is regarded by its proponents as beyond criticism, there is enough evidence here to correct that stereotype. Our question, surely, must not be *whether* ritualists engage in ritual criticism but *what forms* it takes and *in what circumstances* it emerges. The first task is to inquire, What kind of criticism is this? A way to begin thinking about the question is to look at the rhetoric that is used. In this document there are many bipolar contrasts, as is probably the case in most informal criticism of any kind. Consider the following list of participants' terms used to evaluate liturgies. The list is mine, not the researchers, and items in square brackets are opposites, not stated but inferred from the contexts:

2.2. Positive and Negative Qualities of Liturgy

Positive	Negative
active, energetic, dynamic, moving	passive, [inert]
	[static]
friendly, warm, welcome, at home, comfortable, personal	[distant, cold, impersonal, formalized]
shared	[private]
communal, assembly-oriented, shared	[individualistic, hierarchical, private]
prepared, planned	[unprepared, unplanned]
participatory	theatrical, dramatic
proclaimed	[merely] read
connectedness	formality
thoughful, reflective, meaningful	habitual, rote
prayerful	[distracted, firvolous]
flowing, graceful	awkward, [mechanical]
responsive	[flat, unanimated]
[innovative], unusual, special	in a rut, ordinary
works	doesn't work
feels right or fits	doesn't feel right or fit
focused	[diffuse]
appropriate (e.g., to season or occasion)	inappropriate
tailor-made	generic
precise	[imprecise]
proportionate, balanced	too long, too much, too slow, too central, [disproportionate]
serious	somber
festive, celebrative	serious
thematic, [coherent]	[disjointed]
relevant	[dated, irrelevant]

Lists never tell us much, but at least one can see from this list that any suspicion that there are no criteria or that they are hidden is unwarranted. The operative vocabulary is nontechnical, nontheological, and not specific to liturgies. The same is true of the "works"/"doesn't work" distinction introduced by the researchers.[29] The actually operative criteria (as opposed to the criteria theologians think liturgists *should* use) are largely aesthetic in the broad sense of the term. Only a few are explicitly religious or theological. Consider what terms are generally absent from the list: theologically correct, traditional, prescribed, divinely revealed, exuberant, ornate, and so forth. Their absence does not mean they are not operative—much is obviously done because it is prescribed, for example—but it does mean that such criteria are not typically negotiated in discussions.

This list of positive and negative qualities in ordinary, participant evaluation could, if studied more fully and contextually, bring to the surface some of the tensions and contradictions that lie beneath the surface. For instance, participants regularly speak of theatricality and drama as negative qualities, yet they want the scriptures to be "proclaimed" without ever considering what such an expectation demands of one who is not in a proclamatory mood or does not have a proclamatory personality; it demands oratory, verbal dramatization. Not only are there tensions between positive and negative expectations but also between liturgical and extra-liturgical values. For example, individualism and privacy-seeking are bad qualities here, but most of the parishioners probably value individual initiative and creativity, own private property, and treasure their privacy at home. So one could surmise that the liturgy serves a compensatory function. When a compensatory function is operative, we have learned from psychoanalysis to expect backlash. One possibility is that cultivating communal spirit in the liturgy may cause community-mindedness to spill over into the larger society. But another is that having an island of communal spirit may be precisely what relieves participants' guilt for organizing the rest of their lives on the basis of individualistic, privatistic values. There is very little in the entire study that tells us how liturgies are related to social concerns such as racial justice and sexism, even though these are major themes in most Catholic liturgical renewal circles.

As in any artistic or performative genre, so in this ritual tradition there are "givens" and "negotiables." An example of a given is the basic order, the sequence of major ritual phases; no one questions it. Few question the book-orientation of liturgy. Examples of features that have recently shifted from being given to being negotiable are the images of God as king and as male.

Much of the discussion among the interviewees concerns the form, rather than the content, of liturgical enactment, perhaps because there is general consensus concerning the latter. The criticism among liturgical leaders does not focus on fundamental assumptions but on the refinement of stylistic or aesthetic details. An evaluation among musicians after a concert would probably not be rhetorically much different.

The dominant kind of criticism in discussions among the ritual leaders is what literary critics call "reception criticism,"[30] that is, discussion of how participants in the ritual "receive" or "read" what is going on. The basic premise of reception criticism is that the meaning of a text or performance does not consist primarily in an author's intentions or solely in the formal structures of a work itself but in the way a work is received or read.[31] Meaning is a function of the interaction between reader and text, not something inherent in a text. In liturgical terms one would say that among these ritual leaders liturgies are evaluated by their impact. Excessive preoccupation with the reception of anything, whether a liturgy or a brand of soap, might reflect a consumer society's preoccupation with consumption. However, many of the parishioners say they reject nonparticipatory modes. In their view, religious consumerism is, or ought to be, overcome by participation. Often there is a quasi-quantitative view of participation: "lots" of socializing before a liturgy is a good thing. "Much" participation in hymn-singing is also good. Sustained discussions of the qualities of participation are much less frequent.

Again, I shall select one interview that stands out from the rest, because of the clarity of its presentation of criteria. It is easier to see in this interview the tension between improvisation and tradition, restraint and emotional display, performance and enactment.[32] Asked how he knows the opening rites worked, the parishioner says wryly and bluntly, "Eyes look up [*laughter*]" (*LR* IX:114, St. Augustine in Washington, DC). Asked how he knows the homily worked, he responds, "I *felt* the connection between myself and the entire assembly. People *responded* often and powerfully. The people *remembered* what I said after Mass and two weeks later" (118, italics added). From the same parish but in a different interview another criterion—just as terse, serious, and humorous—is stated:

> That is a sign it works, by the way, that the collection increases. Not by whether the music is better one day or another, but the collection; people will respond. It's the kind of thing where [if] people see that something is effective, they're willing to pay for it [*LR* IX:106].

These are not necessarily better criteria than those stated in other interviews, nor are they "correct," but they are clear and candid. In the same interview there are others, clearly stated though impossible to quantify, namely, intuition and attunement (*LR* IX:115,120). These are cited as qualities that this parish requires of its ritual presiders. Passion, emotion, and rootedness in the Word [i.e., scripture] are expected of its preachers. These signs of effective liturgy and preaching are not unique or absent from the other interviews, but they often remain tenuous and hesitant in them. Often one has to infer them and then wonder about their status or rank. Whereas there is a great deal of ambivalence about performance among some of the leaders, there is little of it in this interviewee's mind:

> My expression was dramatic and personalized. . . . I try to say the words as if they're coming out spontaneously . . . and put some affect into my voice . . . . I try to do that, make it sound like it's spontaneous prayer. It's not though [*LR* IX:125–126].

The interview also reveals the presence of nontheatrical spontancity during the liturgy on the part of both presider and congregation. And it narrates their deliberate efforts to cultivate emotion. So spontaneity and the deliberate cultivation of emotion are not seen as contradictory attitudes. Even though emotional, verbal, and gestural creativity are encouraged in this parish, the interviewee is hesitant to "patch" (*LR* IX:138) relevant contemporary concerns into the Eucharistic Prayer. He allows us to see the tension between innovation and tradition, criticism and creativity, in leading liturgies.

To summarize some of my major reservations about the text of the study:

1. It opts for short-term survey rather than long-term field study.

2. It utilizes short-answer questionnaires more often than probing interviews that pursue implications and associations.

3. It assumes interviewees both can and will offer candid and penetrating critiques on the basis of questions posed by relative newcomers.

4. There is no working assumption that people have unconscious motives that must be inferred from repeated observation or that people regularly dramatize themselves according to what they think interviewers want to hear.

5. It assumes liturgy is experienced, recalled, and thus evaluated in terms of distinct, linear phases. Thus it tries to get at the discrete meanings of symbols rather than the sense of ritual.

6. It assumes the primacy of auditory and visual sensoria and makes no systematic attempt to assess kinesthetic, gestural, and postural dimensions of liturgy. It attends primarily to the exegetical meanings of symbols (that is, what people say about those symbols), and it ignores their operational

and positional meanings. For this reason crucial social context and issues such as those presently surrounding ethnicity, war, and gender seem to be missing from parishioners' concerns, but they, in fact, may not be.

7. The study's conception of liturgical context is narrower than that of either ritual studies or the anthropology of ritual, both of which would want to know more about the social, political, geographical, ecological, and economic parameters of liturgical enactment.

8. The study inquires into internal processes such as planning, but never treats the planning process as inherently political as well as religious. The masters of ceremonies, homilists, and presiders do not jockey for power or compete for recognition. They do not envy one another or resent authority.

In sum, the success of the study is compromised because its aim is split views that pursue implications and associations.

3. It assumes interviewees both can and will offer candid and penetrating critiques on the basis of questions posed by relative newcomers.

4. There is no working assumption that people have unconscious motives that must be inferred from repeated observation or that people regularly dramatize themselves according to what they think interviewers want to hear.

5. It assumes liturgy is experienced, recalled, and thus evaluated in terms of distinct, linear phases. Thus it tries to get at the discrete meanings of symbols rather than the sense of ritual.

6. It assumes the primacy of auditory and visual sensoria and makes no systematic attempt to assess kinesthetic, gestural, and postural dimensions of liturgy. It attends primarily to the exegetical meanings of symbols (that is, what people say about those symbols), and it ignores their operational and positional meanings. For this reason crucial social context and issues such as those presently surrounding ethnicity, war, and gender seem to be missing from parishioners' concerns, but they, in fact, may not be.

7. The study's conception of liturgical context is narrower than that of either ritual studies or the anthropology of ritual, both of which would want to know more about the social, political, geographical, ecological, and economic parameters of liturgical enactment.

8. The study inquires into internal processes such as planning, but never treats the planning process as inherently political as well as religious. The masters of ceremonies, homilists, and presiders do not jockey for power or compete for recognition. They do not envy one another or resent authority.

In sum, the success of the study is compromised because its aim is split between compiling data and portraying lived liturgical life. Personally, I wish it had pursued the latter.[33]

A CRITIQUE OF POST-VATICAN II LITURGY

The grounds for liturgical assessments by outsiders obviously cannot be those of theology, liturgiology, or other such disciplines of faith. But they ought not be merely private or personal. And they ought to be explicit. Mine arise from the secular discipline of religious studies generally, and from ritual studies specifically. Ritual studies has been deeply influenced by symbolic anthropology and the experience of participant observation of various kinds of ritual. My approach to liturgical renewal reflects a cross-cultural, interreligious interest in the problem of assessing rites.

Whereas I am not hesitant to criticize studies of ritual, I walk on glass if I heed Jim Lopresti's advice after he read the chapter on which my presentation here is based. He urged me to go beyond criticism of the text of the study to risking an assessment of the rites themselves. I have two major limitations in performing such a task: I am not a participant, and I did not observe these rites. The former can be used to disqualify my comments on religious grounds; the latter, on scholarly grounds. My only option then is to tender a critique of an imagined post-Vatican II liturgy based on piece-meal observations done elsewhere and on the written data presented to us respondents.

Initially, I tried to write an imaginary participant-observer's report to parallel those in the study; I called it "A Nonparticipant, Ignorant Observer's Report on an Imagined, Generic Post-Vatican II Liturgy." You will be relieved that I shall not present that ironic, pseudo-visionary ethnography here, but only summarize under three headings the desiderata that were its aftermath.

The Politics of Liturgy

As I sat in this imaginary parish listening to announcements delivered in an upbeat manner, I fancied the economy was still expanding; something "new" seemed to be afoot in this generic parish of Nowhere. Sitting in chairs that could be oriented toward any of the four directions and singing from xeroxed song sheets (not hardbound hymnals) all things seemed possible there. People acted as though the house had been cleaned and it was spring, although it was really winter outside. I imagined peering into the dumpsters out back to see what had been thrown away and sniffing in the closets to see what was stashed in them. How much of what has been cleaned up liturgically, I wondered, was really repressed rather than worked through? And how much of what was repressed will return?

The Vatican II liturgical reform was predicated on a fundamental paradigm shift that affected everything from the way worshipers attend to

sensory data to ecclesiastical politics. Whenever authority is heavily invested in a hierarchy or authority figure, mystification is inherent in that
process. And it was, in the old days, easy to substitute political mystification for ontological mystery. But when democratization sets it, as it has in
North American liturgical renewal, it is typically accompanied by demystification. And the temptation in the demystified situation is to lapse
into a managerial model with its committees, team leaders, presiders, and
ministers of hospitality. However, liturgy can no more be managed demo-
cratically than it could be dictated royally or pontifically. Just as we should
be suspicious of corporations when they bill themselves as their employ-
ees' "family," so we should wonder about the wisdom of speaking of huge
religious bodies as communities or trying to make cordiality and warmth
the hallmark of worship. There is a fundamental tension in my imagined
contemporary parish between the rhetoric of intimacy and the scale of a
multinational denomination that seems to be courting a managerial model
for liturgical planning.

Accompanying the obvious tension between hierarchy and democracy is
tension between structure and spontaneity. But managing spontaneity does
not produce it any more than commanding it does. It is embarrassing to
watch some liturgists trying to generate and structure spontaneity. One has
the distinct impression of a group trying too hard. The self-conscious effort
undermines the very thing it is supposed to produce.

One can only wait without expectation. Spontaneity, like grace, comes
in its own good time, if at all.

The Environment and Elementals of Liturgy

These "political" tensions between "royal" and "democratic" modes and
between structure and spontaneity inform the aesthetics and liturgics of my
imagined American Catholic parish. To take a simple example, lack of
screwed-to-the floor pews in newly constructed liturgical environments
suggests an incipient poly-directionality. Participants can worship facing
any of the four directions. But what does this poly-directionality suggest
about a group's sense of its own direction? If spirituality follows spatiality,
and if in this case no direction is better than any other, the vertigo that
results would seem to call for a kaleidoscopic liturgy. But the reformed
liturgy is streamlined and comparatively linear. Environment is not ancil-
lary to liturgy; it is generative of it. Or, at least, it ought to be. Is there a
noncentripetal liturgy sufficiently polycentric to make sense out of such an
environment? The loss of a unicentric sanctuary has staggering implications that parallel those attendant upon the loss of a geocentric universe.

And many liturgies have not yet caught up to their new environments.

But how seriously does the liturgical renewal movement want to take the possibility of an environmentally integrated liturgy? Or is liturgy, by its very nature, destined always to be called indoors by the peal of a bell promising shelter from the elements? Is there more than token liturgical use of nonenclosed environments, of the outdoors? Merely transporting the liturgy outside only emphasizes its disaffiliation with its own geography and climate. What would happen to a liturgy that, like the Pueblo Corn Dance, was regularly celebrated in the face of, and in concert with, the elements?

I do not know how to answer my own questions, but I believe the Vatican II liturgical reform ought to continue deepening its commitment to localization in every respect, because local knowledge is the only truly universal knowledge.

Mobile seating is just one example. Consider another from my imagined visit. Using freshly baked bread and homemade wine, as uncanonical as this may yet be, now obviously goes on in some parishes. Using "the real stuff," clearly signals an important recognition that taste and texture actively shape meaning—that "the elements," "under both kinds," should be truly elemental. But how serious is the church about making elemental acts and objects central? How does the removal of the Eucharist from actual feasting and ordinary eating transform its meaning? When does the elevation and stylization of the ordinary lapse into rarification? It seems to me that the process of elementalizing, as opposed to rarification, should continue; it has much further to go if the liturgy is to be grounded in earthen flesh, which, we are told, the Word became.

My concocted minister of hospitality pumped my hand and led me to the basement after my participant observation. There we had a "second communion," the junk food one, and it was no less real than the first one with its natural/supernatural food. Having coffee and doughnuts after bread and wine is, in my fantasy parish, a perfectly sensible, but unfortunate, expression of the desire for more sustained contact with things elemental in the communion rite.

The same is true of holding hands during the Lord's Prayer, handshaking during the Peace, and the decorous gestures of hospitality ministers and others. As done in White, middle-class churches these gestures strike one as self-conscious contrivances either too intimate for groups of five hundred or too abstract to be anything other than formalized friendliness. These gestures cannot bear the load that people heap upon them. These are the gestural equivalents of the second communion—the one that transpires in the basement rather than the sanctuary. They express deep and authentic desires for sustained physical contact and social interaction, but we ought to be saddened when people speak of them as highlights of the service, just as we would be dismayed if a child said her favorite food was potato chips. Cordiality, however nice, does not nourish, and it is no substitute for spiritual connectedness, social interrelatedness, and the kinesic congruence that comes from sustained bodily engagement together. One suspects these are more fully operative in celebrations where ethnic and gender issues are active.

The Sensorium Organization of Liturgy

The sensorium organization (Walter Ong's term, 1967) required by the liturgy has yet to be developed. I believe it must give more attention to the kinesthetic, tactile, and olfactory senses and less to visual and auditory ones if ritual knowledge is to be actually embodied. As it stands in my ignorantly observed liturgy, word and thought dominate. "Themes" are required to unify the parts such as the readings and the homily. But the connections are largely intellectual. Thought out theologically, they demand to be received in the same medium. Whereas they are presented orally, they nevertheless imply and require pages and print to be received.

Not only are some liturgists tied to intellectual thematizing, they are wed to direct, didactic statement. This gives the entire liturgy, especially the liturgy of the Word, a didactic tone, which easily suffocates the role of the arts in liturgy. Working on a very different principle from artists, liturgists are sometimes afraid to be suggestive lest their meaning be missed. So instead they assert and state: the homily tells us what the readings mean. In neither reading nor homily is the story felt to be sufficient unto itself. A model that requires the application of one thing to another, still holds—in this case the homily *applies* the readings to life. The result is a nagging heteronomy that implies that the readings themselves are not life but above or beyond it. And wisdom, not to mention salvation, seems to be something that enters the ear and eye only, requiring reflection and direct action in order to be digested.

But I question the efficacy of this intellectualist, activist epistemology. The alternative posture, of which I daydreamed when I should have been taking notes on my imagined rite, is that of empty receptivity, which is best cultivated by sustained silence, practiced stillness, and kinesthetic engagement with the liturgical and ecological environment. I am not referring to the occasional addition of liturgical dance in order to enhance Gospel readings. I am referring to serious meditative practice as the essential core of liturgical celebration.

What I longed for most at the end of my imagined participant-observation of a post-Vatican II liturgy was sustained silence, genuine stillness, and the curvature of liturgical indirection—either this or an unthrottled exuberance, unbridled improvisation, and kinesthetic exertion. Everything I observed in my mind's eye was swift, clean, decorous, and aimed at the middle range of human emotions. The extremities were forgotten. The liturgy was cordial, friendly, open, upbeat, and more or less democratized. But neither God nor the world is cordial, friendly, open, upbeat, or democratized. The "scandal of Christianity" is largely displaced by such a safe, comfortable environment.

There is indeed a noble simplicity in the new liturgy; everything is up front, out in the open; nothing is hidden, nothing extra. But such an environment requires new forms of ritual knowledge, a new style of embodying mystery. Do not mistake me—I have no patience with the sort of mystification that feeds authoritarianism. But I do imagine a less self-conscious, less didactic, more suggestive liturgy. There is something about focalized attention and trying too hard that causes worshipers to miss sideways glances that feed the unconscious. And if ritual does not feed the unconscious, then ideology and advertising will. It does not require multiple altars, extended hierarchies, and an iconographic glut to evoke mystery. The simplest thing—a stone, a loaf of bread, the sound of a single water drop—is mysterious if attended to fully.

What worries me most about post-Vatican II liturgical renewal is the kind of attention and bodily attitude it cultivates. By this I do not mean that participants cannot recall the Mass in which they have just participated. I mean that so much is aimed at eye and ear and so little at belly and foot. The liturgy, as well as the architecture and artifacts it inspires, calls upon participants to think, reflect, decide—all of which is good and necessary. But where does the worshiper have either the time or space or bodily inclination to meander in the spirit? Always erect, never on the floor, seldom in the dark, never truly hungry, never really sated, how does a people develop a physiology capable of being in the presence of a God who shakes no hands and speaks only in conundrums or in flesh?

It is tempting for the slim, trim, never-overweight Vatican II liturgy to become disembodied, because so little—beyond clumsy old pre-Vatican buildings and ineffective sound systems—pulls it down; so little calls it to the chthonic depths. Shorn of the weight of the ages, a great deal of liturgical and architectural attention of necessity gravitates to the surfaces of things. Having opened up the Gothic closets and stripped off the Baroque trim, worshipers now must attend to clean lines, ungilded surfaces, and a streamlined liturgy in which each part efficiently contributes logically and theologically to the whole. Such a liturgy requires a new quality of attention that is capable of "reading" surfaces. But who will teach this new braille, this language of the surface, this sense for the texture of meanings that are touched rather than spoken and heard?

RITUAL CRITICISM AND LITURGICAL ASSESSMENT

Since I have little doubt that in the future the church will be conducting further research into the effectiveness of its own rites, it might be helpful to conclude with some reflections on the broader parameters of liturgical criticism. Recently, in North America social-scientific writing has begun to function as the prime dialogue partner for liturgical study, as philosophy once did for medieval theology. Not long ago the editors of *Worship* wrote:

> While we do not intend to provide facile or popular answers to the many liturgical questions that arise these days, we do hope to concentrate on the interface between worship and the actual cultural situations in which communities live on local and regional levels. We want our authors to mine the resources of the modern behavioral sciences and arts in an effort to determine which cultural forms best express and communicate the sacred mysteries celebrated by worshiping assemblies [Editors, *Worship* 1987:81].

The idea of culture and the notion of cultural adaptation are central, not only for these editors, but also for the entire post-Vatican II liturgical discussion. The title of John Paul II's address in 1980 to UNESCO makes this fact obvious: "Man's Entire Humanity Is Expressed in Culture" (John Paul II, 1985). Hervé Carrier (1985), secretary of the Vatican's Pontifical Council for Culture, is obliged to discuss definitions of culture and to recommend an anthropological, as opposed to a "classical," approach to it. Anscar Chupungco (1982:3) argues that adapting the liturgy to culture is not a recent novelty but is the way one remains faithful to Christian tradition, which from the beginning was adapting itself culturally.

Not only must liturgies be adapted to cultures, but liturgy itself is an expression of culture—of "Catholic culture" and also of ethnic and civil cultures. It is not enough for liturgies to be relevant to the cultures of participants, because it is too easy to lapse into a liturgy/culture conception that sounds like the old church/world dichotomy. Liturgy does not just answer culture's questions, to use Paul Tillich's terms, but liturgy is itself a cultural artifact, cultural treasure, and cultural question. However authentic, authorized, or revealed the liturgy may be, it is also incarnate in history, so it is not above culture. In this respect, then, liturgy is one of the primary means of enculturation. Because of this role, liturgies, in addition to functioning as agents of revelation, also serve to support class interests, national agendas, and ethnic stratification. Therefore, not only must liturgies criticize cultures, they must undergo constant criticism by cultures. This necessity does not invalidate theological, historical, or other kinds of criticism, but it does mean that a liturgy is not above either popular or scholarly critique. It does not occupy a privileged position, and its means of inspiring insight or criticizing unjust structures are the same as for any other cultural form, at least initially. For this reason aesthetic, cultural, and other forms of interpretation are no less valid than theological ones. In short, it is imperative that liturgy not only be believed and practiced but appreciated (in the technical, aesthetic sense of the term) and understood (in the social-scientific sense of the term).

The study of ritual, whether conducted by religiologists, liturgiologists, or anthropologists, seldom concentrates on the twin problems of ritual creativity and criticism. It should, even though the notion of creativity is fraught with romanticist presuppositions that are difficult to deal with. The idea of creativity is especially problematic in the context of liturgy, because we imagine that we do not create or invent liturgy. Rather, we receive, revise, and enact it.

The notion of criticism is just as formidable. It reminds us too much of parental discipline or grading in school. Only intellectuals engage in it as a profession, and they swarm around the arts like vultures. No one likes the critics or wants to be the object of criticism.

Yet, what is documented in *Liturgical Renewal, 1963–1988* is the way creativity and criticism transpire in relation to an ancient and venerable tradition. In it we glimpse people in the process of trying to adapt creatively and criticize constructively. Usually we do not attribute either creativity or criticism to the Roman Catholic liturgy, but this is a function of our misconstruing both these processes. Whether we speak of creativity and criticism or renewal and reflection, the point is that liturgical revision is an ongoing process, as any historical or social scientific study of ritual can easily show.

Having criticized this study because of the way it makes a reader view liturgy through a glass darkly, I feel obligated to conclude by saying how liturgy could be better studied in the future.

First, there should be more direct access to indigenous language and expression. It should be less manipulated, framed, formed, summarized, and homogenized. We should be able to infer what participants' categories are, not simply see how they respond to the categories of the research instrument. It is not enough to hear how they answer someone else's questions, we need to know how they frame their own questions.

Because of the kind of interviews that were done, the documents contained in *LR* are self-portraits of people trying hard. They have a high investment in this image of themselves. Such an investment does not make the image false, but it keeps the picture from revealing anything of importance. There is nothing unusual about wanting to be photographed in the best light; we all do it. But the most revealing pictures are those snapped when self-consciousness is not so high and posturing is lower. Candid portraits are never the outcome of questionnaires and other such sociologically respectable devices, but of long-term, locally focused, intense participant observation, the staple of anthropology. The instrument—the "camera" if you will—sometimes makes these Catholic participants look dead.[34] A good contrast are the Jews of Barbara Myerhoff's *Number Our Days* (1978). Even though bent with old age and tottering at death's door, they are remarkably alive. They fight. They shout. They disagree.

Of *LR* one wants to ask, Where are the arguments about who gets to put flowers on the altar or why the ushers do not sit down and shut up?[35] One does not get at the human quality of ordinary parish life by asking, "What are the three most troublesome things about the way the liturgy is done in your worshiping community?" (*LR* V). The intention is correct, but the instrument is dull. My aim is not to debunk the document or to suggest that professional social scientists should have done the study;[36] I believe in the value of self-evaluation. My intention is to call attention to the nature of the instrument—to the patterns on the stained glass through which we have to peer at the liturgy—so we can construct more effective tools for self-evaluation of ritual efficacy.

Second, the instruments and circumstances of study and interview need to be fully disclosed. We should not have to guess what the questions were, nor have to infer how many hands have formed the original data.

Third, the identities of participants should be made clear and overt. If researchers think it necessary to protect anonymity, names should be systematically suppressed or changed. As it stands, we know the names of a few participants. Whether or not the names and places are changed, we should know in an interview what sort of person is responding. People need to be identified in some systematic way, for example, by profession, by age, by gender, and so forth.

Fourth, there should be brief profiles of all who write or shape the data, in short, full disclosure of spiritual and social vested interests. A fundamental strategy of *LR* was to have one set of persons observe and document and then another set interpret and evaluate. This tactic allowed for the inclusion of fifteen parishes, perhaps saved us interpreters and evaluators some time, and maybe ensured a system of checks and balances, but it forced those of us in the last loop of the study into redaction criticism, the attempt to distinguish the various hands that shaped the report.

Fifth, even in ecclesiastical self-studies, liturgies should also be studied by at least a few who have no vested interests in the liturgy, and no religious acculturation in the tradition. Many of the participant-observer/interviewers in *LR* overtly reinforce particular kinds of responses and ignore others. We need to see some other biases at work. The interviewers do not use their insiderness to tell us anything that only an insider would know. They do not use their outsiderness to tell us anything that only an outsider would observe. Good field study depends on maximizing the tension between inside and outside points of view so that the dialectic of distancing and empathizing can take place. This tension is repeatedly collapsed in *LR*. We are left with compromise and mutual dilution more often than with genuine dialogue between participants and observers. There is too little tension between commitment and critique.

Sixth, liturgies and the parishes that are their contexts require long-term field study, at least a year in length, to supplement this kind of sociological survey work. We might learn more from one or two in-depth studies than from fifteen short-term ones. Our conclusions about American, English-speaking Catholic liturgies ought to be built on locally focused studies.

The easy universalism of ideas, nation-states, and religions that we could once assume in such notions as that of a "world religion" is no longer viable for both methodological and ethical reasons. Christianity and other multinational religions became such by marketing locally grown produce, and scholars can no longer afford to short-change local-level religion to pay attention solely to the universal level with its sometimes pretentious grand generalizations.

Seventh, there need to be sustained, detailed prose descriptions of the liturgies and parishes emphasizing their styles and implicit rules (see Kavanagh 1982a). If not, then at least a few carefully made films or videos. The process of describing is itself one of the most effective critical procedures, and should be done before the task of active evaluation is undertaken. Profiles of parishes, rites, and individuals should "show" us rather than "tell" us; they should be concrete and nonhomiletical, thus evoking, rather than prescribing, interpretations.[37]

Eighth, the Catholic Christian conception of liturgy, which informs *LR*, needs to be related to theories employed by social scientists such as Roy

Rappaport (1971, 1979, 1980) or religiologists such as Jonathan Z. Smith (1978, 1987). *LR* illustrates one of their most strongly argued claims, that those who study ritual tend to overlook its surface, its "bare facts," thus ignoring the obvious. Many of the interviewers press interviewees to search "deeply" for symbolism, whereas Rappaport, Smith, and others such as Dan Sperber (1975) argue that ritual is not entirely or primarily symbolic. Considerable thought needs to be given to the theory of ritual that informs the instrument that is used to elicit information.

How we study and present ritual depends largely on our sense of it; participating in ritual and studying it are not unrelated. So I would like to conclude with some brief reflections on the nature of ritual itself. Barbara Myerhoff (1978:86) observes:

> All rituals are paradoxical and dangerous enterprises, the traditional and improvised, the sacred and secular. Paradoxical because rituals are conspicuously artificial and theatrical, yet designed to suggest the inevitability and absolute truth of their messages. Dangerous because when we are not convinced by a ritual we may become aware of ourselves as having made them up, thence on to the paralyzing realization that we have made up all our truths; our ceremonies, our most precious conceptions and convictions—all are mere invention, not inevitable understandings about the world at all but the results of mortals' imaginings.

The three epigraphs quoted at the beginning of this paper have their own way of expressing the inevitability and fallibility of ritual, and they, I believe, should have the last word.

"We kind of have to do this because if we don't, we're not," says one participant. "It [the liturgy] is highly familiar and easily ignored," says another. And, "Everyone never does everything together," observes a third.

What originally constituted the opacity of each of these statements later became signals of their profundity. "What do you mean, '. . . kind of have to . . .'?" I scribbled in the margins alongside the first. "Either you do or you don't," I contested. Eventually, I came to understand the ambivalence that suffuses this statement. On the one hand, people do not have to engage in liturgy; no one compels them. In the United States the church is not a state church. On the other, there is a sense of urgency about participation. What sounds like waffling at the beginning of this person's comment becomes pointed by the end of the it: ". . . if we don't, we're not." Nothing less than being itself is at stake. The church staff member does not say, "If we don't [participate in liturgy], we'll not feel good," or something of this sort. The importance of what is being evaluated here is inestimable: without the liturgy this participant would not be.

Even so, the liturgy is "highly familiar and easily ignored." Again, I argued with the respondent: "Ignored? Certainly neither you nor anyone else in this study is ignoring the liturgy. "What do you mean, 'ignored'?" I wanted to know. But the more I reflected on the document the more I was plagued by perverse questions I have not been able to let go of: What if the most important issues are being ignored? What if those things most reflected upon in this study are the least determinative? And what if those least reflected upon are the most determinative? I began to ask myself what was *not* being said and what was *not* being considered. What is it that is so absolutely familiar to these worshipers that they have little choice but systematically to ignore it? No one asks the basic questions such as, Why bother at all? Why have a building at all? What does the liturgy effect? By what authority are these things done or changed or revered? How would we know if they were not "working"? And so on.

Entertaining such questions would create dissension, and besides, they are hard to answer. This is why they are seldom raised. The Roman Catholic liturgy is the "sacrament of unity." Even so, "Everyone never does everything together." Liturgical unity is not to be identified with rigid uniformity. I wondered, "Why doesn't this respondent say, 'No one ever does anything together'?" Because he means "everyone," of course. *All* of us, *all* the time, are only truly together *some* times and in *some* places. It is human nature, even in the midst of sacramental unity, to be drawing apart. And diversity is also to be celebrated.

It is terribly important—maybe more important than fostering the impression of post-Vatican II liturgical success—that someone keep alive recognition that all is not well. This person and others remind us of this fact. In the interview with the leadership of St. Gregory the Great (in Brooklyn, NY), for instance, there is dissatisfaction with the White European models that shape the music, building, and liturgy. Cultural dislocation leads to an underlying desperation in parts of the interview. The interviewee complains that such questions have been talked about *ad nauseam* (*LR* IX:230). This largely Caribbean-American congregation is not happy with southern Black gospel music or liberation theology either. The priest uses an entrance procession, knowing that it has roots in courtroom ritual. He has had it with clericalism, and yet his Black congregation is suspicious of anyone Black in the role of priest-preacher.

Complaints arise from St. Mary's of the Isle too. Parishioners "hug their misalettes" (*LR* IX:245) and are "not into Liturgy 101," that is, do not care much for the participatory ethos of Vatican II collective liturgy planning. In this liturgy leader's view the people could care less whether he does the readings correctly, holds up the host perfectly, plans excellent music, or looks them in the eye during the distribution. They do not comment on these matters, but they let him know in short order what they thought of the homily.

These are only examples of the hundreds of annoying problems that plague those who conduct liturgies. Whether or not the problems are ever solved—many of them are probably endemic and perpetual—they need to be given voice. People's petty complaints and small dreams are part of what make us human. So, however true it is that if we don't do it, we are not, it is also true that everyone never does everything together, and even if they did, it would soon become so familiar that it could easily be ignored. This is why the liturgy must be subject to ongoing criticism and why it is the occasion for our most strenuous exercises in creating tradition.[38] And it is why the question is not *whether*, but *how*, to study liturgies critically.

3

RITUAL CRITICISM OF FIELD
EXCAVATIONS AND MUSEUM
DISPLAYS*

Are we then to give up their sacred graves to be plowed for corn? Dakotas, I am for war!
— Red Cloud, 1866 (in McLuhan 1971:94)

They stumble all night over the bones of the dead
And feel they know not what but care
And wish to lead others when they should be led.
— William Blake, 1794, *Songs of Experience*, plate 54

The distance between Roman Catholic liturgy and the sort of ritual we now examine is considerable. No one questions whether the Mass is a rite. But many will be puzzled and intrigued that we now examine archaeological excavation and museum display as ritual processes. However, the jux-

---

*On three occasions I have been invited as a consultant, critic, or contributor to museum-related activities involving indigenous people or Native artifacts. These three consultations have been occasions for critical reflection upon the relation of ritual to power in archaeological fieldwork and in public spaces, particularly museums.

In 1982 I participated in a project directed by anthropologist Victor Turner, who served as a guest curator for the Smithsonian Institution's display, "Celebration: Studies in Festivity and Ritual."

Then, in 1985 I was invited to Washington, DC, by the American Anthropological Association to respond, along with half a dozen other scholars, to pleas from Native Americans to respect the sanctity of burial sites and mortuary remains. The first part of this chapter was delivered at that meeting and subsequently published in the *American Indian Quarterly* 10(4):304–318; it is reprinted here with the permission of the Native American Studies Program, University of California, Berkeley.

In October 1987 several consultants were asked by National Museums of Canada to evaluate and make proposals regarding the use of rites and performances, especially those of Native people, in the new Canadian Museum of Civilization in Hull, Quebec, just across the river from Ottawa, Ontario, the nation's capital. The second part of this chapter grew out that consultation and was subsequently presented in 1988 at a workshop on "Ritual and Power" at the University of California, Santa Barbara.

taposition of a highly differentiated rite and a scarcely differentiated, largely tacit ritualization process follows from our initial characterization of ritual in chapter 1. What qualifies as ritual depends not only on the qualities of the action involved, but also on the ways it is perceived and understood. Here, we shall not so much be critically assessing a traditional rite as using the concept of ritual for a critical lever against what appear to be non-ritualistic processes: digging up burial remains and displaying artifacts in museums.

Ordinarily, we think of museums as service institutions oriented to the general public. Even though this definition of their role and orientation may be true, it is not the whole truth. Museums are also quasi-religious and quasi-political institutions, which is to say, they espouse ultimate values and mobilize power in the interests of specific groups. The fieldwork necessary to acquire objects for display is inherently political. Even though museums may aim to be cross-cultural in scope and to challenge ethnocentrism, they are also arenas in which one culture displays another. The power to display to another, as other, is considerable. To display is not merely to show or to make visible but to create. A display, particularly when it is effective, is a performance; it is active rather than inert. Perhaps we can go even further. An effective displaying of cultures is an enactment, a putting into force, much as a society enacts legislation, only in the case of museums it is culture rather than law that is enacted. Because the power of display has the force of enactment, it is important that displays, performances, and rites in museums be critically analyzed with special attention to their modes of exercising power.

Michael Ames and Claudia Haagen (1988:119) have summarized the situation well. Regarding Native peoples and museums, they write:

> Native people are taking control of their own histories. They are claiming the right to present themselves, in school texts, in university programs, in public media, and in museum displays, to correct what they consider to be incomplete, stereotypical, and incorrect interpretations. They are claiming for themselves a right that White people have taken for granted ever since they came to the new world, the right to construct for themselves and for outsiders their own version of who they are, where they came from, and what they wish to become.
>
> . . . [This claim] challenges the very foundations of anthropology and museums, including especially the beliefs in the principle of scientific freedom and the validity of knowledge derived from scientific research, and the rights assumed by anthropologists and their museums to represent other cultures.

Rites are often a nexus connecting religious cosmologies and political ideologies, hence their embeddedness in power struggles. Power, like space, is never neutral, never abstract except in inadequate philosophical conceptions of it. Conceptualizations of power are secondary to specific embodiments and enactments of it. Power is always "power to" and "power of." We desire and judge power on the basis of its intentions and origins.

The subject matter of religious studies is the sacred, and sacrality is often closely associated with power. In religious studies it is widely assumed that differences between religions are fundamentally rooted in divergent ways of naming and conceptualizing power, for example, *mana*, *taboo*, *anima*, *tapas*, *ṛta*, or *tao*.[39] One scholarly strategy has been to appropriate and generalize these terms for theoretical use. Another has been to employ the rhetoric of power itself. Gerardus van der Leeuw in *Religion in Essence and Manifestation* (van der Leeuw 1963) made the notion of power central to his understanding of religion, thus implicitly challenging the separation of religion from magic and calling attention to religion's interest in the capacity to effect, cause, and originate events. Mircea Eliade (1957) coined the term "kratophany" to refer to any appearance of the sacred characterized by power, especially when such power is derived from origins.

But neither van der Leeuw nor Eliade had much to say about the relation of sacred (i.e., cosmic or meditative) power to social or political power. This link is made explicitly by Max Weber who, in *The Sociology of Religion* (1922), developed the notion of charisma, which denoted the convergence of personal and/or spiritual power with social-political power of influential leaders. One of the main preoccupations of recent scholarship in religious studies has been to maintain a conceptual connection between sacred and social power without reducing the former to the latter.

This connection is nowhere more evident than in the current struggle of Native people to control the display of indigenous burial remains and sacred artifacts. Because of charges by, and pleas from, Native people, it is essential that White people reflect critically on the ethical and religious implications of their own actions in supplying, maintaining, and visiting public sites such as museums where sacred artifacts and mortuary remains are displayed.[40]

Controversy over the disposition of Native burial remains has been in the public eye since at least 1971. Two examples illustrate the issue as it has appeared on both sides of the United States/Canada border. In 1971 members of AIM (American Indian Movement) disrupted a dig outside Minneapolis-St. Paul. Even though there were no burials at the site, the symbolism of the confrontation was important to AIM members who felt the excavation was proceeding without consideration of Native values and beliefs. According to the Arlie House Report (McGimsey and Davis 1977:90) the public was largely sympathetic with Native people while archaeologists were not.

In 1977, after a controversy over a burial site at Grimsby, Ontario, and a sit-in by Native Canadians at the Royal Ontario Museum, a meeting was convened among representatives of Native and archaeological groups in order to begin the formulation of ethical guidelines to ensure "proper dignity and reverence for the remains" (Douglas Tushingham, cited in Savage 1977:35). In this case a number of archaeologists, including the president of the Ontario Archaeological Society, were sympathetic and insisted that the permission of the nearest Native band should be obtained before any excavation begins. Despite the passage in 1978 of the American Indian Religious Freedom Act, desecration of burial sites and unceremonious methods of handling excavated remains continue today.

THE REBURIAL CONTROVERSY IN WASHINGTON

At a brief forum held in Denver in 1984 at the American Anthropological Association's annual meeting Native representatives asked scholars to formulate professional guidelines against excavation of Native burial remains. Repeatedly, they insisted that the issue is a religious one, but the responses they received—even the most sympathetic ones—were of the political-legal variety.

With Jan Hammil, head of AIAD[41] (American Indians against Desecration), present in 1985 the forum continued, this time formally and on a larger scale. There were two meetings, one conducted largely by scholars; the other conducted largely by Indians. Many physical anthropologists and archaeologists stayed away from the meetings, though a few attended, along with a number of cultural anthropologists. As one might expect, the first meeting was cool and low key; the latter was laden with emotion.

Three main questions were at issue: Should researchers excavate burial sites at all? If so, how should they be treated and the remains handled? Who has, or should have, the power to make decisions on these questions? As the epigraph by Red Cloud illustrates, the roots of the conflict are old and deep.

The problem as articulated by scholars appears complex. A common position among anthropologists was that the desire for repatriation of burial remains was merely a political ploy to gain national attention, that it had little or nothing to do with the maintenance of religious or ethnic integrity.

In the scholarly view the issues are thorny and seldom solved by being reduced to the question, Should non-Natives be allowed to dig up Native cemeteries in the name of science? A list of some of the recurring questions illustrates this complexity:

1. Are the remains historical or prehistorical? And are they identifiable as relatives of existing Native groups? If so, which one(s)? How related, genealogically and ritually, are the living to the disinterred dead?

2. What is it that is sacred, and thus subject to desecration? All land in general? A specific site? Human remains? The location and position of the remains? Burial goods? Who owns the land on which the remains were found? Who owned or used it at the time of burial?

3. How were the remains initially interred, if at all? Ritually? By slaughter? Abandonment? What is the history of the care of the site? How should this history influence present practices?[42] What if the contentious grave sites were unmarked, neglected, or the result of mere disposal rather than ritual burial? Should they not fall in the public domain?

4. Was the exhumation deliberate or accidental? If deliberate, for what purpose (e.g., secondary burial, research, looting)? What consultations were held and permissions obtained? What if sites are accidentally disinterred by developers? Isn't it better that archaeologists rather than construction crews or vandals excavate the remains?

5. How will the remains be treated? How long will they be kept? How and by whom will they be reburied, if at all? If by AIAD or some other intertribal group, where should they be buried? By what authority does such a group act? What will be the disposition of sacred mortuary artifacts? Will they be used in museum displays? What Native attitudes and practices does such handling contravene? What if there are no direct, living descendants of the deceased? Does a Native group, especially one that was historically at war with the exhumed, have any more right to claim the remains than a non-Native group?

6. Whom does the research on human remains and sacred sites benefit? How much does it benefit them? What about the rights of North Americans to know their past? Would not repatriation and reburial violate these rights? Don't Indians benefit from archaeologists' reconstruction of the prehistoric, indigenous past? Aren't rights notoriously culture-bound? Why should Whites accept the Native view of the dead rather than their own? Isn't this really a legal, rather than an ethical or religious, issue?[43]

7. Do the dead have rights? How do the various groups of the living define the transitions from person to corpse to skeleton to remains to earth?

8. What are the religio-ethical values and practices of the researchers,

and how significantly do these figure in deciding whether and how to dig or retain possession of remains? How long is it justifiable to store remains in anticipation of new research techniques? To what extent is the issue the sacrality of sites and remains, and to what extent is it the power to decide what happens to them?

Many of the questions are themselves ethno- or religio-centric.[44] In addition, any one of them could tie those who debate them in such intellectual and emotional knots that they might be tempted to avoid the hard decisions at hand. It is unlikely that one can untangle all of them before being called upon to make further decisions about policy and action.

RELIGION, RITUAL, AND REBURIAL

As in the case of the Indigenous People's Theatre Celebration, here there are conflicting definitions of the situation. Clearly, one party in this debate considers the issue a religious one. Native people defined the issue as essentially religious, not just political or scientific; they spoke of burial sites and remains as "sacred" and the act of excavating and doing research on human remains as "desecration." Many felt that the issue was simpler than Whites made it out to be. The resort to complexity was viewed by some Indians as a political tactic typical of academics. AIAD insists that it is a religious, ethical, and legal one. AIAD has convened conferences, made appeals, initiated legal proceedings, and provoked confrontations on the issue of the disposition of Native mortuary remains.

What has religious studies generally and ritual studies specifically to say about this issue?[45] There seem to be three related tasks:(1) from the point of view of the history of religions to discuss conflicting mortuary attitudes of scholars and Natives and to account for the "neutral" attitude of the former; (2) from the point of view of comparative religion to define desecration and show how it is a function of this neutrality; and (3) from the point of view of ritual studies and ethics to offer some brief reflections on the notion of ritual responsibility.

As it has appeared in anthropology, the controversy over the treatment of Native North American burial sites and human skeletal remains has seemed to be either a legal question, a matter of professional ethics, or a science-versus-religion debate. However, from the point of view of religious studies it appears differently in three respects:(1) North American intertribalism and scholarly humanism are seen as conflicting religions or parareligious ideologies; (2) desecration is understood to be the result of a historical process and defined independently of the intentions of those accused of committing it; and (3) the act of exhumation and the procedures for doing mortuary research are considered tacitly ritualized processes for which scholars must assume responsibility.[46]

Matthew King, a spiritual leader and a chief of the Lakota nation, when asked to comment on the excavation of human skeletal remains, said:

> This is nothing new. After the immigrants came into our country, they started digging for graves, I don't know why. They have no respect. They show their ignorance. They don't know God.
>
> Religion is praying with all the heart, mind, body, and soul, nothing else. You could know a lot of things, but if you change your whole life, that's religion.
>
> Let the people sleep in peace. It [the land] is a burial ground and also a church, for our Indian people [Hammil and Zimmerman 1983:3–4].

To illustrate the communication problem that arises when Native people and scholars discuss burials, consider the following passage. Notice the rhetorical parallels and divergences between King's plea and this summary statement made by two respected archaeologists (Chapman et al. 1981. 1,23) on the archaeology of death:

> The archaeology of death is not a new subject. An interest in the mortuary practices of past human cultures has been evident throughout the development of archaeology to its present disciplinary status. Indeed there is little to match the discovery of an impressive new grave assemblage in generating both professional and public enthusiasm and demonstrating "the universal impact of death."

> Among the shortcomings of social analyses published in the last decade we have discussed the insufficiently explicit attention given to the formation and transformation of the archaeological record, the inadequate treatment of symbolism, the relative neglect of spatial patterning in the location of disposal areas and the absence of a regional perspective in the analysis of mortuary practices.

King says digging up other people's graves is not new. Chapman and Randsborg say the archaeology of death is not new. King complains that he does not know why non-Natives are digging up Native bones. Chapman and Randsborg note that mortuary data are central to the archaeological enterprise. King bemoans the lack of respect. Chapman and Randsborg put "the universal impact of death" in quotation marks and note the enthusiasm that greets an impressive mortuary find. King accuses excavators of not knowing God and implies that knowing lots of data is of less worth than religious knowledge. Chapman and Randsborg are silent on the matter of their religiosity. King regards the earth not only as a burial ground but as a "church." For Chapman and Randsborg the earth is a "disposal area" in which graves display "spatial patterning."

These two passages have little in common except the topic of burial, and it seems that comparing them is as futile and misguided as comparing snails and doorknobs. King is speaking religious language, while Chapman and Randsborg are speaking scientific language. So one might argue that communication would be better served if King would speak scientifically or Chapman and Randsborg, religiously about human burials. But what would have to happen for this to occur? What sort of magic or confrontation could bring about a situation in which physical anthropologists and Native people could stop talking past one another? One possibility would be for one party to speak the language of the other. But King already speaks English, the language of the dominating culture. Have we any right to expect him also to speak scientific language? Would that really change the outcome of the debate or just extend it? What if we required Chapman, or any physical anthropologist for that matter, to respond religiously? What sort of face, credibility, and reputation would archaeologists lose if they responded religiously to what Native people insist are religious issues? The worst possible situation is one in which the debate gets reduced to the polarity, "science versus religion," especially if this sort of terminology is thought to imply non-Native science versus Native religion. The situation seems to require interlocutors, Native archaeologists and anthropologists, for example. But there are very few of these.[47]

A religiologist must consider not only the so-called "world" religions or major denominations but also examine the interplay and conflict between several sources of mortuary attitudes that are likely to lie behind local controversies: Jewish, Catholic, Protestant, scholarly-humanistic, civic-professional (e.g., funeral-directing ethics), tribal, and inter-tribal. Some of these overlap. For instance, some Natives are Catholics and some civic practices have become standard in distinctly religious institutions.

The disagreement between Native North Americans, on the one hand, and archaeologists and physical anthropologists, on the other, is not a science-versus-religion controversy but a clash between conflicting religions. No doubt, there will be immediate and vigorous resistance to this claim: Which religions? Is AIAD a religion? As an intertribal group, whom does it represent? Is it an example of Lakota religion? Also of Pueblo and Ojibwa religion? After all, aren't there important tribal and individual differences that ought not be glossed over by an inter-tribal plea?

As a result of recent North American religious history a religiologist would consider it as proper to speak of an inter-tribal religion of indigenous people as it is to conceptualize either civil religion or ecumenical Christianity, provided one does not claim too much for the term. On certain issues— and desecration of the dead seems to be one of them—the consensus among tribes and factions, along with the moral weight of the appeal, outweighs the differences. Just as one can be, say, a Presbyterian and at the same time an ecumenical Christian, so one can be a Pima and an intertribally religious person. AIAD may not speak for every single Native person or equally well for every tribe, but neither does the World Council of Churches or the pope speak for every Christian. Modern intertribal religiosity has the same religious (or parareligious, if you prefer) authority (and problems) as modern ecumenicity does. Denominationalism and tribalism are social realities no scholar or religious person ought ignore, but so are intertribalism and ecumenism. It is a political tactic, not a matter of scientific principle, when scholars focus on tribal differences as an excuse for ignoring an intertribal appeal.

So much for the kind of religiosity that motivates those who plead for reburial. What about the religiosity of archaeologists and anthropologists? There are those who espouse humanistic codes of professional ethics, thereby rejecting explicit religiosity, and they, no doubt, would prefer to speak of conflicting "ethics" or "value systems" rather than "religions." My argument is that the term "religion" is appropriate, because it includes not only values and ethics but myths, symbols, and rituals as well. But let us not quibble about terms. It is enough if one can arrive at the point of admitting the clash is between competing value systems rather than religion and science (two different kinds of systems). If we speak of the "religion" of social scientists, we can, for the sake of the discussion, put the term in quotation marks.

Let us assume that, despite the reputed agnosticism of social scientists, some are Catholics, Jews, Protestants, and "other." How has this religiosity anything to do with their scholarship, since, as a matter of principle, they intend to bracket it out of their research—at least insofar as it is written and published in scholarly books and journals? We would be claiming too much if we were to imply that archaeologists, as archaeologists, when they are excavating burial mounds, are doing so as Southern Baptists, as Reformed Jews, or as Zen Buddhists. Everything hinges on the mysterious "as," a grammatical symbol that one is wearing this hat rather than that hat.

Hat-wearing, or if you prefer the more respectable term, role differentiation, is a cardinal tenet in the tacit religiosity of many scholars, including

archaeologists. This religion[48] one might call "universalistic" or "scientis-
tic" humanism. If archaeologists are Hindus or Christian Scientists or
atheists, they are also likely to be humanists.[49] So, to be precise, the
conflict as presently focused is between two religions, Western humanism
and North American intertribalism, both of which have distinct histories
with relatively recent origins.[50]

Humanism usually assumes, and occasionally argues, that its practices
are universal and therefore neutral. But research is not value-free. It may
be true (though I doubt it) that the rules of scientific procedure are. But the
motives, side-effects, and consequences of research are not. Consequently,
scientists, especially social scientists, formulate codes of professional behavior, for example, the American Anthropological Association's "Statements on Ethics and Professional Responsibility." To the religiologist such
statements should not be understood apart from their historical derivation
from identifiable religious traditions (notably, Judaism and Christianity)
and longstanding cosmologies and epistemologies (especially classical
Greek ones). Although not reducible to these traditions, the ethics of
scholarly humanism are secularized derivations from them. If one does a
textual analysis of general statements on professional responsibility or
specific ones on reburial, they are recognizable as documents of a specific
culture, era, and ethos. One needs only to count the number of times words
like "sensitivity" and "communication" occur in the Arlie House Report
(McGimsey and Davis 1977) and its appended code of ethics "as promul-
gated by the Society of Professional Archaeologists" to notice how culture-
bound they are. Along with terms such as "reasonable," "dignity," and
"preservation," there are the old humanist standbys "universal" and "human." These virtues are treated as if they were the moral equivalent of
travelers checks. Even though we have the illusion that they can be cashed
anywhere in the world market, they are (to pursue the analogy a bit further)
drawn on a national currency. American Express is still very American. As
values they have their limits, because "human" is precisely what is at issue.
In the eyes of Native people it is inhuman to disinter skeletal remains,
while in the eyes of archaeologists and physical anthropologists it is human
to want to expand the horizons of scientific understanding.

Scholars who would never assume the universality of their research
conclusions, do assume the universality of their codes of ethics. But claims
to universal ethics have the same status as religious claims to universality.
When Christian evangelism, Jungian archetypalism, or Bahai inclusivism
claims universal validity, this claim usually means that some local, regional, or historical symbols are being *imposed* on others or, euphemistically,

said to "encompass" all others. The tacit religiosity of scholarly humanism is no different in this respect. Its universalistic aspirations easily become universalistic pretensions or platitudes. To a religiologist vagaries like "dignity" and "respect" are meaningless until we see the shape of the practices they engender. Many scientists do not consider it undignified to put skeletal remains in bags, because they have been trained to believe that they serve humanity by doing sound research. But this belief is being flatly contradicted by those Native people who insist that exhumation does not serve them.

Alongside the claim that research has universal value is the assumption that it is neutral. In comparative religion a "neutral" attitude toward the dead is anomalous, a rarity in the 70,000 or more years people have been burying their dead. Neutrality, not veneration needs explanation or, if not explanation, then historical context to be comprehensible. We ought not busy ourselves with doing further studies of Native spirituality to account for their attitudes if, in fact, ours are the peculiar ones. Our skeletons, not theirs, need to come out of the closet. How have we arrived at the attitude that scientific exhumation of other people's burials is not desecration or, if it is, that it is worth it? I cannot hope to answer such a question in so short a time.

Philip Aries's (1981) history of Western attitudes toward death is probably the best single treatment, but it does not directly address the topic of attitudes toward *other people's* dead nor toward the land that contains them. So the best one can do for the moment is to list some possibilities, which, by the way, are not *causes*; they may simply be *expressions* of this so-called "neutral" attitude:

Early Christian eschatological indifference ("Let the dead bury the dead") and subsequent beliefs in the immortality of the soul may have led eventually to indifference toward the fate of human remains.

Various dualisms (body/soul, mind/body, body/spirit) that directly encourage indifference toward the body may have precipitated the objectification of the body that became obvious by the eighteenth century.

The nineteenth-century removal of the dead from churchyards and the centers of town to "gardens" on the edge of towns, along with zoning laws that disallowed funeral homes in residential areas, may have contributed to the modern alienation from death and the dead.

Symbolization of the earth as an object or machine may have fostered
a sense of disconnectedness between the human body and the
earth.

Ideas of "private" and "public" property, that is, belief that land must
be either owned by individuals or else equally open to all, may
have encouraged a feeling that the prehistorical dead are public
property.

The privatization of death and the professionalization of funeral-
directing may have desensitized us to communal bonds with the
dead.

The parochialization and folklorization[51] of death in anthropology
itself may have contributed to social scientists' indifference.

Aries has chronicled the process by which Euro-American culture repressed the reality of death. People alienated from their own deaths are
likely to vacillate between objectification of, and fascination with, the
dead.[52] Much more historical research would have to be done to demonstrate this or to prove that any of the factors isolated has, in fact, led to our
own "neutral" attitudes toward sacred burial sites. Such neutrality is probably compounded of objectification and fascination, two attitudes that exercise considerable torque on one another.[53]

An important question is that of the Lakota elder who asked, "What
good will it do anybody?" (Hammil and Zimmerman 1983:3). What do the
bones, mortuary goods, and grave sites tell us? Scholars say the archaeology of death can provide information about the age, sex, social position,
stress level, fertility, marital status, profession, religion, health, and diet of
the deceased. Current American archaeology, if one may take Chapman
and others' (1981:8) summary as accurate, relates the disposal of the dead
to the reconstruction of social organization (not of religious beliefs, as
many British archaeologists do).

Suppose that it *might* do Matthew King some good to know more about
the social organization of his prehistorical ancestors. We must say "suppose," because he clearly says such information will do him and his people
no good. Even if it did, he would probably still object that data gained in an
unholy manner cannot lead to understanding. He might also respond ironically, as one Native spokesman did in one South Dakota discussion (Hammil and Zimmerman 1983:20–21), that authentic understanding of bones
best comes from ritual divination of them, or, as other spokespersons have
claimed, from oral traditions about burial. In short, however useful the
information is to humanistic scholars, its mode of acquisition is an affront

to Native religious values. There is no denying that archaeologically gained information about mortuary practices is useful. The question is, Useful to whom? And the answer to that question in most cases is clear, although some Indians, for example, Zunis, have instituted projects that indicate that archaeology of some kinds is in fact useful to them.

DESECRATION AND RITUAL RESPONSIBILITY

The charge leveled at scientists is that exhumation and subsequent analysis and handling of human remains constitute desecration, that an attitude of neutrality is, in fact, an ethic spawning practices that amount to covert or unwitting sacrilege. To assess such an accusation, we would need to know whether accused persons (1) maintain on principle that desecration is impossible, (2) claim that in such-and-such a case they did not desecrate, or (3) believe that scientific discoveries are worth the cost of admitted desecration.

But this kind of information is just the beginning. The seriousness of the charge demands that attention be paid to the definition of desecration. Doing so is essential for legal as well as scholarly purposes. Since the literature on the concept is almost nonexistent, our discussion will of necessity constitute a proposal rather than a consensus. Much more energy has been spent in describing the sacred and modes of sacralization than in understanding profanation, desecration, and other forms of ritual negation.

To begin the work of understanding our own anomalous attitude, we need some basic concepts. Several terms require distinguishing: profanation, desecration, desanctification, and to a lesser extent, secularization and taboo. "Taboo" refers to an intrareligious avoidance. As I propose to use the term here, one must be an insider to violate or observe a taboo. When some act, place, object, or person is taboo, it is too holy to approach directly.

"Deconsecration" applies to an intrareligious act. For example, a priest may desanctify an altar when the destruction of a church building is necessary.

When something becomes "secularized," it is part of a historical process whereby a religion becomes differentiated, leaving it in either a compartmentalized or a covert relation to other cultural domains. Whereas the tabooed is so positively charged that it exerts a negative effect, the secularized appears to be simply neutral. Archaeological excavation in cemeteries is the outcome of a long process of secularization, which functions as a powerful "invisible religion" (Luckmann 1967). When a researcher is capable of suspending fear, reverence, and awe in order to treat human remains as data, a remarkable transformation has occurred. Secularization as such is not desecration, though it may lay the groundwork for it.

The two most important terms for the present discussion are "profanation" and "desecration." "Profanation" implies a charged relation to the sacred. When people profane, they take the sacred seriously but invert or violate it. For example, in the case of profane language one draws upon the sanctity of religious or sexual imagery for the sake of the power that this sanctity provides. The one who profanes is not necessarily an insider or a believer, but by definition the profaner is not indifferent to the power implicit in the violated object. When someone chisels out the name of the deceased from an Egyptian tomb, this is an act of profanation.

"Desecration," I suggest, is an interreligious violation in which one discounts or ignores the sacredness of what is violated. It is, one might say, a ritual blunder even though perpetrators may deny that they intended to violate or to engage in a ritual act. Desecration is not counterritual, as is the case in profanation; nor is it a "neutralization" of ritual, as in instances of deconsecration. Rather, it seems to arise in two sorts of circumstances: when one is ignorant of ritual consecration or when one refuses to admit the sacred as a relevant category. Desecration is a possible ritual consequence of the historical process of secularization. There may be varying degrees of desecration ranging from the ignorant to the willful, but, just as ignorance of the law is no excuse, choosing to overlook sacred zones and remains is not either. The cultural milieu in which desecration is likely to occur is one in which a highly secularized society (in which religion is compartmentalized and/or covert) and a more traditional one (in which religion more thoroughly permeates other cultural domains) impinge upon one another.

Little has been said about the purely ethical dimensions of this conflict, namely, that those who have power also have responsibilities to allow the living to bury their dead without fear. Since few would disagree, at least in principle, with this view, we need to look at the ritual dimensions that parallel the ethical ones that bear on direct dealings with the long-buried dead. From a point of view within ritual studies, desecration must be interpreted as a form of tacit ritualization. Whatever scientists' *intentions* may be, the *consequences* of exhumation include ritual ones.[54]

The ethical and ritual traditions of most White North American scholars predispose us to desecration, which may occur *despite* (perhaps even *because of*) our noblest intentions. There is no point in claiming that all exhumation constitutes desecration. Nevertheless, our religious heritages make the likelihood of it high. Because of this predilection, we are obliged to assume a higher degree of "ritual responsibility," an ethic that bears directly upon habitual practices and bodily comportment in sacred places and in the presence of sacred objects and skeletal remains.

It is a mistake in discussions of mortuary behavior to make too absolute a distinction between tacit ritualization, codes of professional responsibility, and scientific procedures. We scholars must assume explicit responsibility for the implicitly ritualistic dimensions of our research. Our professional and scientific conduct at burial sites is itself a form of mortuary behavior. Whatever its practical consequences, it has inescapable symbolic and quasi-ritualistic dimensions.

As a bare minimum, full consultation and proper permission should be obtained from Native descendants or spiritual kin, and, if denied, no excavation whatever should occur. However, we should go further. If permission is granted, or when no such descendants are found, leaving archaeologists free to dig, fieldworkers have an obligation to develop minimal practices that are in keeping with the most reverent we know—whether or not we are "believers" in any orthodox sense. In addition to our ethical responsibilities to obtain permission, we have ritual ones that bear on bodily comportment. And we are ill prepared for the latter because humanism has been so notoriously oblivious to the ritual implications of its ethics.

Certainly, in any field study of the rites of another culture we would typically show our respect for indigenous sacredness by walking softly, as it were, and other means of handling with care. In short, we should behave with ritual decorum—either by drawing on our own gestural canons of sanctity or by imitating those of others on whose sacred precincts we tread. We should allow ourselves to be tutored; we should suspend or modify our usual manners out of respect for our hosts. The same decorum is appropriate when visiting a "society" of the dead. If we neither have conventions of our own nor are sure what were the practices of the prehistorical people we may have unearthed, then we may have to invent ways of embodying our ritual responsibilities. I emphasize the idea of ritual, rather than merely ethical, responsibility in order to remind us that in situations of cultural conflict the importance of symbolic gestures escalates, because we can no longer assume a shared moral consensus. It would be a mistake to assume that exhumation of Native burials is analogous to autopsies or research carried out on donated cadavers. In the latter instances the dead have shared the value systems of the living; they are bound by a common legal, ethical, and ceremonial code. But in cases characterized by intercultural conflict, recourse to ritual is sometimes a necessary prelude or accompaniment to moral negotiation. If we show no respect (a ritual quality), how can we expect to be taken seriously (a moral necessity)?

Probably these suggestions, if taken seriously, will at first result in awkwardness. Archaeological digs are not noted for their air of sanctity but, rather, for their sweat, bawdy humor, and iconoclasm.[55] We have little other than our aesthetic sense of "appreciation" and some vague sense of "respect" to draw upon. We approach grave sites in a state of ritual ignorance; we may not even know, as an ethologist might put it, how to display respect. Most of us have never known how to walk in a sacred manner, so we can expect considerable self-consciousness until we relearn what we may never have known, namely, how to let those whose bones we transmute by a strange alchemy into data rest in peace.

The conflict that surfaced in Washington and elsewhere continues in many regions, though there have been some piecemeal resolutions. The most militant statement of the Native case insists that no further digging be done in Native cemeteries, that accidental disinterments (e.g., by bulldozing for subdivisions and roads) lead to immediate reburial, and that all remains presently in museums and laboratories be returned for ritual reburial. More moderate positions call for full consultation with nearby Native groups and for reburial once archaeological analysis is complete (within a specified time, say, a year or two). Some government bodies and professional associations (e.g., the American Association of Museums) have already formulated guidelines. As far as I know there are no ethical statements regarding the ethics of research on dead subjects that parallel those on living subjects (e.g., by the Social Sciences and Humanities Research Council of Canada 1983), and there should be.

The resolutions have been largely local, focused on this museum, that Indian band, or such-and-such professional society. In some places the practice now is to consult with the Indian band nearest the site. In other places it is to refrain from excavation altogether or to continue digging unless public protests force the work to cease. However, the question of the disposition of human remains presently in White hands is largely unsettled. Some institutions steadfastly refuse to give up "their" bones and associated burial residue, insisting that they may be needed for scientific research in the future, since new techniques are always a possibility.[56]

Near the end of the consultation we were read a letter sent by the director of the Smithsonian Institution outlining his reasons for refusing to give up its Native mortuary holdings. Curators typically feel powerless to authorize repatriation of museum holdings, because they have a charge to serve the entire public, not just one group. The question is, Who has the power to decide, when groups differ in their opinions about whether they are being served by museum displays and practices?

Rebuttals of my position have pursued several strategies. One is to argue that information gained in excavation and laboratory research is valuable to Native people—that the "responsibility for interpretation and presentation of Native cultural development" (Dean Knight in Wilfrid Laurier University 1988:13) rests on archaeologists' shoulders—but this approach ignores blatant Native questioning of the usefulness of the information and the need for scholarly interpretation. Another is to appeal to a lesser-of-two-evils principle: better the archaeologists than vandals or bulldozers. No doubt this is true, but one doubts that there are typically only two alternatives. And a third has been to argue that we have no way of knowing what the deceased may have valued, therefore we cannot argue that reburial reflects their wishes. In some cases this is probably true, but we can probably make well-educated guesses, and these are not likely to include the moral equivalent of Native peoples' willing their bodies to science. The clear tendency among anthropologists and archaeologists who attack the idea of returning remains held in research facilities is to posit an ethical relativism and use it to justify continuation of their practices. On what basis, they say, can one claim that the rights of the dead supersede those of the living to know their past? In response I question the moral validity of a Faustian quest for knowledge, which amasses knowledge without assimilating it. Though I have never heard the statement in public, anthropologists sometimes claim in private that the reburial controversy is "pure" politics, nothing but a ploy by Native people to gain media attention. Asked for evidence, none is ever forthcoming, so one has to assume this is a prejudgment of some sort. No one would deny that the controversy has political dimensions—certainly a key issue is the power of the living to determine who controls the fate of the dead. Nevertheless, the "nothing but" logic of this "argument" reeks of White reductionism and prejudice.

THE PERFORMANCE CONSULTATION IN OTTAWA

We turn now to a second consultation in which many similar issues and values came to the surface. In October of 1987 National Museums of Canada invited a small number of participants to a three-day consultation on anthropology and performance. The number was limited, because the meeting was designed as a task force to consider policies and practices regarding performance, ritual, and public events in the new Canadian Museum of Civilization (CMC), which was then under construction and scheduled for opening in 1989. Participants included staff from several museums, scholars from a variety of disciplines, and theater personnel; among these were several indigenous people.[57]

One of the main questions proposed for the agenda was how "to support a dynamic, on-going program of Native participation" (from the agenda). One of the reasons for this question's importance was that the CMC's director and his staff considered indigenous cultures essential to the development of Canada. This conviction was literally to be enshrined in stone. The centerpiece of the museum is the Grand Hall, through which visitors make their first entry into the museum. It is a series of façades in the style of various West Coast Indian architectures.

The architecture of the museum itself—an astonishing sculpture that reminds one of windswept snow or sand—was designed by Douglas J. Cardinal, a Metís from Alberta. A brochure speaks of the building and Grand Hall in tones bordering on religious enthusiasm:

> The hall is an open cathedral-like space featuring a dramatic back-drop almost three storeys high, evocative of a Pacific rain forest. Ranged below in village fashion is a group of recreated Northwest Coast Indian housefronts, embellished with characteristic paintings and carvings representing six major tribes. Six soaring totems, among the Museum's most prized artifacts, stand sentinel, mutely speaking of kinship, spiritual values, and relationships to nature.[58]

In the same brochure the director speaks of the CMC as "a treasure house for cultural objects which possess power as enduring standards, icons, and reality anchors."[59] Given this view of material culture, it is not hard to understand why one of the major questions we had to face was the nature of ritual, one species of human performance, and its relation to others such as theater. If artifacts function as "standards, icons, and reality anchors," handling them is likely to evoke ritualized behavior and power struggles.

One of the first questions asked to the director was about the Museum's position on the reburial controversy. He surprised us—or me, at least—by informing us that he thought the Smithsonian Institution's director had expressed his willingness to turn over its skeletal remains. If this had been true, it would have been a landmark decision in the history of North American archaeology, one that would have established a precedent hard to resist elsewhere. The director also said that presently the CMC retains its Native mortuary remains. Pressed about why this was the case, he indicated his sympathy with the movement toward reburial and said the reason was simply because there was no demand at present and that he hoped to get the new museum open before such a demand was pressing. In other words, the politics of funding a new museum requires low-key handling of potentially controversial events. He said he would be willing to support repatriation if he could do so without fanfare. He did not specify precisely what holdings would be implicated.

In general the CMC staff were less bureaucratic and more visionary than many of us had presupposed. The CMC has a mandate in its charter to engage in advocacy, which means that, like the Canadian Broadcasting Corporation, it does not have to reflect the status quo but can actively criticize it, even though it is a government organization. Consequently, it is invested with the power to work for change. It had been actively soliciting Native input long before we arrived.

A major aim of the CMC is to become an interactive, as opposed to a passive, museum. The plan is to animate spectators to interact with displays, not merely peer at objects in glass cases. The staff said it wants symbolically to shatter the glass barrier that separates people from artifacts and the cultures they embody. The Ontario Science Centre and the fortress at Louisbourg, Nova Scotia, are examples of this sort of approach. One of the most widely visited "living museums" is Walt Disney Enterprises' Epcot Center in Florida, which attracts twenty-five million visitors a year to its international pavilions. Like Epcot, the CMC would be animated by "real" people, many of them representatives from the cultures on display. The CMC's director had visited, studied, and written about Epcot. Both his humor and his dream are evident in the following excerpt:

> . . . My very best slides of the Temple of Heaven were taken under sunny Florida skies, and I show them in preference to those I took of the real thing later in Beijing under leaden skies and years of neglect during the cultural revolution. My Epcot slides portray the Temple of Heaven as the Emperors would have dreamed it [MacDonald 1987a:10].

No doubt, the director's irony and wit protect him from confusing the Epcot temple set with the real thing. But what if the magnificent totems at the CMC overpower or outclass the real ones on the West Coast? What is implied if Northwest Coast people cannot afford to possess the best products of their own labor? How does one ensure that "museum reality" does not overshadow reality beyond the confines of its walls? Do not imbalances in economic and political power threaten the integrity of sacred power?

The director knows well that trips to museums, camera in hand, are "validation of experience ritual[s]" (MacDonald 1987a:10). And such ritually validated experiences can either transform or confirm oppressive social structures. He admits, "The image of museum directors as the high priests of abandoned cathedrals of culture haunts us all . . ."(14). What he proposes to change, however, is not the part about priests and cathedrals but the phenomenon of the abandoned museum. He unabashedly speaks of museums as "centres of initiation." In his view the museum is the only institution in society in which individuals and icons can interact in a process of "lifelong learning and lifelong initiation."

What strikes one first about the "Vision Statement" of the Canadian Museum of Civilization is its scale—its grandeur if we like it, its grandiosity if we do not. A million visitors per year are expected. It aspires to be *the* Canadian showcase and a key player in the "world class tourism industry" (1987:5). The statement is highly reflexive, its authors worried not just about what the CMC will be but how it will be seen. One can, perhaps, attribute much of this self-consciousness to the obvious political and economic problems of starting and sustaining and a new museum. But some of the self-consciousness reflects what actually is transpiring, namely an attempt to re-imagine Canada by way of artifacts and enactments. It is a lofty aim; parts of it are perhaps even noble. But we typically fail at our strongest points, not our weakest. So what are the possibilities for power conflicts in carrying out the CMC vision? There are at least four obvious trouble spots: sacred objects, rites and performances, the structure and definition of the building itself, and the modes of displaying objects.

THE DISPLAY OF OBJECTS

Some of the holdings of the CMC were no doubt purchased in good faith and thus are the property, both legally and morally, of the institution. But much of what one sees on display, particularly if it is of indigenous origin, is booty. Thus, a sacred pipe, for instance, was not only *once* a fetish for Indians, it remains a fetish (in the Marxist sense) of our materialistic culture. Sacred objects in museums function as "symbolic capital" (Bourdieu 1977:177–183). A museum piece cathects (to use a psychoanalytic term), or condenses, bygone centuries and distant cultures, thus generating a market value strikingly out of proportion with the original. Such things are all the more valuable if the people who made and used them have been exterminated. So the question is, Whose reality does the peace pipe in the glass case anchor?

One of the proposals made to the CMC by our group of consultants was a kind of "truth in labeling" policy. Insofar as it is known, the history of acquisition of each item should be made part of its exhibit. If an object was purchased, the museum should say when, from whom, and how much. If it was stolen, it should specify the circumstances. If the CMC were to accept this proposal, it would be a significant contribution to demystifying its own quasi-ecclesiastical functions.

The stories told about objects and the stories objects tell are crucial, and the power to decide which story is told is therefore important. Most museums are designed to reassure visitors of their perceptions of reality, so they typically tell only one story, not multiple, dissonant stories. Why is the CMC called the Canadian Museum of Civilization (in the singular), not Civilizations (in the plural)? Probably because the illusion of unity tranquilizes and reassures us.

Some of us argued that museums should also juxtapose, and thus relativize, cultural realities. Museums, like universities, should be encouraged to display dissonant narratives and performance, thus calling into question any single definition of reality.[60] Typically, museums do not represent the present, dominant culture, because it is, as it were, backstage displaying the "other" cultures. This is why one may find a Salish totem pole but probably not a Catholic steeple or Lutheran church front in the CMC. One way to juxtapose cultural realities might be to commission Native people to depict White people's religions—to encourage those displayed as others to display those who display them.

Dead indigenous people have been routinely displayed as "remains." One may be able to comprehend why Indians might regard the displaying of their ancestors' bones behind glass as a violation. But it is probably harder to understand that the preservation ethic, to which curators are bound by law, might violate a Native worldview. To preserve under glass is an implicit denial of the decaying and dying processes. In many Native worldviews people, power, and objects are not only used but used up. A Navajo sand painting, for example, is not an artifact but a sacred tool that is used and then dispersed. Certain West Coast masks and dances are used once, and no more. One Native group is said to burn its masterpieces so the young will not see them and be intimidated but, rather, only hear of them and be inspired to make their own.

I am not claiming that Native people never preserve sacred objects, but only that when they do, the objects are more like beings and less like mere things. Such "object-beings" are either returned to the elements or kept alive with use. So when we Whites control humidity, install glass to filter out the sun's rays because they fade colors, and encase objects in glass, we, in effect, deny both life and death to a sacred item. Perhaps we do with our fetishes what we do with our corpses: preserve them so we can ignore them.

At the consultation we proposed two ways of dealing with this dilemma. One was repatriation and the other was limited ritual access. It may sound absurd to propose repatriation of sacred objects to an institution whose very existence depends on conserving those objects. Since some of the museum's holdings were fairly and legitimately purchased, there is little moral obligation to repatriate them. But those taken as booty might, we argued, be returned—if not all of them, then some of them as an opening gesture. Some indigenous groups, we suggested, might choose to leave them on loan with the museum, which would label them "On Loan, with Gratitude to Such-and-Such a Band." Another possibility would be co-ownership shared by the CMC and an indigenous community. In short, repatriation would not necessarily mean the permanent loss of all pilfered objects.

THE STRUCTURE OF SPACE AND
THE POSSIBILITIES OF PERFORMANCE

We were shown several miniatures of the new CMC. One was of the Native Peoples' Hall, which is behind the Grand Hall. Its several areas consisted of stylized environments and various Native groups, for example, an animal skin-clad man with a spear raised toward a mastodon. There was not a single twentieth-century urban or reservation scene among them. Many of us felt the depictions were of a golden age, either in the past or in some mythic realm. One could not know from this sort of exhibit either that Indians live in the present or that they live in cities. Museum staff insisted that they were not going to reproduce the miniature literally, but we were unable to determine what they were, in fact, going to depict. In any case the miniature illustrated what most contemporary museums will undoubtedly be pressed to overcome.

What is not shown or seen in a museum is a fundamental determinant of visitors' perceptions of reality. Behind the scenes of one of the architectural miniatures we saw the batteries that run the little show—an apt metaphor for the locus of structuring power. The power to animate objects, structure exhibits, and choreograph performances is considerable. Museums, like churches and universities, invent reality by re- and de-contextualizing it. Usually, this inventing of reality takes the form of decontextualizing objects. The most important aspect of recontextualizing is not the information on the labels, because much of it is not read anyway. Rather, it is in the mode and structure of display. Here is where the subliminal, thus efficacious, messages are hidden.

One of the most questionable features of the CMC is the structure of its floors, or rather, the academic definition of that architectural structure. On the bottom floor are the Grand Hall and the Native Peoples' Exhibition Hall. The second floor houses the Folk Art and Traditions Hall. And on the third is the History Exhibition Hall. Museum staff insist that Native people have an important history and that it should be known, but the model did not indicate that the Native Peoples' Hall was to be historically organized. The separation of the history floor from the Native/anthropological floor could reinforce the prejudice that Native people have no history. This division of labor institutionalizes the White world's nature/culture dualism. Literally, bodily, visitors will ascend into history and descend into nature. What are we to think—that one ascends from nature and Indians through culture and immigrants to history and . . . and what? This is the question. And . . . those with power to determine the structure? Assuming that animators from the various groups do in fact work at the museum, will the floor definitions not tempt them to continue their segregation? If the animators do resist organizing themselves into first- and second- and third-floor cliques or subcultures, they will have to do so despite—not because of—the proposed structure.

Since the Grand Hall is the grandest, it could be interpreted as an architectural recognition of the primacy of indigenous cultures. But the danger is that it will function like those gorgeous, expensive books that sit on coffee tables and never get read. That it will have immense visual power is unquestionable, but whether that power will be used to undermine or reinforce stereotypes remains to be seen.

And who belongs on the folk floor? Italians, Vietnamese, Chinese, Irish? Jews? And if this is the case, who are the makers of history on the top floor—English and French? Pressed with questions and criticism, the staff admitted that the division of labor among the three floors arose in part because of turf concerns among anthropologists (first floor), folklorists (second floor), and historians (third floor). This three-storied universe, this supposed microcosm of Canada, is really a microcosm of academic fiefdoms just at the point in our history at which the rigid separation of these disciplines is being called into question.

Finally, what are the possibilities and dangers regarding rites and performance in this space? There is little problem with outdoor folk festivals and powwows except the usual ones of how to import talent and orchestrate such massive events. We did not discuss the possibility of outdoor demonstrations such as rites of protest.

As presently conceived, the only possible large-scale performance spaces are the Grand Hall and the roof. The Grand Hall was obviously conceived first for visual effect, not for performative flexibility. The rooftop has astonishing possibilities, not overlooked by the architect, but as yet not scheduled for creative use. By default many events and performances will take place in the Grand Hall, which means that West Coast totem poles will have to witness a great deal that may tire them. The fact that they will become scenic background for all sorts of events is ironic because, as one museum director noted, many West Coast peoples are rather private in their ritual enactments.

Regarding private ceremonies, we also proposed that those objects that are kept by the museum might be made accessible in some limited way to the groups from which they came.[61] The museum is going to operate on a day and a night cycle. The day cycle will be free or inexpensive, and its emphasis will be on education. The night cycle will cost more, and its emphasis will be on entertainment. The latter will help pay for the former. We suggested a third cycle, beginning at around midnight and ending at, say, 7:00 A.M. During this after-hours period a Native group might be allowed access to museum space, where, for example, masks and pipes could be made available for use in actual ceremonies. We saw no reason why all rites enacted in a public institution had to be public. After all, the night cycle will be open only to those who can afford the cost of tickets. One of the Native consultants inquired whether earth was accessible from within the Grand Hall, the most likely scene of ceremonies. Since it is not, and since the space is generally thought of as public rather than sacred, it is not hard to imagine indigenous peoples' rejecting offers to use the space for sacred rites.

Many of us in the non-Native majority come from religious traditions in which the sacred is identified with what is public or universal. Christianity, for instance, is supposed to be spread everywhere and announced to all people. There is very little in Christianity to contradict the North American ethic of display; free and unrestricted access is of high value. Many Native traditions, however, regard the most sacred activities as private: to publicize is to profane. Sacred Native ceremonies are not private in the White, individualistic sense, rather they are "tribally private," not open to those who have no kinship ties or religious obligations to the people engaging in ceremonial activity. For many Native people displaying sacred power in non-Native ritual contexts is a sacrilege.

The CMC will do more than display objects. It will animate them and surround them with performances. It plans to use animators such as those we are familiar with at Louisbourg, Williamsburg, Epcot, and Disneyland. One danger is "the real Indian" syndrome. The history of Indians' being expected to play Indians, that is play themselves, is a long, painful, complicated one, and it includes everything from Black Elk's performing with Buffalo Bill before Queen Victoria to Pueblos' enacting their own defeat in the Santa Fe Fiesta Pageant. Typically, such performances of Indians performing themselves in public spaces have been in terms of White images.

Thus this sort of enactment has reinforced, not disenchanted, those images. The images begin to create the reality, rather than vice-versa. So, for example, a "real" Indian wears a plains war bonnet, lives in a tepee, and hunts for a living. Even though most of us know these things are not true to Native life, they still determine White expectations and condition our disappointments when we do not get what we want.

Of course, the presence of animators could lead to the reverse, the shattering of stereotypes, but doing so will require deliberate, sustained effort. Some of us argued against the exclusive use of actors as animators and of actor-training methods that lead to role playing.[62] The main reason is that in situations of potential intercultural conflict, we need less, not more, role playing and posturing. Another is that the successful examples of animation typically require people to impersonate the historic dead (as in Louisbourg and Williamsburg) or mythic characters (as in Disneyland). Indians are neither a dead people nor a mythic/fantastic people, so Whites ought to avoid the treatment of Native people as living artifacts, which too easily happens if they are expected to play, rather than be, Indians. So perhaps animators need training, not in acting but in intercultural decorum and diplomacy and in interreligious reverence.

If the CMC is successful in attaining its goals, it will provide powerful images for the next generation. Not only does it matter *what* things are displayed but also *how* they are displayed and what things are not displayed. A museum is an odd place because it is unusually dense with once-powerful objects rendered powerless. Yet, paradoxically, in museums objects become actors, whereas in life, in history, objects are usually the shadows of actors, the residue of events. So taking steps toward re-immersing objects in contemporary events by animating them is an enormously important move fraught with dangers and possibilities. For one thing, the very notion of animating objects and/or visitors presupposes that they are dead or lifeless in the first place. Adding animators to museums can be a little like adding "enrichment" to white flour after processing has taken out the enriching ingredients in the first place. I am not opposed to animation; I simply want to be aware of whose culture it presupposes.

There remain many unanswered questions—all of them interesting: What ceremonies ought not be permissible at the CMC? Aside from non-sacred opening ceremonies, folk and ethnic festivals, and powwows, what about weddings, child-namings, and funerals or even evangelistic meetings? Who decides, and on what basis—practical or ideological?[63]

Is consultation with Indian bands and ethnic groups enough? How can we ensure the hiring of non-Anglophones and non-Whites in directors' positions so that nonmajority people are not merely the objects of display but its agents?

If a museum functions as a ritual center of some sort, what is the shape of its implied cosmology? What else besides the quasi-religion of pluralism is part of the package? What are the differences between museum rites and, say, Voodoo bars in Port-au-Prince and tourist trance in Africa? Have we any right to assume that temple, church, and synagogue rites are better than these? In short, what counts as ritual authenticity or ritual failure?

We consultants saw two performances during the conference. In one a Native director introduced us to "The Rez Sisters," lotteries on reservations and off, rape by screwdriver, and other deeply painful tragicomedies. In another a White performer led members of the consultation in an allegorical, slapstick lottery in which the winner got to smash a glass display case with an ax in order to free the skull (fake, of course) imprisoned in it. The "winner" was a Native woman who protested that she did not want to be the executioner. She was shy about breaking the glass, clearly an iconoclastic act, but she finally yielded to peer pressure and slapstick badgering. After three tries, the glass barrier shattered. We were supposed to be jubilant, because in our various ways we were all supposed to want to free dead artifacts from their glass cages so they could live and thus shape our sense of Canada's multicultural heritage. But I still wonder if anyone else is haunted by the feeling that a violation, a metaphoric "rape" of some sort, had occurred unwittingly in this second play. Whose job is it, anyway, to break the glass barrier? And whose ritual heritage is it that requires such iconoclastic hyperboles in order to right historic wrongs? If in some instances we Whites have violated sacred objects and human remains by hedging them about with glass barriers, do we escape or do we perpetuate desecration by smashing them?[64]

4

RITUAL CRITICISM OF A

MODERNIZED MYSTERY PLAY*

The difference between animal ritual and human ritual is that animals are always performing what they are, while humans almost always perform what they are not.
—Richard Schechner (1981b:7)

On May 25–26, 1985, the Towneley Cycle of Mystery Plays was performed in Toronto by twenty-six groups from Canada and the United States. The cycle consisted of twenty-seven plays dramatizing the full sweep of the Bible story from creation to judgment. The stated aim was to present them as nearly as possible in the manner that they might have been performed in 1475 in England's West Riding of Yorkshire.

Having been asked to observe and to respond to the plays from the point of view of ritual studies, a discipline still very much in a fledgling state, my immediate problem was how to view the plays. Medieval scholars, most of them employing literary-critical and historical methods, were also participating in the event as respondents. So questions arose prior to attendance upon the plays: What is "a ritual studies point of view?" Is there anything distinctive about it? Is there only one viewpoint? What ought a ritologist notice that literary critics and performance critics do not?

Prior to the performances it was easier to say what a ritological approach ought not attempt. It ought not be primarily concerned with making judg-

---

*This chapter is based on study of the text of the Towneley Cycle of Mystery Plays and, more significantly, on participant-observation of the cycle sponsored by the Poculi Ludique Societas (Drinking and Playing Society). The society's artistic director and administrator, David Parry, produced the modernized text, on the basis of which Garrett Epp directed the production. Since the event was confined to a weekend, so was the period of observation. However, interviews with the artistic director and selected performers preceded and followed the production.

The field study and consultation were conducted at the request of members of the Modern Language Association who were planning a panel on the cycle at their annual meeting (Chicago, 1985), at which a summary of this chapter was presented. Part of the chapter, reprinted with the permission of the Canadian Corporation for Studies in Religion, was published in 1988 as "Ritual in the Toronto Towneley Cycle of Mystery Plays" in *Studies in Religion* 16(4):473–480.

ments about the aesthetic and dramatic qualities of the plays; it is not theater criticism. And it ought not be preoccupied with the literary-historical questions, Do the performances adequately reflect the medieval texts? or, What do the contemporary performances teach us about reading these medieval texts? At the very least a ritological approach should describe the whole event, which extends beyond the plays themselves to the cultural occasion and social circumstances in which they were embedded. Such a description ought to make explicit the worldviews projected by this event. And it should try to infer the genres of action implied by the events observed without assuming that there is anything permanent or normative about a genre and with an expectation that what we call rites often represent the bleeding or melting of several other genres. By explicating worldview and genre, a critical perspective should emerge that allows us to see the conflicting interests negotiated by the production.

FRAMING AND WORLDVIEW

Clifford Geertz (1973:113) theorizes that "any religious ritual, no matter how apparently automatic or conventional involves [a] symbolic fusion of ethos and world view." Ethos consists of a people's moral and aesthetic attitudes (89); worldview, of its cognitive and existential ones. In performative circumstances worldview and ethos are strongly fused, though not identical, because, after all, actors can perform aesthetically what they are not existentially.

Performances, like texts, construct "worlds." A performance creates a microcosm in gestural and concrete form. The temporary cosmos generated by a rite or a play is a way of condensing the plural realities of a people. Cultural performances can unify what threatens to break apart as well as pluralize what threatens to become too solidly entrenched. The Toronto Towneley cycle is best understood as a temporary "heterocosm," because in many respects the values within the plays were other than those of the actors and audience. The relations between the performed world and the real world were dissonant; multiple realities were negotiated. They did not mirror one another; the actors performed what they were not.

It is all too easy when interpreting a performance to fall into the unquestioned assumption that a performance "expresses" in some simple, mimetic fashion the values and worldview of the participants. But performances not only mirror social structures and cultural values, they also transform them. So an interpreter cannot assume that the dramatic world *in* a performance is identical with the social world *around* that performance. Therefore, when examining the world *of* the Toronto Towneley plays, we must consider both worlds, the one in it and the one around it. In addition, both of these worlds are plural; each is at once medieval and modern. Diagrammatically, the situation looks like this:

4.1. **Worlds of the Toronto Towneley Cycle[65]**

The medieval world in the Towneley	The contemporary world in the Towneley
The medieval world around the Towneley	The contemporary world around the Towneley

How does one get hold of such a plural world in order to examine it? Cultural performances of any kind, particularly those with ritual qualities, are especially dense with symbols that help establish the tone, character, and quality of people's lives and undergird their most comprehensive ideas and images of order. The most reliable indicators of a worldview are those symbols most taken for granted. Even though they lie on the "surface" of a culture, we often speak of them as "deep" structures, because their very pervasiveness makes them almost invisible or unconscious to participants, though they may seem obvious to others. These dimensions of a performance are more likely to be by-products, not the outcome, of explicit aims in the minds of its organizers and proponents, but this does not make them any less effective. Symbols of space, time, and identity are among those most fundamental to performative world construction.

Erving Goffman (1974) developed a method he called "frame analysis." Put simply, frame analysis is an examination of the ways people define social situations. For example, if a woman takes an old shoe and puts a wooden frame around it, she will be interpreted as trying to convince viewers to define the shoe as "art." If she puts that same old shoe in a five-gallon drum and deposits it in front of her house, she is inviting the sanitation man to define the shoe as "garbage."

The largest, or most inclusive, frame is that of a worldview. And the most important frames are not wooden ones but metaphoric ones, because from these we build up perceptions of reality and construct worlds. Frame analysis is the study of boundaries, boundary conditions, and boundary crossings. What it requires of fieldworkers is a rhythm, either physical or conceptual, of moving in and out of some cultural domain—in this instance a performing space—while noticing both in themselves and in others what transpires. The point is to discover the "boundaries" or "defini- tions" by which experience is being organized. Perhaps the point is not strained too far if we imagine that frames are to ritual criticism what genres are to literary theory; they determine the bounds within which ones plays. Like genres, frames are not eternal; they change through time and overlap. It requires a high degree of self-consciousness to become aware of them, because they encode the meta-commentary of a performance. Frames are, almost by definition, those aspects of a performance that are most perva- sive, therefore least visible to insiders and most visible but opaque to outsiders. To study them one has to assume and cultivate the posture of an outsider—to see with an uninitiated eye.

Time, space, and identity are key components of any framing that is on the worldview, or cosmological, scale (see Kearney 1984:chaps. 3,5). There are several ways to answer the question, When did the Towneley plays take place? Among the answers are: circa 1475; May 25–26, 1985; on a weekend; at the end of school; on the sabbath; *Anno Domini*; in the postmodern era; during the day; springtime, and so on. The temporal framing of the event was multiple, a typical feature of much ritual and drama. Not only did official publicity say the cycle would be performed "as it might have been performed in the West Riding of Yorkshire in the year 1475," audience members themselves actively cultivated this definition of the situation. A typical remark was, "I forgot where we were. I felt what it was like to be a medieval peasant."

Temporal and spatial categories are among people's most constitutive frameworks and, if they alter their sense of time or space, they alter their worlds. Of course, neither audience nor performers thought they had liter- ally shifted worlds. Rather they participated in a temporary, subjunctively framed sub-world. The smaller one, 1475, was contained in a larger one, 1985; the latter remained the primary (or "real") frame. Some participants spoke of the play as "timeless," but it seems better to regard it as "timeful"—full of its times, both 1475 and 1985.

Director and actor David Parry spoke of his version of the Middle English Towneley text as a "modernization." But he preserved as much of the rhyme and rhythm as he could, and sets, costumes, and gestures all indicated that the aim was to minimize, not maximize, the modernity of the performance. Modernization of language served the overriding intention to restore, re-create, and preserve a medieval sense of the performance. The organizers and scholars held "faithfulness to the text" as a primary value. Nevertheless, the audience took particular delight in rare occasions when actors slipped modern place and street names ("Montreal" and "Spadina") into their lines.

Another bit of modernization was evident in an interpretation of the play. Some academics, including more conservative ones, singled out Cain (from "The Killing of Abel") as a kind of lens through which to view the whole cycle. One might account for this choice by referring either to the obvious high quality of the performance or to the fact that Parry himself played Cain. But its modern, existentialist tenor was also a crucial factor for making it the key play in some viewers' estimations. The audience did not seem to agree with Elanor Prosser (1961:82–86), who regards the Cain of the medieval text as "an over-grown gargoyle who almost totally obscures the cathedral, the religious purpose." Or, if the audience did agree, it did not care.

Other time frames were also evident. May is spring, end-of-school-time, rebirth-renewal time. For whatever practical reasons the date may have been set, the symbolic dimensions of the season were not ignored; they were pervasive. There were Morris and Maypole dances during breaks with frequent references to fertility, rain, and new life. May weather, besides having practical consequences (e.g., rain), played an important role in Toronto cycle lore, a point on which I shall elaborate later.

Setting the plays on a weekend framed the two days as "time off," not work time. And having the play end on Sunday no doubt helped define the the resurrection and the judgment as religious events, particularly for church groups that had furnished players.

People often commented on the length of the plays (about fourteen performing hours) largely to express their weariness. But the collective exertion was crucial to generating the obvious sense of communitas that had developed by Sunday evening and to allowing the images to bypass conscious defenses of either the secularized or pious sort. Ritual images often require repetition to be absorbed, and the Towneley text is replete with outright repetitions as well as modulations of themes and images. Hence it was easy to leave the performing space for a while and return without having to worry that something essential would be missed. Like that other form of popular drama, soap opera, these mystery plays provided concise, retrospective summaries that allowed latecomers to catch up. Taking periodic times-out is part of the genre.

Some participants were quite aware of the complexities of temporal framing, so I am saying little that is new to them. However, audience members (though probably not production staff) were less aware of the spatial framing, probably because the ethos surrounding the play was generally historical, not geographical, in orientation. Officially, the plays were advertised as occurring in the University of Toronto, Victoria College Quadrangle. This definition implies that what transpired elsewhere, say, in restaurants and hotels, was defined as out-of-bounds. Consequently, cameras were capped and recorders off in these areas.

Having initially defined the Toronto Towneley cycle as an "event" that included plays but was not exhausted by them, it was necessary to include participants' frames within mine. When, for example, other photographers moved closer to cut out the Park Plaza Hotel sign from their pictures of Jesus on the cross, I moved back to be able to include the Park Plaza sign, as well as the media people and buffs with their cameras.

Other people probably knew about—but likely did not reflect upon—buildings outside the quadrangle. Beyond it are the Royal Ontario Museum, the Ontario Parliament, and Queen's Park government offices such as the Mowat and MacDonald blocks. The plays were situated in one of the densest concentrations of governmental, educational, and economic power in Ontario, if not Canada.

Immediately surrounding the six playing scaffolds were the neo-Gothic and Victorian revival buildings of Victoria University, the first degree-granting institution in Upper Canada (now Ontario). Dominating its large commons room is the flag that covered Queen Victoria's coffin—an apt symbol of the royalist tenor of the architecture and geography. The site is replete with architectural and spatial symbols of established, generally conservative, religious, educational, and political power.

It is important to notice where the celebration did not happen. The plays were not performed in England or the United States, not in a working-class section of the city, not on a small town college campus, and not in a churchyard. This selection of a playing space contributes to the generation of a distinctive ethos that one might label, with only slight exaggeration, as "Upper Canadian" or "Anglican Tory." A less exaggerated way to characterize it would be as an example of upper-middle-class biculturalism, a point to which I shall return.

Because the quadrangle was so fully utilized by the performance, one could not hope to uncover all the tacit, proxemic[66] messages implied by its use but only to call attention to a few examples. Internal to the quadrangle were six performing spaces: heaven, hell, a hill, a palace, a temple, and an undefined scaffold. Some of the places underwent dramatic redefinition. The hill, for example, was Eden, then Moriah (where Abraham takes Isaac), and finally Golgotha (where Jesus is crucified). The locations for heaven and hell, however, did not change their definitions. Heaven was the only location that utilized existing architecture. The spatial world *around* the play was mostly bracketed out, but there were strategic inclusions in which the boundaries between the world-within and the world-around bled into each other. Significantly, heaven was constructed to include the large, imposing administration building of the university. One might ask what difference it made to students' definitions of the administration building to see it identified with heaven rather than the palace or hell.

The quadrangle tended to contain the sound and energy of the crowd and probably contributed by its location to a sense of the event's importance and by its size to a sense of community. Symbolically, it became a center of convergence, which was suggested by the posting of a fake road sign built of wooden arrows pointing to the home towns of participating groups: "Hamilton: 43 km., Boulder: 2200 km.," and so forth.

In ordinary proscenium drama, space defined as "offstage" is beyond the curtains—in the wings but not in the place where the audience sits. Offstage in the Towneley plays meant something different. After their performances characters were often found, still in costume, among the audience watching the other plays. Since costume still conveyed the aura of a character, even when an actor was out of character, one effect was to raise identity questions. Is that Pilate standing next to that elderly gentleman? The gentleman looks at him with disdain even though the actor is offstage and not in character. Is this offstage Judas my "neighbor," whom I am supposed to love? Standing next to Moses, now offstage but in the audience, should that lady take off her shoes? For many of the participants, watching performances alongside nonperforming but costumed actors heightened the sense of participation in a cosmic drama and the feeling that the event was a ritual of some sort.

One feature in the framing of identity was having characters played by more than one actor. There were several Gods, Jesuses, Herods, and Marys. Modern social attitudes were reflected more in casting decisions than in the lines of the text. For instance, there were no female Gods even though Satan, another mythological character, and one of the archangels were played by women. All the Jesuses, except the one who, at age twelve, debates with the doctors, were male and of predictable body type. There were no obese Jesuses or Marys, but there were obese demons. Demons were often costumed with exaggerated genitals, played in drag, or made bisexual—all of which contrasted with the asexuality of the "good" characters.

The effect of multiple Gods and Jesuses was to open up the audience's imagination and perhaps its understanding of the biblical canon, but this effect was counteracted by selecting actors who fitted established types. So, in general, identity framing and role definition supported the culture's existing racial and gender types—no female Gods, no asexual demons, no sexed Jesuses—a striking fact when we remember that the performers came from twenty-six groups across North America.

The identities of many characters were conveyed in opening speeches that put into the mouths of these characters evaluations and attitudes appropriate to other characters or later times. For instance, God often praised himself and Judas condemned himself—both acts more appropriate to Christians than to the characters themselves. The audience was impatient with this sort of homiletical anachronism but not with anachronistic objects (e.g., Eve's pearl ring) or anachronistic place names.

The most evidence of active social criticism in the performance was probably the handling of "the wicked Jews." The Towneley text, particularly the three postresurrection plays, is rife with anti-Semitism. The modernized script made "wicked men" rather than "wicked Jews" the object of repeated condemnation. This decision was echoed by playing corrupt religious authorities in Christian rather than Jewish vestments.

Misogynistic passages, however, were left intact, I was told, on the assumption that the audience would recognize and reject them. Women booed and hissed at Adam for blaming Eve, at Noah for his crass generalizations about women, and at Joseph for his views on how to take a wife. But one has to wonder if leaving sexist passages intact really indicates that we are so far beyond sexism that laughing at it is a better sign of our liberation than flatly rejecting it. Anti-Semitic remarks were deleted because the audience would not have tolerated them. The *motive* for leaving the sexist ones was probably to enhance historical authenticity. But their *function* was probably to allow people to substitute amusement for rejection.

SENSORIUM ORGANIZATION

Any culturally constructed world, especially one enacted by ritual or performed in drama, does so by invoking and reorganizing sensory data. Walter Ong (1962:6) says that different cultures attend to the senses in differing ways. A culture's distinctive way of organizing sensory data he calls a "sensorium." Organizing the senses, like framing the world, is something we usually do rather than something we think about. Ordinarily, sensorium organizing and world-framing are what we are conscious *with*, not what we are conscious *of*. So we can learn a great deal about the Toronto Towneley cycle by examining examples of the ways it organized the senses by employing various media.

Visual data are closely connected to the spatial frames already discussed; and they are useful in helping get what we call metaphorically "perspective" on the cycle. The quadrangle lent itself to dramatic figure-ground reversals. God loomed and boomed, drawing attention to himself with gold masks and tin thunder, only to be forgotten as the action shifted to another stage. But every now and then audience members sneaked glimpses back at God, across the quadrangle, sitting there, staring out into space or across a great distance at the play. The fact that spectators could see one place through, or from, another (for instance, Calvary's hill through the structure of the palace) meant that they were led spatially into metaphor, just as they were led temporally into typology (by, for example, seeing the "tree" of crucifixion at the same place as the tree of temptation). In addition, being able to stand at the sides of performing scaffolds and see characters both on stage and backstage emphasized the humanity of the players (like us, they wanted to know how they did) and the fictionality, or constructedness, of the action. This visual perspective allowed people to witness mystery making actions one minute and demystifying ones the next. Simultaneous mystery-making and demystification did not encourage naïve belief but what we might call "second naïveté" (Ricoeur 1967) or "make-belief" (Neale 1969).

Evaluations of performances ("I loved that Mary, didn't you?") were often a function of visual and auditory distance. Audience members said they felt one way when they were so close to the action that swords flew over their heads and sweat dropped on them, another when standing on a chair to see, across several hundred umbrellas, Joseph ranting about Mary's infidelity. To a large extent viewers could choose their perspectives, and they chose them according to their "perspectives," that is, their own values and interpretive predispositions. A number of adults moved closer to children in order to see, as it were, through their eyes. Some pursued the opposite strategy to avoid the running commentary of child-babble. The positions of viewers' bodies literally and fundamentally determined and expressed their interpretations of the play.

Whatever else it was, the Toronto Towneley cycle was a media event. People (mostly men) with equipment were allowed easy access to the front, and they were treated as "culturally invisible" (like Bunraku puppeteers who appear hooded in black and are ignored by Japanese viewers). Jesus on the *via crucis* had a host of cameras in his face, and most seemed to feel this was no sacrilege. One of my most interesting photographs is of a photographer who boldly approached the sweating Jesus on his way to Golgotha, snapped a picture, then fell to one knee, wept, and clapped his hand over his mouth in awe.

Even though media equipment may provide a way of remembering and re-presenting an event, it can also distance the person operating the equipment. But apparently such equipment is becoming part of modern religiosity, not merely functioning as a deterrent to it. As Schechner (1981:12) has put it, ". . . Media create action." One wonders whether the photos, slides, and tapes that eventuated from the performance would be shown more than once or twice. No doubt, in many instances the act of photographing is more significant than the pictures themselves. Photographing is a way of classifying the event alongside birthdays, holidays, and other times-out. Photographing, like applause, is an ambiguous gesture. On the one hand, it elevates an amateur play to newsworthiness. On the other, it demeans the cosmic to a mere news event. Not photographing and not applauding might have been the appropriate gesture of homage had the audience classified mystery plays in the same category as worship.

Apparently, the audience came expecting an event more worth recording visually than aurally. The large number of cameras outnumbered a small number of tape recorders. This visual attentiveness may have been because people assumed they could buy a copy of the text if they desired and also because in our culture the visual sensorium captures the "real" event.

The same large but enclosed space that allowed for dramatic vistas and metaphoric peering through sets at actions occurring elsewhere created auditory problems. Anger and ranting, particularly of male voices, were more audible than intimate scenes played by women. This fact may have unintentionally amplified the misogyny of the text.

After a few hours audience members were incapable of focalized, Western-style attention, so it became diffuse. As a result, rhythm and rhyme took over, and the language began to function more as music than as rhetoric, communication of information, or any of its other possibilities. Auditory data are more "circular" than visual data; sound surrounds. Aurally considered, there were two zones, close enough and too far back; other distinctions did not matter much. In contrast visual meanings changed drastically depending on where one stood. One could lounge, as it were, in the sound, but had to lean forward, peer, and twist this way and that in order to witness the dramatic interaction.

The Towneley plays, like other cycles, are especially effective in condensing the Bible into a single, oral narrative. Most participants were probably used to encountering only passages consisting of a few verses. Only Bible story books, read largely by children, present anything like an integrated, whole narrative. During the play, instead of hearing passages read to us from a focal point such as a lectern in a church, we were surrounded by the story. As the narrative theologians (see Goldberg 1982) have said, a myth is a story "big" enough to contain our "smaller," auto-biographical stories. This the Toronto Towneley cycle did quite literally. And it could hardly have been an accident that the production was discussed in a hall named after Northrop Frye, whose *Great Code* (1982) is a major exposition of the theory that the Bible is the single most important narrative and imaginative resource for the Western world. Both his book and the Toronto Towneley cycle emerged during a time in which it was evident how little this is the case. But perhaps this dissonance between ritual reality and social reality is part of what ritual is about. As Schechner (1981b:7) says in the epigraph that opens this chapter, "The difference between animal ritual and human ritual is that animals are always performing what they are, while humans almost always perform what they are not."

One spectator, a doctoral student in New Testament, said half jokingly, half seriously, that seeing the Towneley plays had changed her whole attitude toward the Bible. For many audience members this was probably the first time they had ever encountered the Bible rendered into a single story. For the most part worshipers hear only verses and short passages scattered throughout a long liturgical year.

The rhetorical and homiletical parts of the Towneley text were long and frequent, and it soon became evident that the audience, whose ear was not used to such, began to define the introductory, self-laudatory speeches as "preliminaries." This interpretation meant they could take their time focusing their attention or could allow it to drift until "the action" started. Actors often responded to audience indifference by intensifying volume and amplifying gestures.

Instrumental music was used to demarcate transitions and turn audience attention from one set to another; whereas choral music was employed to heighten the sense of sanctity, for example, at creation and judgment. And drumming, contrary to the "percussion and transition" hypothesis (Needham 1967), did not mark transitions but conveyed a sense of suspense or danger. Announcements and the like were noticeable because of their lack of rhyme. One exception was an announcement concerning the location of donation boxes. Besides evoking laughter, delivering the plea for support in medieval rhyme and rhetoric emphasized the urgency of the need.

Audience members clearly took well to being yelled at to get back or make a path as long as it was done so in a way that sounded like lines from the Towneley text; momentarily, they could be insiders.

Olfactory and gustatory elements in the Towneley cycle were limited.

Unlike Hispanic fiestas and Germanic Oktoberfests, in which eating good-
smelling food is essential to the genre, this event was for eye and ear more
than tongue and nose. When the shepherds on Christmas eve threw away
their chunks of bread, audience members scrambled for it as they would for
a baseball in a major-league playoff. Some clearly defined the bread as
"souvenir." At least one person appeared to be defining it as "communion." When Adam threw the apple into the audience, it was ignored, if not
deliberately avoided; it retained its poison even outside the officially defined playing area.

Smells were used in at least two instances. Sulphur (not formaldehyde)
poured out of Lazarus' tomb—in direct contrast to the ecclesiastical incense flung into the air at Jesus' resurrection. Even though visually and
conceptually the resuscitation and resurrection were typologically related,
the two odors were used to define them as distinct in value. The use of
sulphur with Lazarus did not so much define the events as having to do
with death—in fact, audience members said it reminded them of "skunk
juice"—as it defined the resuscitation as different from Jesus' resurrection.
He rose with a pleasant odor.

The kinesic sensorium alone would be worth an entire study, but doing
such research well would have required a filming team. Both ritual and
drama depend on overt action. Consequently, posture and gesture are ut-
terly essential to them. Gesturally considered, one of the most interesting
features of the Toronto Towneley cycle was its kinesic congruence. Ordinarily, this phrase refers to the way in which individuals who spend time
together begin to develop gestural styles distinctive to that group; one
begins to move "Christian" or move "upper class," for example. It is
striking that members of twenty-six groups that did not rehearse together
achieved such remarkable gestural consistency. Clearly, there was no way
to direct such consistency over the phone or by mail. Nevertheless, there
was a quasi-medieval style that became instantly recognizable: arms
spread, hands lifted to heaven, hands folded, and so forth. There are two
obvious ways to account for this congruence. One is that players watched
other players' performances or had seen other cycles or films of them.
Another is that some were imitating postures and gestures from iconic
sources such as paintings, stained-glass windows, and sculptures. There
are no mystery-play manuals of gesture that parallel, for example, the
gestural codes for classical Indian dance. So gesturing with a medieval
English accent is probably a hybrid: imitations of ecclesiastical practice,
some current kinesic Briticisms gleaned from film and personal acquain-
tances, clichés borrowed from *commedia dell'arte*, and a few techniques

picked up from liturgical drama circles. If one attended to the profane gestures performed at hell's mouth, they were mostly of the instantly recognizable, current street variety, not the classical ones catalogued by Desmond Morris and others.

A second kinesic feature, one that bears directly on spatial framing, had to do with seating and seating expectations among the audience. The requirement that we move to see the actors as they migrated from stage to stage undermined territoriality. But chairs were generally regarded as legitimate declarations that a space was taken. Such respect for private property was a clear indication that the audience was middle class. The assumption that such chairs belonged to the elderly was only partly true. The chairs seemed to belong to those with enough money, foresight, and willingness to be seen as "above" those seated on the grass.

Compared to a Hispanic fiesta audience in New Mexico, the University of Toronto audience, including the children, would have to be described as recessive, decorous, and appreciative but not very demonstrative. By its body language it asked to be played to. It did not—as one could expect of a Southern black Pentecostal congregation—attempt to cue the action or lead the actors.

CEREMONY, CELEBRATION, AND LITURGY

Genre definitions are one device that scholars use for framing academic worlds, so they parallel ritual symbols inasmuch as they determine what is noticed and assumed to be real. Sometimes criteria for determining genre are explicit; sometimes they are assumed, taken for granted as obvious or undebatable. On some occasions they are formal; on others, informal. At one of the symposia on the cycle of plays one of the elders thanked the performers for "this feast of academic entertainment." This is an informal genre definition. Although it represented a widely shared way of characterizing the event, it was not a formal specification of genre. More formal tags were theater, drama, mystery plays, and festival. These are not mutually exclusive, and there is no reason why an event cannot be considered a mixed genre. There was little debate over any of these labels, though medievalists do theorize about the differences and continuities among mystery, morality, and miracle plays. Rather than enter this debate, it would be more helpful to notice some of the other genre possibilities.

The event had ceremonial functions. The ceremonial elements in a rite are those processes that are concerned with negotiations of power between groups or that attempt to defend and extend a social ideology. Ceremony consists of the symbolic means by which a group maintains cohesion and establishes its own mystique. Ceremonially considered, the event served to consolidate the interests of at least three—probably more—kinds of social groups: academic, "Anglophile," and national.

The Toronto Towneley cycle was performed during the day. During the evenings the text and production were discussed publicly by scholars, production staff, and interested audience members. The presentations typically took one of two forms—either analyses of the text in its fifteenth-century setting or responses to aesthetic qualities of the production itself. Only a few comments were made about the entire event, and those were largely impressionistic and laudatory. There was very little general discussion about the politics of contemporary performance or the specific social issues and statuses being negotiated in Toronto, rather than Yorkshire.

In addition to the obvious architectural symbols of academic power that surrounded the performing space, there were other obvious ceremonial elements that deserve notice. For instance, the title page of the program was set up as follows:

4.2. **Title Page of the Toronto Towneley Program**

THE TOWNELEY CYCLE
In a New Modernization
by David Parry

Produced by *Poculi Ludique Societas* in association
with Victoria University and
Records of Early English Drama

THE PRESIDENTS' PLAYERS OF THE UNIVERSITY OF TORONTO

Innocuous as they may seem, the order, size of type, and placement are symbolic condensations of complex negotiations that lie backstage to the performances. Why the redundancy of "new modernization?" Are there, perhaps, other competing modernizations? Why is the modernizer's name, and not the director's, the only one to appear on the page? What is the significance of a group's having the patronage of the president of the university? Why "presidents'" rather than "president's?" Were several presidents involved? And if so, sequentially or simultaneously? And if simultaneously, how was such cooperation achieved? What kind of concord and/or discord obtains between the University of Toronto and Victoria University on the issue of medieval theater? Is their relationship one of equality or of sub- and super-ordination?

A longer, more sociologically inclined study would have to answer some of these questions. Presently, it is enough to raise them in order to illustrate the way that local politics are not irrelevant to the shape, direction, and fate of local performances, a fact that every theater person knows only too well.

One commonly heard university-affiliated persons refer to their trips to Toronto as a "pilgrimage" and to performing in the plays as an "initiation." But pilgrimage to where? And initiation into what? The answer some interviewees gave was this: pilgrimage to the seat of academic authority on medieval English drama, and, initiation into the public and popular aspects of its study. Participation served as a quasi-initiation rite for students interested in teaching English or medieval and renaissance studies.

The director, artistic director, and others in Poculi Ludique Societas circles were sometimes spoken of as "younger" (whether they actually were or not). The "elders" were professors, often specialists in the study of medieval dramatic texts. So, among other things, putting on the plays was a way of validating the more obscure, less popular work, of the textualists, as well as demonstrating the competence and imagination of the more performance oriented. Given these values, it is no accident that the modernizer of the text rather than the director, a graduate student, would be given top billing.

A particularly potent academic rite is "testing hypotheses." In this instance, hypothesis testing was as important to professors of English and medieval studies as it was to the excavators in chapter 3. Testing is a notion borrowed from the sciences but bearing heavily on the humanities despite its incongruence with many of the tenets of the humanities. Several authorities said that the performance was done in order to test the hypothesis that the Towneley text was not unified.[67] Conclusions differed on whether or not the performance had, in fact, revealed a unified text. And there was the expected wry comment that those who wanted to find unity found it.

This debate raises a more basic question: In the estimation of scholars (who are the "indigenous people" of this study), does the performance exist for the sake of the text or vice-versa? There was tension between older academics who assigned priority to texts and younger ones for whom performance was primary. One ceremonial function of the event was to produce symbols of mediation between these positions. This resulted in a more dialectical view: neither is primary, each needs the other. This view exercised the social function of holding together two generations of academics and ensuring the succession between those generations. As serious as the symposia were, there were nevertheless highly reflexive, ironic observations to the effect that such meetings constituted a second disputation with the doctors (the first being that with Jesus at twelve).

One could go on with this sort of analysis by recounting discussions about finances and internal power struggles, but there is little point in it, since the primary point is already made, namely, that performances and enactments embody factional interests—whether they emanate from ethnic groups, ecclesiastical institutions, or academic communities. Ritual criticism involves attending to the ways these interests are ceremonialized.[68]

After watching several children imitating English accents while playing roles they had just seen performed, it became necessary to attend to the ceremonialization of "Anglophile" interests. The density of English accents in the quadrangle and seminar rooms was much higher than is characteristic of the city of Toronto in general, which calls attention to the ethnic and class interests encoded in the event.

Had a formal sociological study been done, a profile of the typical audience member based on such observable features as dress, gestural codes, and accent might have suggested that the audience contained an unusually high proportion of people who were highly educated, middle- to upper-class, middle- to high-church in ritual preference, and Anglophile. "Anglophile" rather than "English" because the former includes people who teach English as well as people whose values are such that they still think of Ontario as "Upper Canada."

When I asked the artistic director of the Poculi Ludique Societas if he thought of the event as "English" in the same way there were Italian or Portuguese festivals in the city, he said emphatically not. He viewed this festival as more universal. But, of course, this is a view that a dominant or majority group can have of itself. Therefore, one might interpret his response as indicating intentions, whereas the question had to do with functions. And one of the functions of the Towneley festival was to consolidate Anglophile culture.

Since the Toronto Towneley cycle enacted what was once an instance of "popular" rather than "fine" art, a word is in order about class interests. The text was lowbrow but the audience highbrow. What are we to make of this? Peter Burke (1978:58–64) suggests that even though there were two cultures in early modern Europe, a popular and a noble one, some of the nobility were "bicultural." A similar social phenomenon occurred in Toronto. Only a few years ago medieval English drama was not considered "fine" enough to warrant widespread, serious study in many North American English departments; now it is crucial. A "high" culture, that is, one that has considerable education, wealth, and access to cultural resources, sometimes renews itself by reaching "downward." Burke insists that cultural forms are not only handed down (like an older brother's clothes) but they rise up as well. As performed, there was little that would be "popular" (in Burke's sense) in the eyes of a contemporary, working-class audience. The language was too archaic. And the piety was too laced with profanity and humor for an unsophisticated contemporary audience. This fact does not make the art of the production "fine" however. No one was bothered by roughness in the performance. In fact, the audience took delight in Adam's fig leaf, which would not stay up, and in the dog that joined Jesus on the hill as he was trying to ascend. Roughness and frame-breaking were interpreted as part of the genre, therefore both qualities were sometimes deliberately cultivated. But cultivated roughness is not, of course, the same as roughness that cannot be helped. The blue jeans of the poor are not the same as the new, pre-faded variety of the upper-middle-class.

In comparison to the academic and Anglophile interests, civic and national ones were less ceremonialized. The civic ones were least visible. There was no mayor's declaration such as one finds in public celebrations in Catholic Santa Fe. "Toronto" in the various publicity materials seemed to mean to most participants "University of Toronto" rather than "City of Toronto." If there is still room for debate whether the Towneley cycle was ever a civic drama in Yorkshire, there is little question about its lack of that function now. Rather, the university community itself functioned as a temporary *civitas* (Grimes 1976:chap. 3).

Some recognition was given to the fact that the event was Canadian, though this was low profile and indirect. Among the groups performing, eighteen were affiliated with Canadian institutions, and eight with U.S. ones; no groups from England performed. However, official responses to the production were billed as "British" and "North American," which says something about the nature of Canadian national self-consciousness in Ontario. Scholars spoke of themselves in international rather than local or national terms. But publicly paid compliments and other gestures of decorum clearly indicated that Canada, in addition to its familiar mediating role, was on this occasion playing a leading role. Some participants boasted that only in Canada, not in the United States or England, would such an event be likely to occur in the twentieth century.[69]

The decorous layer of a rite concerns face-to-face behavior. Erving Goffman (1967) calls such decorum "interaction ritual." Having already alluded to decorous concerns, for example, exchanges of scholarly courtesy and the treatment of chairs as private property, I shall note only two examples here. The first illustrates how decorous rites imply particular ways of framing space.

Patrons of the Poculi Ludique Societas, officially designated as such by the amount of their contributions, were seated on a special platform between the hill (joined by a walkway to heaven) and the palace. They were not placed, significantly, by hell. The location was obviously intended to be a place for privileged viewing, which it failed to be. Because it was higher than the crowd, the platform was most exposed to sun and blowing rain. Because it was not in the center, viewers from the platform were often, like God, so far removed from the action that they could not see or hear well despite their height. As Goffman might say, the frame was "broken." Once this became obvious, some patrons simply joined the crowd. Others, however, appeared to feel on display, as if they were obliged by virtue of their honorary office to remain where they could be seen. Under duress privilege was transformed into obligation.

A second illustration that shows how decorous and ceremonial ritual shade off into one another is that negative criticism of the production was noticeably softened. Ordinarily, drama criticism is overt, and in newspapers it has a reputation for being caustic. But on this occasion the public symposia put scholars on display, and they muted their criticisms. This public muting was clear by contrast. After the symposia, in small groups and parties the business of serious assessment began in earnest. The symposia were not scholarship pure and simple but scholarship performed, and performance of any sort requires that one not jeopardize the sense of teamwork while it is in progress.

Decorum is on the low end of the ritual scale; it is not highly differentiated.[70] On the high end is liturgy, the explicitly religious dimension of ritual. Some of the plays (e.g., *The Prophets* by Wilfrid Laurier University) were directed by religiously motivated artists, while others (e.g., *The Judgment* by Brock University) were more secular and theatrical in intent. The aesthetic decisions made by the director were flexible enough to accommodate both types, as well as serious and comical or parodied interpretations.

Several factors might lead interpreters to treat the event as only drama and not also ritual. One factor is that five hundred years separated the text from the performance. Another is that the performances were called "plays."[71] Another is that a "drinking and playing" society affiliated with a university (not a church) organized the event. Another was the use of applause as a gestural marker after performances, including the buffeting of Jesus. Another is that some of the Poculi Ludique Societas-sponsored plays have been performed at folk festivals alongside other forms of popular entertainment. The dramatic elements were undeniable; the ritual ones debatable, especially if one claims that some of the ritual sensibilities were celebratory in a religious sense.

Conventional wisdom has it that religion is believed, whereas drama is played. Our usual way of imagining society as consisting of clearly delineated "sectors" ("the private sector," "the business sector") might tempt one to classify the Toronto Towneley cycle in the same category with productions at the Stratford Festival Theatre or the St. Lawrence Centre. But to do so we would have to overlook some crucial points about the nature of religion. Religion is sometimes—perhaps often—played. Robert Neale (1969) has shown that faith is more akin to make-believe than to what we conventionally consider belief. It is not at all unusual to find instances of religious entertainment (e.g., the Hindu *Ramlila*) and religious games (e.g., sacred race-running among the Pueblos). So regarding the Toronto Towneley cycle as ritual celebration makes better sense than treating it as mere secular drama. The celebration contained mystery plays, a mixed medium sometimes referred to as "ritual drama." Imbedded within the ritual-drama were fragments of "liturgy" (rites that people use as paradigms of value ultimately).

Celebrations and festivals are typically marked by "inversions" (see Babcock 1978). A slogan circulating during the Towneley celebration was "Medieval Madness." The usual association with things medieval is not madness but hierarchy and order, but the slogan suggests that in our day, at least insofar as this celebration represents it, medieval images and ideals are marginal and therefore possibly subversive "possibly" because they were not so in Toronto. The inversions were safely contained by the space and decorum of participants. But it is not hard to imagine situations in which, or groups for which, the medieval juxtaposition of piety and profanity would be so "liminoid" (Turner 1974b) that they would threaten to subvert the structures that contain them.

Jonathan Z. Smith (1980:125) defines ritual as "a means of performing the way things ought to be in such a way that this ritualized perfection is recollected in the ordinary, uncontrolled, course of things." Although perfection was hardly being performed in the Toronto Towneley plays, it is easy to see that "medieval madness" is one thing contained and another thing outside its ritually established bounds. It is tempting to stand Smith's definition on its head and suggest that for the University of Toronto community the plays were a way of introducing a little chaos into a very controlled and ordered environment. This is what celebrative, as opposed to liturgical, rites do.[72]

One of the first cues for pursuing such a definition of the event was a bit of lore heard in several variations. To recount one version, one man said to a group of friends, "During the Chester cycle [Toronto, 1983] it rained all day. But when it came time for the Judgment, the rain stopped, the clouds parted, and the sun shone through. And I said, 'Where's a church? I am about to be converted!' [*laughter*]."

Similar stories were told about people deeply moved by playing the part of Mary or Jesus or about being found standing a few inches to the left of the dividing line when the judgment came. The celebrative consciousness is a fascinating one. Consider two examples. A child watching the crucifixion: "It's Okay, Mommy, it's not real." And one adolescent to another: "Jesus will get pneumonia in this rain." The child, demonstrably disturbed, was repeating to her mother what her mother had said to her. She "believed" but was trying hard not to. On the other hand, the adolescent did not believe, but the tone of his voice made clear his genuine concern, not just for the actor but for "Jesus." He was believing despite what he knew about the dramatic fictionality of the occasion. Perhaps an even better illustration of ludic belief, which accompanies celebrative ritual, was when one academic dared to say in front of two hundred others, "Piety and goodness have got to win, folks," and no one laughed or offered a rebuttal. An interesting comparison could be made between the Catholic parishes of chapter 2 and the Towneley audience. The former believe but do not remember the liturgy. The latter remember but do not believe the play. Is one of these attitudes any more authentic than the other?

At the Towneley cycle some viewers were just spectating, to be sure. And some probably believed, period. But most seemed to be playing with or at belief. They believed in a subjunctive mode. Ludic belief is not quite the same as aesthetic "appreciation," though it may include that. Nor is it the same as the belief one has during conventional worship services in churches. The attitude is typical of celebration rites but probably not of liturgical ones. "Celebration is social and metaphysical fiction. When we are in the midst of it, questions about the reality of its characters (gods, heroes, tutelary spirits, incarnations), along with questions about its continuation, authenticity, and origin are irrelevant" (Grimes 1982a:49).

Whereas liturgy is religious work, celebration is religious play. During liturgies people wear clerical vestments and their Sunday (or Sabbath) best; during celebrations, T-shirts sporting a drenched Noah's ark. Certainly not everyone at the Toronto Towneley cycle was playing religiously, but it was one of those rare occasions in our society when such is possible. Most of the time we are forced to make a choice between sacrality, profanity, and humor. Not so on this occasion.

5

RITUAL CRITICISM

OF EXPERIMENTS IN WORKSHOPS

AND CLASSROOMS*

. . . In modern man, [for whom] collective rites no longer exist and the problems relating to these transitions devolve upon the individual, his responsibility and understanding are so overburdened that psychic disorders are frequent. This is the case not only in childhood but also in puberty, in marriage and mid-life, at the climacteric, and in the hour of death. All these stages in life were formerly numinous points at which the collectivity intervened with its rites; today they are points of psychic illness and anxiety for the individual, whose awareness does not suffice to enable him to live his life.

Erich Neumann (1973:86)

Ritual is typically conceived and defined in such a way as to exclude rites self-consciously invented by individuals. Psychologists have treated private ritual as synonymous with neurosis. Theologians have regarded self-generated rites as lacking in moral character because they minimize social responsibility. And anthropologists have thought of ritual as traditional, collective representation, implying that the notion of individual or invented ritual was a contradiction in terms.

---

*The account of Jerzy Grotowski's paratheatrical phase is based on participant-observation of the Theater of Sources Project in 1980 and on written sources.

The account of Ken Feit is based on two summers of team-teaching with him and on repeated participant-observation of his performances and workshops between 1976 and 1980.

The discussion of Welfare State International is based on a week of participant-observation in 1981, subsequent interviews, and written sources.

Data concerning the ritual experiments of Victor Turner are from conversations with Victor and Edith Turner, as well as Richard Schechner, and from written materials on their collaboration.

The account of the Ritual Studies Lab is first-person, based on my experience as director of the lab from 1975 to the present.

Portions of this chapter were delivered as "Ritual Creativity," the Sibley Lecture of 1988 at Alfred University, Alfred, NY; others were presented as "Parashamanism and Performance" at a conference in 1977 on "Ritual and Performance" at the University of California, Santa Barbara.

Nevertheless, in recent years workshops have been the scene of an increasing number of self-consciously invented, individually practiced rites. These workshops have many of the features of scientific laboratories and artistic studios. Like labs they are places for experiment, trial and error, testing, and questioning. And like studios they are protected spaces set aside for creative exploration and the incubation of new forms. Some of them are marked by the ethos of popular psychology with its attendant focus on the self and interpersonal processes. A few ritual workshops occur in mainline institutions such as universities and theaters; some in alternative institutions (e.g., Mimesis Institute, Naropa Institute, Esalen Institute, the Foundation for Shamanic Studies); and many more, on what one might call "the workshop circuit," a loose network of individuals and small groups that meet for occasional short-term engagements with ritual. Virtually all of them are involved in either inventing or borrowing rites. They have various emphases. Some are feminist; some, anthropological; some dramatic; some quasi-religious; some psychological. They regard themselves as "new age" or countercultural.

The distinction between conventional and countercultural[73] attitudes is a relative, changing one. What is against the mainstream of culture today may be scooped up and carried along by that mainstream tomorrow. What seems alternative today may be conventional tomorrow. For this reason criticism is essential in countercultural contexts. Otherwise, how is one going to distinguish specious from authentic uses of ritual? How can one distinguish what is genuinely creative from what is exploitative and manipulative?

Two representative examples of countercultural interest in ritual are the essays in the collections *Betwixt and Between: Patterns of Masculine and Feminine Initiation* (Madhi et al. 1987) and *The Politics of Feminine Spirituality* (Spretnak 1982). In the vaguely Jungian orientation of the former and the strongly feminist stance of the latter are three recurring ideas used to explain the nature of ritual: self, experience, and creativity.

There are no scholarly treatments of ritual and the self, though the theme of selfhood is important in Western thought generally. The usual scholarly argument is that ritual has little or nothing to do with the self and everything to do with the group. The omission of any scholarly research on the matter might seem surprising given the proverbial individualism of North American culture. A number of factors have contributed to this situation. Among them are the Protestant suspicion of ritual, social conceptions of the self in the social sciences, corporate conceptions of the self in theology and ethics, and the psychoanalytic view of personal ritual as pathological. Even psychologists, whom one would expect to have the most interest in the impact of ritual on individuals, have left the topic almost untouched, except in the negative treatment by the psychoanalytic school. No one doubts that rites can contribute to the formation of personal identity, but most question whether individuals as such have any role in ritual.

Precisely the opposite is the case in the widespread experimentation with ritual that marks countercultural ritualizing. Here one meets the repeated expectation that ritual function as a self-enhancing, self-enriching activity capable of wedding the best of religion with best of therapy. Ritual is offered as a means of "working on oneself" that now rivals other methods such the introspective ones of medieval and Puritan spirituality, the talk-based therapies of the late nineteenth and early twentieth centuries, and the hands-on techniques of more recent times.[74]

No matter how narcissistic one may think countercultural spirituality is, it is challenging the studied refusal of academics to consider the power of ritual as a tool for exploring the self. As a result we are seeing the rise of an "anthropology of experience" (Turner and Bruner 1986), studies of the physiology of ritual activity, the emergence of theologies of play, and revisions of attitudes toward ritual within the Freudian ranks. All these trends indicate the permeation of the academic establishment by counter-cultural themes that take seriously the individual and bodily dimensions of ritual.

In North American popular culture the search for self through ritual is allied with what we might call "experientialism." Experimenting with ritual is an expression of a specifically North American ethos, one that posits experience as a primary value. For most of us the meaning of the word "experience" is so self-evident that it needs no definition. Experience is merely whatever we undergo or do: one has a heart attack and experiences pain; one goes to Europe and has a wonderful experience. We might assume that, since experience is universal, literally anything could be spoken of an object of experience. But this is not so. Outside counter-cultural circles ritual is seldom thought of in this way.

In ordinary usage "experience" suggests depth and inwardness, as well as something capable of accumulation. The connotation of depth appears in phrases like "religious experience," "sexual experience," or "experience of pain." We do not normally say we "experience" a flat tire. We say instead, "had" a flat tire. The connotation of accumulation arises when we speak of "work experience" or call someone a "man of experience." (Unfortunately, "woman of experience" does not connote the same thing.) Experience is supposed to be deep, and we should learn—even become wise—by having more of it.

Popularly, the term connotes something good to have. "Habit," on the other hand, has come to suggest something boring, if not evil. As a result, it is very difficult for us to imagine what "ritual experience" might be, since we usually associate ritual with dispirited routines. Experience, we suspect, is what we undergo only insofar as we can overcome habituation. Thus we come to assume that experience is to be had only outside ritual contexts.[75]

Along with self and experience, creativity is another theme arising from countercultural ritual contexts. In these circles not only is ritual a means of self-expression, it is the outcome of imaginative activity. No matter how traditional ritual may seem in mainstream circles, in countercultural circles tradition is but a repository to be mined for the purpose of creating new rites. Traditional liturgiologists and anthropologists shudder at the thought, but this does not prevent practitioners from approaching the data and texts of comparative religion and cross-cultural anthropology with a religio-aesthetic attitude that sees no contradiction between experimenting and devotion.

In polemical moments countercultural ritualists see ritual criticism as the enemy of ritual creativity: whereas the latter is a way of saying Yes to creation, the former is preoccupied with No-saying. But there is no *necessary* contradiction. Creation is not out of nothing. Even the God of Genesis does not create from nothing. Rather, all creativity is a matter of saying No to something in order to say Yes to something else. Creativity is a mode of selectivity. It is a way of reordering and thus reorienting. Criticism needs creativity and creativity, criticism. At least, philosophically this is so. Whether socially the creators and critics can stop pretending one is superior to the other is another question.

EXAMPLES OF COUNTERCULTURAL RITUALIZING

A recent flyer publicizes a week-long "vision quest experience" led by David and Karen Knudsen, an American couple. Claiming to follow the Lakota holy man, Black Elk,[76] they argue that vision questing should not be restricted to any one age range or, one assumes, any specific ethnic group. They take small groups to Windshift Island in Lake Temagami, Ontario, a site from which they can see Maple Mountain, "where ancient Ojibwa dream fasts have been practiced."[77] Before individuals engage in their private quests, they take a traditional sweat bath together, a ritual practice borrowed from the Lakota. Describing the conclusion of the quest, the publicity brochure tells us:

Everyone is returning, paddling in pairs. "What a difference in their faces," someone says. The nourishing solitude seems to show in their eyes. Is this the "inner light"? Some had gone without water, all had fasted, but didn't even mention it. Now is the time to reflect on the inside stories, as well as their meanings.

We have experienced a Vision Quest, a rite of passage. We modern day people have participated in one of the most ancient rites, valued by the traditions of the great religions, a real retreat. Our primitive ancestors knew what we have long forgotten—that at times of crisis and transition, whether it be entering adulthood, choosing a profession, marriage, death, divorce, mid-life, man needs a ritual that reconnects him with all of life.

Another example of ritual invention is that of Rites of Passage, Inc., run by Steven Foster and Meredith Little (1987) at the School of Lost Borders in Big Pine, California. For fifteen years they have led nearly a thousand young men and women, usually seniors in high school, through a two-month vision-quest course. It is followed by a three- to four-day trek in the wilderness in which each adolescent fasts alone in search of a vision. No mere weekend lark, the process involves each person's community, particularly friends and family. Foster and Little identify ten components of the process; these are traditional possibilities for symbols and actions:

5.1. Components of Initiation

1. Finding one's own place
2. Building a stone pile and forming a buddy system
3. Crossing the threshold
4. Fasting
5. Self-conferral of a medicine name
6. Listening with an intuitive ear for natural/supernatural guidance
7. Dreaming
8. Fire tending
9. Entering a "purpose circle" to attract power
10. Emerging: giving birth to oneself

The vision quest is followed by returning home and giving away part of what was received, for example, songs, words, or feelings. A feast follows. And two weeks later there is a reunion to discuss reintegration and direction problems.

One may have several reactions to these two versions of the vision-quest procedure. It is easy to blast them with accusations: "This stuff is just glorified Boy Scout behavior. It is cultural theft; the quest belongs to Native peoples. This is no real vision quest; it is self-deceived spiritual consumerism. It is outrageous to think you can 'incorporate' rites of passage." I am tempted by all these responses; each contains some truth. But some of the experiments are serious, sustained attempts at developing alternatives, and some are mindful of the possibilities for self-deception, cultural imperialism, and spiritual consumerism. It is too easy to indulge in the well-worn tactic of labeling and dismissing. Students of religion contribute nothing by tagging the phenomenon "pop culture" or applying the usual brands of sect-and-cult sociology. Any ritual criticism of it must take into account its cultural and social context.

In 1981 Anna and Lawrence Halprin conducted a series of community workshops called "A Search for Living Myths and Rituals through Dance and the Environment" (see Halprin 1989 and Schechner 1989). At the same time a series of brutal murders occurred on Mt. Tamalpais, near the San Francisco Bay area of California. The group decided to try cleansing the mountain ritually. They did so and the killer was captured a few days later. Not long afterward the Halprins' group was joined by José Matsuwa, a Huichol shaman, who said that the group must continue its purification rite for five years if they wanted it to be effective.

For their fifth year (April 6–14, 1985) the Halprins organized an event called "Circle the Mountain: A Dance in the Spirit of Peace" to be conducted on the mountain. The purpose of the ritual was to "find a dance that inspires us to keep the earth alive." To prepare for it, full-time participants paid $150 for a week-long workshop followed by a complex of events, including ritual running by a team from Deganwidah Quetzalcoatl University (a Native American educational institution) and a performance by a hundred dancers for a selected group of "witnesses." The time of the race was April 7, Easter Sunday, Buddha's birthday, and the day after Passover.

Anna Halprin, founder of the Dancers' Workshop, received the American Dance Guild award in 1980. She, along with Jerzy Grotowski of the Polish Theater Laboratory and Peter Schumann of Bread and Puppet Theater, have deeply influenced North American theater to move in a ritualized direction. "Circle the Mountain" contains a number of elements that characterize contemporary parashamanic experiments with ritual: (1) the presence of, or collaboration with, a Native shaman; (2) a concern with ecology and world peace; (3) religious pluralism and eclecticism; (4) an artistic or performative orientation; (5) a training period that is relatively short in comparison to those required in traditional initiation rites; and (6) the creation of an event marked by temporary communitas rather than ongoing social structures such as a church or a community.

In such a context religion, art, and performance are fused into a single cultural domain, which, because of its occasional nature, is often segregated from the ongoing routines of its participants. No matter what the organizers' intentions, ritual is typically experienced as a powerful but isolated and unintegrated force. Even though it aims at ecological and cosmic integration, its traditions are not those of the ambient culture, so it is short on social integration. The segregation of ritual is a major problem in all postmodern rites, not just "Circle the Mountain."

Jerzy Grotowski, director of the Polish Theater Laboratory, has been involved in events that seem at first to resemble the work of Anna Halprin (see Grimes 1982a:chaps. 10–11). His "paratheatrical" experiments, are known popularly, though obliquely, in North America through the film, "My Dinner with André." Grotowski's "Theater of Sources" in 1980 had little to do with theater and everything to do with ritual. There were no performances for witnesses, much less for paying audiences. However, like "Circle the Mountain," which received National Endowment for the Arts money, "Theater of Sources," despite its religious overtones, was supported in part by UNESCO. Religiously significant ritual in the postmodern world is no longer the sole purview of religious institutions.

Just as members of Sufi, Native American, and other communities participated in the Halprins' event, so Grotowski's involved Haitians, a group from India, and members of other "traditional" groups. Clearly, some ritual experiments utilize the resources of many cultures in order to generate an archaic, primal, or ritual atmosphere. Unlike the Halprins, Grotowski and his staff imposed a rule of silence so that all collective public attempts to rationalize or analyze actions would stop. Gesture or, on occasion, nonverbal sound became the sole means of communication and exploration. One was free to make running in the forest, whirling, crawling on the ground, holding onto trees, and other such activities as mystical or as ordinary as he or she pleased. No aims, such as finding a "dance that inspires us to keep the earth alive" (the Halprins' stated goal) were postulated. If there were goals at all, they were individual or tacit. The resulting atmosphere was one of being in solitude together. The "group grope" that often typifies North American workshopping was absent. The ethos was noticeably a-personal and unpsychological. Unlike the California event, the Polish one was low profile. Credentials were not published; there were no glossy publicity materials or printed descriptions of the order of events.[78]

Another, quite different example of parashamanism is that of the late Ken Feit, who gave "fool" as his occupation when asked at border crossings. He was probably the most widely known Christian fool, or clown, in North America. He may have been the only one actually to have made a steady living at it. Although he lived a life of poverty, owning little more than a change of pants, shirt, and underwear, he once confessed that he was no fool. He made, he said, $18,000 a year, bought children's books with a bit of it, and the rest he put away for retirement. "I no longer have the Order to look after me in my old age," he said, dreading the onslaught of forty.

Feit had been in training as a Jesuit, and when he dropped out in the mid–1960s, he decided to continue celebrating Mass but did so in white-face. His "Fool's Mass" was celebrated out of a paper bag containing a banana, scissors, thread, a paper unicorn, and a host of other tiny paraphernalia.

Feit was a wandering storyteller, ritualizer, and teacher who averaged 200,000 miles a year across several continents. Although he trained for a while with a circus company, he never thought of himself as a clown any more than he considered himself a Jesuit. Unmistakably marked by both traditions, his Christianity was as ragtag as his clowning was religious. He never hesitated to borrow stories, symbols, or objects except when he thought they lacked portability. Although he would "perform" his brown-bag communion for others, he refused to think of it as a mere performance. It was his ritual staple. It alone remained as he added and subtracted items from his repertoire. A typical workshop would include: learning to mime haiku poems, dancing part of an African initiation rite, telling stories around selected themes such as wind or eggs, and so on. He carried with him a single suitcase containing hundreds of tiny items for impromptu and scheduled performances such as a flea circus or making paper cut-outs. Packing and unpacking the suitcase was a deliberate and carefully executed rite, during which he seldom socialized. Aside from a few props such as a head scarf, which he used in his role as [Ms.] America in travail, his "ecclesiastical" robe consisted of a threadbare jacket covered with a bricolage of things people gave him and which he in turn gave away: a baby's pacifier, a broken watch, a piece of knotted rope, and a host of other indescribable items.

In his piecemeal way Feit trained or inspired hundreds, perhaps thousands, in ritual-making and storytelling skills. In comparison with the Halprins, Feit's experiments were smaller in scale. He worked with small groups and preferred traveling to establishing a center. The ethos of his workshops was earthy, not mystical. Although at times authoritarian, he hated hierarchy, including the hierarchy of ritual expertise, so he emphasized a do-it-yourself, borrow-it-from-where-you-can-get-it attitude, not just toward techniques but toward the sacred itself. The objects and gestures he sacralized were seldom central to other religious traditions but were more likely to be the castaways of our own society.

What Feit aimed for on a small scale, Welfare State International achieves on a large one: a good-natured but iconoclastic "magic." Although John Fox and other members of this collective of ritual artists are British, they, like Grotowski, have exercised considerable influence on North American ritual experimentation. Whereas the Halprins and Grotowski are serious about their parashamanism, Fox, like Feit, is playful and humorous about his. Drawing heavily on British mumming, puppetry, and traditions of the circus, fairground, and music hall, Welfare State designs both performances and rites that remind one of the paintings of Bosch and Breughel. Although they have done research on funerals, because of legal complications they have so far confined their "stage-managing" skills largely to child namings and weddings. Because of its love of incongruity, Welfare State's style might be described as that of "epic cartoon" or "civic magic." Using huge, primal puppets and brassy music, they regard themselves as ritual "plumbers." Like Feit they are intensely practical but have no sense of copyright or ownership concerning their techniques and art. They are the only group I know to have produced a good how-to-do-it book, *Engineers of the Imagination* (Coult and Kershaw 1983). There is nothing arty about their art; it is thoroughly left-wing and populist. Again like Feit, they search rubble for things to transform into ritual objects.

Nowhere does the shamanic model appear more deliberately and overtly than at the Center for Shamanic Studies founded by Michael Harner who did fieldwork among the Jivaro of the Upper Amazon forest. Later he began appropriating some of their techniques and teaching them to his students. And he plans to "reintroduce" his form of shamanism to "traditional" shamanic cultures that supposedly have lost the techniques. Now he has trademarked his technique. His experiments and techniques are recounted in *The Way of the Shaman: A Guide to Power and Healing* (1980). For example, you learn to "dance your animal," a way of luring and retaining a zoomorphically imagined guardian spirit. Harner writes, "I remember one young Westerner trained in shamanism who worked weekdays in a bookstore and on Sundays went to a regional park where he took his [guardian spirit] Cougar for lopes over the hills. No one ever stopped him, and he found it more satisfying than going to church" (68). At the center Harner teaches people to find their "power songs," shake rattles 180 times per minute, beat drums, paddle spirit canoes, and retrieve vital souls. Those who searched for Carlos Castaneda or Don Juan but found neither, often locate Michael Harner much more easily: he advertises in *Shaman's Drum*.

Whereas the rites of Ken Feit and Welfare State International are invented, pasted together from the remains of a spendthrift culture, and those of Grotowski and the Halprins are constructed to seem as if they emerge from a mysterious depth "below" culture, those of Harner and Starhawk (1979) appear to be "imported." Starhawk, like Harner, draws on traditions that are not of the "Great" sort that figure so heavily in typologies of "Eastern" and "Western" religions. Harner borrows from the Jivaro, a group hardly known except to anthropologists, and Starhawk depends on what she calls the "faery" tradition of witchcraft. Although the activities of Starhawk's covens may fall outside the topic of ritual experiment and belong instead in the arena of competing sects, I think it crucial to mention two examples, one that North Americans generally fear and one that is conservative, almost mainline.

In *The Spiral Dance* (1979) and other works, Starhawk (Miriam Simos), a minister of the Covenant of the Goddess and founder of two covens, provides an introduction to witchcraft as a viable contemporary form of goddess religion. She describes the role of Compost Coven thus:

> The coven is a Witch's support group, consciousness-raising group, psychic study center, clergy-training program, College of Mysteries, surrogate clan, and religious congregation all rolled into one. In a strong coven, the bond is, by tradition, "closer than family": a sharing of spirits, emotions, imaginations. "Perfect love and perfect trust" is the goal [Starhawk 1979:35].

This version of witchcraft ritual is quite different from the dark, melodramatic rites of Anton LaVey's (1972) satanism. Like Harner's book, Starhawk's volume is a ritual manual. Even though Starhawk leads a coven, the manual clearly presupposes the possibility of solitary individuals privately engaging in the nature religion she advocates. The rites, which she sometimes describes and at others prescribes, clearly show the influence of the human potential movement and popular psychology. She insists that the 'Craft depends on a poetics rather than a theology; it emphasizes what she calls "starlight vision" (i.e., right-brained orientation) and relies heavily on guided imagery and the deliberate cultivation of interior imagery. Some of the practices for which she offers guidelines are sensing auras, inducing trances, consecrating tools, purification, banishment, moon meditations, and various spells such as attracting a lover or "becoming friends with your womb."

Starhawk is a respected feminist practitioner of witchcraft and a writer mentioned frequently in religious studies, particularly by feminist theologians. She is in dialogue with Christian, Jewish, and secular theologians and is presently on the staff of the Center for Creation-Centered Spirituality founded by Matthew Fox.[79]

Since I am male, white, and a professor, it would be easy to land in the same spot while discussing her feminist rites as the two critics did while assessing Native performances in Peterborough (see chap. 1). On the one hand, I can be blamed if I criticize what I have not participated in or, on the other, accused of patronizing if I do not treat the rites as worthy of critical attention. So I propose that a better beginning point in such cases is to take note of, and describe, the criticism implicit in the group itself.

In *Spiral Dance* ritual criticism is expected to serve ritual creativity. Having found no coven that suited her, Starhawk founded one of her own. The exercises she developed were an eclectically gathered patchwork of psychological exercises, artist-training techniques, traditional practices inherited from her teacher, and collective inventions of the group. No matter how much she emphasizes the "starlight vision" of 'Craft practice, the group process itself clearly includes discrimination, judgment, rejection, and selection. An emic criticism is at work. Not only is the very existence of coven ritual an implicit criticism of existing ritual options, but the prolific nature of its ritual experiments are such that the group must reject much more than it can keep of all the options it tries out. Criticism occurs on at least three levels: the social and religious critique implied by the group's continuing practice; the ongoing criticism within the group that enables it to choose this and reject that; and public criticism by observers of the rites and readers of the manual in which they are described.[80]

For the last twenty years or so feminism has been a consistent source of ritual creativity; it provides an ongoing context for ritual experiment unparalleled in any other sector of North American society. This phenomenon is regularly and, I think, wrongly ignored by most theorists of ritual. Some of the more important writings about ritual among women are gathered by Charlene Spretnak in her anthology, *The Politics of Women's Spirituality* (1982). For instance, E. M. Broner's article in this collection offers a brief description of a women's Passover first celebrated in 1976. Broner is Jewish and many of the rites she is involved in designing are attempts to de-patriarchalize Jewish practices. She and others have been instrumental in constructing rites for international gatherings in which women, for example, Jewish and Arab women, attempt by virtue of gender-solidarity to transcend what they take to be male warmongering. The fictive rites in her novels are marked by the same interweaving of poetry and ritual, Judaism and feminism, that characterizes the actual rites in which she participates.[81]

Kay Turner (in Spretnak 1982:221) argues:

> Generally, men have held the rights to ritual use; in fact, the participation in ritual by men has been their most profound display of cultural authority and their most direct access to it. The performance of ritual in most societies, "primitive" and "civilized," is a simultaneous acknowledgement of men's warrant to create and define culture and, by exclusion, a sign to women to keep in their place, a place which we have already designated as outside culture and without the symbolic or real attributes of power.

The sacred/profane distinction, so crucial to both anthropology and religious studies, has, Turner insists, served the vested interests of men. Until recently women have been forced to live in a largely profane world, while men have had open access to the world of the sacred. Among many feminists rites now have a privileged place as a—sometimes *the*—primary mode of claiming power to invent, control, and interpret the symbolic resources of their traditions and cultures. Turner (Spretnak 1982:226) suggests that ritual is the basic means of celebrating the validity of feeling as a mode of revelation, communication, and transvaluation.

Three recurrent questions among feminist ritualists are (1) how authority should be constituted, (2) to what extent hierarchy can be transcended, and (3) how individual interests can be balanced with communal ones. These are perennial questions, especially in counterculturally oriented groups. Though they are not restricted to ritual, the issues clearly bear on the sociology and politics of ritual criticism and construction. Claims to have overcome authoritarianism, hierarchy, and individualism are severely tested when a group undergoes a transition between generations and is faced with the problem of transmitting ritual lore and knowledge. Self-conscious feminists preoccupied with ritual experiment and struggling to find new answers to these questions are currently undergoing this test.

One could go on describing ritual experiments conducted in the interstices among artistic, educational, religious, and therapeutic institutions, but perhaps these examples are sufficient to suggest the outlines of an emergent ritual sensibility. Many of the groups will be dead in ten years; much of what they do is riddled with faddishness, self-deception, pretension, and general lack of perspective. Nevertheless, some of the experimentation is conducted with great integrity, at considerable risk, and with a great deal of promise. But how shall we conceptualize the staggering diversity of countercultural ritualizing?

PARASHAMANISM AND RITUAL

In an earlier work (Grimes 1982a:chap. 15) I introduced the idea of parashamanism, a way of identifying the religiosity of countercultural movements. Parashamanism is not popular in the sense that it is typical of mass culture; it is not a majority religion. But neither does it follow the usual configurations of sects and cults. It is much more tentative, exploratory, and experimental, and it seldom fosters the same kind of leadership dynamics as the so-called "personality cults." Seldom does parashamanism eventuate in lasting groups. And the conference-table model of the respectable interreligious discussions (e.g., Christian-Buddhist dialogue, Jewish-Christian dialogue) does not apply. The aim of these inventing, borrowing ritualists is not empathetic theological discussion, and they do not function as representatives of longstanding traditions. Instead they aim to reinvent tradition. That the traditions they reinvent may never have existed to start with may not make much difference.

Whether one considers the popular or the professional versions of this phenomenon, and whether one calls it parashamanism, paratheater, or pararitual, three interlocked themes recur: ritual, performance, and healing. An often expressed aim is to unify these manifestations and thereby transcend their division into ecclesiastical, theatrical, and medical institutions.

The most distinctive characteristic of parashamanism is its penchant for inventing, borrowing, and performing ritual in search of healing, which is understood holistically or ecologically to be a state of integrated selfhood. Parashamanism is not the same as shamanism, but without an understanding of the latter, the former makes little sense. The idea of shamanism is itself a scholarly construct, and there are debates about whether it is a useful one. The literature on shamanism is immense, so I will not attempt to review it here.[82]

Originally a Tungus term from the Siberian Arctic, the term "shaman" has been used by Eliade and others to denote a technique of ecstasy in which shamans enter a trance, leave their bodies, and ascend or descend to a region of the spirit. The technique is part of a widespread, cross-cultural pattern. Some of its most commonly recurring features, compared with those of parashamanism, are as follows:

5.2. Comparison of Shamanism and Parashamanism

Shamanism	Parashamanism
1. A revelatory call, usually in the form of illness	1. Call by self-selection
2. A visionary experience of descent, death, dismemberment	2. Workshop experience of togetherness
3. Replacement of bones or organs with special ones	3. Special reverence for the body, coupled with social alienation
4. Helper spirits or animals derived from socially sanctioned myths or rites	4. Helper spirits or animals derived from art, dreams, or books about other cultures
5. Use of a special spirit language	5. Use of psychological or aesthetic language
6. A multileveled cosmology with narrow passages, mountains, or trees connecting the levels	6. Interiorization of cosmos, mythologized as "the unconscious" and populated with archetypes
7. Use of ritual or hunting instruments, typically bow, arrow, and drum	7. Use of musical instruments, especially drums and bells
8. Use of herbs and/or hallucinogens for healing	8. Use of herbs, "health" food, and/or crystals for healing

Parashamanism, as distinct from shamanism, appears in contemporary postindustrial, postmodern cultures. Here our concern is with the North American version of it. Scholars generally treat shamanism as distinctive to hunting cultures. At least it had its origin in such cultures, though it continued in modified form into agriculturally based societies. Presently, it is undergoing a further transformation into a postindustrial idiom. We are witnessing an unprecedented desire among the religiously disfranchised to appropriate the model.

From the 1960s to the present, experimental ritual has grown steadily. By "experimental ritual" I do not mean primarily the ritual practices of new religious groups, sects, or cults even though one certainly finds ritual experimentation in them. Rather, I refer to groups and individuals in search of ritual specifically. These groups may or may not have names. They do not typically have charismatic leaders claiming special revelations on the basis of which new religions with prescribed rites are founded and propagated. Their approach is more tentative; they invite a try-and-see-for-yourself attitude. Those interested in their work usually pay to attend workshops. Seeking initiation into an ongoing membership is rarely a possibility. Often such groups deemphasize belief, cultivating an open or eclectic atmosphere. The result is not a new denomination but a workshop circuit informally and unofficially linking centers like Esalen (Big Sur, California) and Naropa (Boulder, Colorado) with churches, educational institutions, societies (e.g., chapters of the C. G. Jung Society), counter-culture bookstores, theater collectives, artists' circles, and various human potential and popular therapy groups. A quick way to sample the spiritual urgency of parashamanic ritual experiment is to look at issues of *Shaman's Drum*, a California-based magazine that began publication in 1985 under the auspices of the Cross-Cultural Shamanism Network. This "journal of experiential shamanism" offers its readers "magical journeys" under the tutelage of such parashamans as Michael Harner, Brooke Medicine Eagle, Natasha Frazier, Sun Bear, and others who promise "a holiday that heals," weekend workshops on the "female roots of shamanism," "Native American healing vocation workshops," "desert vision quests for women," "shamanic drumming circles," "shamanic survival skills," and "guides to working with . . . spirit helpers."

Parashamanism is an emergent form of religiosity, but we must qualify the statement. Parashamanism consists of an effort to unify what are separate cultural domains in North American society: religion, art, education, medicine, and therapy. So we could have just as easily described it as a contemporary form of art, education, medicine, or therapy. Although para-shamanism has collective dimensions, it emphasizes individual religiosity. The rites it borrows, invents, and performs are not part of some theologically coherent system. The parashaman's use of ritual is ad hoc and eclectic. Likewise, it is just as Eastern as Western, just as "primitive" as "modern."

A CRITIQUE OF COUNTERCULTURAL RITUALIZING

Invented rites, like authorized ones, have their liabilities. One of them is spiritual consumerism. The spiritual consumer hungers and thirsts after ritual, drifting from workshop to workshop, event to event, without ever being satisfied. Rituals are eaten but never digested; one becomes a galloping gourmet, tasting this and that without being nourished.

Spiritual consumerism was already linked to the search for experience in the nineteenth century. By emphasizing the value of experience as an end in itself, late-nineteenth-century ritualism laid the foundation for a twentieth-century culture rooted in therapy and consumerism. Religious art objects were acquired less for their moral worth and didactic usefulness than for their psychological effect, and worship became increasingly conditioned by a demand for tastefully dramatic qualities; ritual was supposed to add "charm" to life. Jackson Lears, one of the most perceptive contemporary historians of this period, writes:

> Yet the link between aesthetics and belief remained problematic. Ruskinian assumptions about the religious value of art and ritual could not be taken for granted. The "instinct of worship" stirred by ritual might be only emotional or sensuous excitement. Religious estheticism could point toward unconscious realms of vitality; it could have a primitivist appeal. *Fin-de-siècle* primitivism revalued ritual for its enlargement of sensuous experience and its aid in cultivating non-rational mental processes. This primitivist approach to ritual contained possibilities for deepening religious experience, but it might also blend with a secular cult of inner experience. And whatever the long-term results of ritualism, the immediate personal impact was sometimes catastrophic. For Protestants who were adrift from older theological moorings and still clinging to liberal formulas, the encounter with premodern art and ritual engendered confusion and even despair [1981:196].

Cultural imperialism, a second version, is the practice of indiscriminate or unself-critical appropriation of the sacred resources of other cultures. Often steeped in Jungian archetypalism, the parashamanically enthused feel justified in "borrowing" these resources, because they are "universal" or "unconscious": no one owns them. Like park land, symbols are open to the public. No copyrights or trademarks hold. Unfortunately, popular artists with this attitude often assume that Native people hold no copyrights, but as soon as they paint a borrowed symbol on a canvas or a T-shirt, it is protected by copyright or trademark.[83]

A third variant results in spiritual experimentalism. One tries this spirit and that but refrains from testing. Rituals are rotated to keep up their interest level. They are regarded as ever-changing processes, never structures to be assumed or facts beyond question. The experimentalist is always looking for a new ritual, assuming that it must be better, and always wary of one that has been around for too long: the only good ritual is some other ritual. Experimenting may be necessary, but when it becomes an "-ism," an ideology unto itself, it runs aground and becomes the rationalization for lacking the courage to make a choice.

These attitudes, along with their attendant problems, run counter to our usual assumptions about ritual, which we ordinarily take to be beyond the reaches of consumerism, imperialism, or experimentalism, beyond the marketplace and the laboratory. I do not claim that these attitudes toward ritual are typical of our culture or that they have replaced the more conventional ones found in mainline Protestantism, Catholicism, or Judaism. But they do represent a new configuration as distinctive as the rise of denominations, sects, and cults in the wake of the Protestant Reformations.

Ritual experimentation is quite recent. Perhaps it is the most typical postmodern form of ritual action. Strictly speaking, experimenting is an activity derived from scientific procedures, particularly those of the laboratory. But it is not confined to sciences; there is also experimental theater. Regardless of its origin, the notion of experimenting ritually implies attitudes far more tentative than those we normally associate with religious rites, which we typically think of as relatively fixed and unquestionable. In a highly technological culture experimenting itself has a quasi-ritualistic quality. So even though ritual experimentation threatens some of the values of mainline religious traditions, it expresses thoroughly Western values. Insofar as experimenting as an ideology compromises the possibilities for commitment and fidelity by evoking mere whimsical tinkering, it is dangerous but no more dangerous than commitment and fidelity, both of which can be perverted into rigid fanaticism. Experimenting *can be*—I do not say, *is*—a means by which humility is reintroduced to established ritual practices. It can lead to attitudes more open and respectful of rites in other traditions and more honesty with ourselves about the values of rites we already practice.

VICTOR TURNER'S EXPERIMENTS WITH RITUAL

Long after his work among the Ndembu, anthropologist Victor Turner reenacted some Ndembu rites in a workshop with theater director Richard Schechner. Ritual experiments such as this one ran parallel to his penchant for the pre-Vatican II Mass. The tension between his Catholic traditionalism and ritual experimentalism is both problematic and fruitful. The problems include his definition of ritual, discussed in chapter 1, and his ambivalence about personal or invented rites. Some fruitful results of the tension were his theoretical attempts to overcome the split between spontaneity and self-consciousness and his influence on actual religious practices, for instance, the Middletown initiation rites (see Roberts 1982).

In "Dramatic Ritual/Ritual Drama: Performative and Reflexive Anthropology" (1979a), Turner reports on his and Edith Turner's two-week collaboration with theater director Richard Schechner and a group of anthropology and drama students. During this workshop the Turners played the role they dubbed "ethnodramaturg" and led the group in a reenactment of parts of an Ndembu ritual called "Name Inheritance" (*Kuswanika ijina*), a ceremony in which they had participated several times during their field-work in Africa. Victor Turner himself gave a "reading performance" and, with characteristic humor, describes his having led participants in a dance "to the best of his arthritic ability" (86).[84]

Since Turner justifies his ethnodramaturgical experiment primarily on pedagogical grounds, most readers are likely to feel justified in reading it as an indirect portrait of Turner the teacher and ignoring its theoretical implications. On the contrary, there is no better way to take either the man or the teacher seriously than to follow both his theory and his practice to their conclusions. The article mentioned above is not the strongest example of his scholarship, but the subject matter, cross-cultural ritual experiment, is crucial to an understanding of ritual criticism, and Turner's instinct to dance beyond the boundaries of learned monographs is instructive for the way we both study and practice ritual.

Like the rationale offered by Turnbull and Garner (1979) for their experi-ments with drama and anthropology, the one proposed by Turner is ped-agogical. He claims students become alienated unless they are dealing with lived experience, unless they are given ways of integrating cognitive, affective, and volitional learning. Understanding, he says, requires empa-thy and intersubjectivity.

These ideas are not new; Turner does not claim they are. One can hardly deny that they are also indelibly marked by their geography as North American and their history as of the post–1960s era. Few people would bother to disagree with them had they remained mere pious abstractions. But their repeated enactment makes them controversial and provocative of further reflection. We are provoked into asking, Beyond their pedagogical relevance, what else was going on? The answer, I believe, was the search for a viable ritology, that is, a coherent understanding of ritual experience, construction, and criticism. Turner was at times torn by the great distance between the academic study of ritual and religious participation in it, especially if academic meant "detached" and religious meant "naïve." So he invoked drama and play as mediating, third possibilities that do not force such dualistic choices. Put a more provocative way, the workshop with Schechner is an example of one side of Turner's own religious prac-tice, that side engaged in liminoid ritualizing.

Many anthropologists will probably shy away from this designation of Turner's involvement as religious. Turner, they might insist, was a Catho-lic. And furthermore, a group that endures for only two weeks in a work-shop is hardly a religious institution. But Turner describes moments that are undeniably religious, even though one may want to think of such religiosity as "subjunctive," to use one of Turner's own terms. In one such moment he asks "Becky" to tell him the name of a recently deceased relative. Deeply moved, Becky, in Ndembu fashion, names her aunt Ruth. Turner then marks Becky with white clay on her brow and above her navel and declares her Nswana-Ruth, "successor of Ruth" (1979a:87). Turner is judicious enough not to recount the intimacies of the effect of the rite on Becky, but it is clear that participants recognize the performance to be in some way "religious." Why the quotation marks? The event was not an example of Catholic religion nor of Ndembu religion, though a Catholic performed the act using Ndembu gestures and symbols. Nevertheless, it was a transcendent gesture and response. Even if we think of it as make-believe, the make-believe "works." It does not work in the Durkheimian sense; it does not glue a society together, but it certainly intensifies the relations in this small, temporary group and links this one woman with an ancestor. Some might prefer to label the event dramatic, but the labels "dramatic," "religious," and "academic" can coexist, disappear, or fluctu-ate rapidly in the course of such ritual experimentation.

As an anthropologist Turner pulls up short of talking about personal appropriation of rites. Even though he was initiated by the Ndembu and participated in many of their rites, neither this fact nor his dramatic re-enactments, as far as I know, ever led him to regard himself as a convert. Nor did he ever say much publicly about the possibility of constructing and actually using Ndembu rites.

Near the end of his life Turner was paying considerable attention to two modes of consciousness: flow and reflexivity. A primary concern was how rituals enable participants to overcome the dualism between spontaneity and self-consciousness; hence his interest in celebrations, those rites in which this tension is maximized. We might borrow Paul Tillich's term and refer to rites that are "broken" (1960:85). In the face of myth, Tillich showed, we no longer believe, yet we do not not-believe. If a myth is broken, we recognize it as a myth but continue to believe in some special sense of the term.

Turner's experimentation suggests that it is possible to invent effective rituals in a critical, self-conscious culture. Yet his work, at least as it is publicly articulated in his published works, stopped short of advocating active ritual construction. But without his theory of ritual process and his analysis of ritual change, ritual studies would not have examined seriously the usual misgivings about personal, tacit, invented, and self-consciously constructed rites.

Another of Turner's articles, "Ritual, Tribal and Catholic" (1976), is also likely to be overlooked by anthropologists, but students of religion ought not ignore it. It is my least favorite among his writings, but I keep returning it. If the article on the collaboration with Schechner is left-wing Turner, this one is right-wing Turner. In it he has nothing but uncritical praise for the pre-Vatican II Mass and little but disdain for the post-Vatican II version. The Mass of Pius V, dating from 1570, he considers an "architectonic masterpiece" (509), a "golden mean" (512) and, surprisingly, a bastion of liminality (524). Why he does not regard it as a veritable hyperbole of the status system he does not say. He considers the Vatican II reforms as jaunty revisionism and seems to imply that ritual experimentation of this sort is merely hackwork or worse, a dismemberment (525). The tone of his article is one of veneration for rituals that are "the work of ages" (524). He concludes it on a homiletical note, "We must not dynamite the liturgical rock of Peter" in favor of "personal religious romanticism" (526). It is impossible to accept Turner's very conservative analysis as "science having its say" (525). Rather, he is expressing a personal preference or making a statement of faith.

The daring facet of this article is Turner's comparing the Catholic Mass to the Chihamba rite of the Ndembu, which he regards as an instance of what theologians call "natural" (as opposed to "special" or "Christian") revelation (1976:519). But his comparison is neither systematic nor critical. And it is not suggestive in his usual manner. As with the former article, one is forced again to read between the lines to discern what the unspoken agenda is. What is Turner struggling with that so ambivalently colors his attitude toward ritual innovation? On the one hand, he reenacts an Ndembu rite with a group of students and dramatists, and on the other, he sounds like an aged cardinal in his nostalgia for the Latin Mass. An easy way to resolve the dilemma would be to claim that he knew how to recognize second-rate revisions of perfectly functional rites. Though one might be open to being convinced that the post-Vatican II Mass is inferior, Turner provides no real arguments that this is the case. Instead, he provides lists of the Mass's symbolic objects and actions for no obvious analytical purpose.

In the two articles considered we meet Turner the religious animal and Turner the anthropologist; both roles are activated simultaneously. In the first article the religious animal is below the surface of the writing; in the second, the anthropologist is submerged. But in both the torque is considerable.

The point in calling attention to this tension is less to chide Turner than to go beyond him. His dilemma is ours. How can a fieldworker *not* bring back some Ndembu gestures? How can a North American scholar *not* make Catholic (or Protestant or North American) judgments and comparisons? How can the study of ritual not have ritual consequences? In ritual studies such questions are central. Although many anthropologists pose these questions, they do not usually do so as part of their methodology. Consideration of the effect of an investigator's own ritual practices is usually subsidiary to treatment of the social context of the rite. And observations about the lived experience of a rite are subordinated to those about the social structures supported or inverted by it.

Victor Turner pulled up short of writing about personal appropriation of the rites of others. Yet he was initiated by the Ndembu and had an Ndembu funeral (conducted by Whites in Virginia, not by Blacks in Africa) as well as a Catholic one.[85] Nor did he ever write much about the possibility of constructing and actually using Ndembu rites.

In "Ritual, Tribal and Catholic" Turner points out similarities and differences between the Mass and the Chihamba rite, but the comparison remains parallel rather than convergent. He does not allow us to see the conflictual dynamics that would set up if a single individual or group were to perform both rites, which was his own situation. He seems to assume what we might call "monoreligiosity," the practice of one religion, not several; or "henoreligiosity," the practice of one normative religion while all others are kept at a distance by some special or subordinating frame. The article never entertains the possibility of "polyreligiosity," engagement in several ritual traditions at once—a phenomenon Turner ordinarily studied with acumen. Whatever Turner *did* personally behind the scenes or off the record, his analysis in this article still plays it safe from both an orthodox Catholic and perhaps even an anthropological viewpoint. He has neither criticized Ndembu ritual nor appropriated it. He suspends normative questions such as "What shall I do to be saved?" or "What dance is worth doing?" Negative ways to pose normative questions are, "What constitutes ritual failure?" or "When is a revision of a rite a poor one?"

Although Turner suspends overt, normative considerations, he nevertheless implies criteria. Pre-Vatican II rites are treated as superior to post-Vatican ones because of their (1) adaptability to local/tribal conditions (1976:512); (2) longevity (517); (3) lack of fashionable relevance (524); and (4) freedom from individual romanticism, collective millenarianism, and political opportunism (526).

Liturgists would probably challenge the accuracy and adequacy of some of these criteria, but the point is simply that Turner does, in fact, have operative ritological values. The work of a ritologist is to identify these values, making them explicit in order to begin the work of cross-cultural criticism. Ritology is committed to the examination of the full range of ritual from the most tacit[86] to the most differentiated, from the most traditional to the most self-consciously invented, ad hoc ones. Turner's theoretical work and his fieldwork attended to this range, but his own religious convictions sometimes made him wary of countercultural liminality.

Originally, Turner's term "liminality" designated something explicit, the transition phase of a rite of passage in traditional tribal societies. Later, Turner coined the neologism "liminoid" to apply to transition phenomena in industrial societies. He summarizes the differences in this way:

> We might say that liminal genres put much stress on social frames, plural reflexivity, and mass flow, shared flow, while liminoid genres emphasize idiosyncratic framing, individual reflexivity, subjective flow, and see the social as problem not datum [1979a:117].

Many of Turner's followers pay little attention to the differences in social contexts implied by each term. What is of interest here is the shift in Turner's own focus from ritual specifically to transition phenomena generally.[87] His usual examples of liminoid behavior are taken from the arts (see, e.g., 1979a:115) or from celebration and other modes of cultural inversion. But one wonders how Turner's suspicion of post-Vatican II liturgy and ritual experimentation could help us understand the pronounced, postmodern tendency to invent personal rituals—for example, those that do not initiate a person into a group but away from groups into solitude; or "baptisms" that draw on both tribal and Catholic, not to mention Hindu and Yaqui, symbolism. Is the transition phase of a postmodern, invented rite an example of the liminal or of the liminoid? Would he advise us to regard invented symbolic actions as "rites"?

Turner's enthodramaturgical experiment was motivated by the desire to overcome the split between the study and the practice of ritual, which he took to be rooted in Cartesian dualism:

> Cartesian dualism has insisted on separating subject from object, us from them. It has, indeed, made voyeurs of Western man, exaggerating sight by macro- and micro-instrumentation, the better to learn the structures of the world with an "eye" to its exploitation. The deep bonds between body and mentality, unconscious and conscious thinking, species and self have been treated without respect, as though irrelevant for analytical purposes.
>   The reflexivity of performance dissolves these bonds, and so creatively democratizes: as we become on earth a single noosphere, the

Platonic cleavage between an aristocracy of the spirit and the "lower or foreign orders" can no longer be maintained. To be reflexive is to be at once one's own subject and direct object. The poet, whom Plato rejected from his Republic, subjectivizes the object, or, better, makes intersubjectivity the characteristically postmodern human mode [1979a:92–93].

One of Turner's most useful distinctions is his characterization of the flow/reflexivity dialectic.[88] He successfully broke the stereotypes of ritual consciousness as rigid (not also flowing) and naïve (not also reflexive). My divergence from him arises when he associates individuality with drama and collectivity with ritual, thus obstructing the possibility of a theory adequate to deal with individual ritual. "In ritual and carnival," Turner says, "it may not be too fanciful to see social structure itself as the author or source of scenarios" (1979a.114). That such a view might be true of either "tribal or Catholic" contexts is unquestionable. But "signed," un-anonymous ritualization is simply a fact of postmodern culture. One might want to argue that "authored" rituals—those constructed deliberately by individuals—are culturally insignificant, but this must be shown, not assumed. Turner has no difficulty accepting dramatized rituals but seems ambivalent about invented ones, especially if they are primarily religious rather than dramatic. He never explicitly says why this is the case. One can surmise that he believes individual ritual is open to easy abuse and fosters ego inflation. Wagner (1981:82) puts it this way: ". . . Neurotic 'rituals' allow the individual to act successfully (to manipulate the self very seriously) by precipitating a motivating and justifying but highly idiosyncratic 'convention.'" The alternative implied by Wagner is "funny" (72,82) ritual, ritual with some sense of humor about itself. In my estimation this is an important criterion. If individuals are able to take an invented ritual both seriously and not seriously, as well as being able both to flow with it and to be reflexive about it, either we have misunderstood the nature of traditional ritual or else a new mode of ritual consciousness has emerged. Reflexivity, however, is not an unqualified good. Turner roundly asserts that reflexivity democratizes. He seems to forget how it also introduces the neurotic self-alienation that Kierkegaard so prophetically anticipated in his book *Repetition*.

What worries Turner about ritual experimentation is more evident in his *Process, Pilgrimage and Performance* (1979b:117–120). After a discussion of theater directors Artaud, Grotowski, and Schechner, in which he describes Grotowski's "holy" theater and its attempt to create rites of passage by dissolving the boundary between audience and performer, he reflects:

As a personal footnote I would like to add that I see the liminoid as an advance in the history of human freedom. For this reason I relish the separation of an audience from performers and the liberation of scripts from cosmology and theology. The concept of individuality has been hard-won, and to surrender it to a new totalizing process of reliminalization is a dejecting thought. As a member of an audience I can see the theme and message of a play as one among a number of "subjunctive" possibilities, a variant model for thought or action to be accepted or rejected after careful consideration. Even as audience people can be "moved" by plays; they need not be "carried away" by them—into another person's utopia or "secular sacrum," to use Grotowski's phrase. Liminoid theater should present alternatives; it should not be a brainwashing technique. As Blake said: "One Law for the Lion and the Ox is Oppression."

Turner's worry is that experimenting with ritual construction will bring with it a loss of the individual, that it will be fraught with anti-intellectualism (of which he accuses Grotowski) and thus inhibit our freedom to reflect before we accept or reject. He seems to prefer Schechner's post-Jewish theatricalizing to Grotowski's post-Catholic ritualizing. What he likes about Schechner's work is its public reflexivity. Grotowski, with whom he did not collaborate, seems to him too esoteric.

Certainly the danger Turner anticipates was present in Grotowski's experiments.[89] But whereas Grotowski sometimes errs on the side of excessive flow, Schechner (an academic as well as a theater director) sometimes errs on the side of reflexivity. He has been known to carry a tape recorder to document his own conversations with others. Grotowski often meets and greets strangers in silence—apt illustrations of emphatic reflexivity and flow respectively.

Before completing this discussion of Turner's own ritual creativity and criticism, it might be interesting to consider a brief example in which ritual innovation and critique inspired by Turner's writings transpire in an ecclesiastical setting. Such an example—and there are others—illustrates the religious effects, or functions, of some kinds of anthropology (see Taylor 1986). Functions, of course, have no necessary connections with intentions.

In *Initiation to Adulthood: An Ancient Rite of Passage in Contemporary Form* (1982), William O. Roberts, Jr., the minister of First Church of Christ, Middletown, Connecticut, describes the efforts of his congregation to construct initiation rites for their youth. Prominent among their motives was a desire to come to terms with the tacit ritualizing of alcohol, sex, and drugs—"self-initiation" (3) Roberts calls it—that was already going on. Their first attempt to fill the void was a cautious ritual revisionism; they tried firming up their confirmation rite. But the attempt failed. The impetus to try something more imaginative comes after a young woman sees "the real thing" in a movie, *The Trial of Billy Jack*. The woman complains to her pastor. This Protestant pastor, under the impetus of Ignatius Loyola's (Catholic) spiritual exercises, has a vision. The vision leads to research in anthropology (including Turner), religious studies (especially Eliade), and developmental psychology. And, finally, the research leads to ritual experiment. This combination—research, vision, meditation, and dramatization—condenses an emergent ritual style increasingly typical of North American cultures and traditions.

Roberts (1982:11) quotes the response of a denominational executive to their experiment: "In Christianity we confirm faith. We do not initiate people." The official treats the situation not in the "tribal and Catholic" spirit but as "tribal vs. Protestant." Robert's response is markedly Protestant. He finds initiation motifs in scripture and builds a case using these images. His counterargument is that the congregation has not invented a rite, much less tacked on a pagan addition to a Christian rite, but rather, has rediscovered a "lost" rite.

Roberts managed to convince his United Church of Christ congregation to design a two-year initiation rite for eighth- and ninth-graders (ninth and tenth-graders by the end of it). His report covers four initiation cycles involving a hundred or so adolescents. The group, typically consisting of twelve to twenty-five youths, a male and a female adult leaders, and on occasion a cadre of other adults, met regularly twice a week and held frequent retreats.

The whole process was far too complex to describe here, and Roberts himself has provided a comparatively full and useful account of it. Of most significance for our purposes were the eight "mystery rites," all of which followed van Gennep's separation-transition-incorporation pattern, and which dealt with four major themes: society, self, sexuality, spirituality. Formulas, of course, are easy to come by and are sometimes tempting for busy clergy, but what is impressive about the Middletown experiment is the congregation's actually having put this ritual scheme into operation. For example, in the first mystery rite, designed to remove symbolically the children from their parents, Roberts drew on Masai (Kenya) and Pueblo initiations as well as on the ceremonies of an honorary society at an eastern university. The rite included blindfolding, taunting, riddle-solving, river-crossing, a meal, and dusting with white powder. In one version of its enactment, it drew these activities together around the story of Jacob's struggle at Penuel (Genesis 32).

Other mystery rites involved masking, silence, fasting, solitude, sleep deprivation, debate, verbal and written examination, singing, game-playing, journeys, guided imagery, statements of faith, physical endurance, baptism, laying on of hands, anointing, Communion, and many others. The rites seem to depend on at least four obvious resources for techniques: psychotherapy and developmental psychology, comparative religion and anthropology, public education, and traditional Christian education and practice. An experiment such as this could easily have become a mere hodgepodge, serving no deeper purpose than providing religiously tinged entertainment, or it could have degenerated into a mere trick for keeping adolescents off the streets—for morality-building and counseling. What makes it remarkable is its cohesion and seriousness *as ritual*.

Anthropological methods do not, as a rule, require anthropologists to be very concerned about the religious implications and ritual consequences of their field and theoretical work. Even Turner, who was quite aware of such matters, was seldom in a position to see how his theories might influence actual religious practice. Roberts's initiation is a prime example of such an influence. He read and cites both Van Gennep and Turner. Specifically, Roberts (1982:98ff.) argues that North American societies have lowered the age of entering adolescence and raised the age of leaving it, producing a prolonged, six- to sixteen-year period of liminality. For this reason he leads his congregation in one of the most sustained experiments in constructing initiation rites in North American Christianity. The Middletown initiation is both an application and an implicit critique of Turner's research. As application, the rite puts the theory of liminality (originally derived from observed practice) back into practice. It appropriates cross-cultural anthropological data and molds it into specifically Christian use. And by implication, it reconnects the generally liminoid to the explicitly ritualistic liminal. The implicit critique consists of the experiment's actually entering the arena of convergent and conflicting ritual traditions, rather than simply noting parallels and differences (as is the case in "Ritual, Tribal and Catholic") or framing them dramatically and nonreligiously (as is the case in "Dramatic Ritual").

Parenthetically, it is interesting to note that whatever the effects of Vatican II were on the Mass and on Catholics like Turner, its effect on the theology and practice of baptism was to open it to "primitive" influence (see Roberts 1982:83–90; cf. Kavanagh 1978). Anthropologists have been more attuned than theologians to the migration of ritual motifs across cultural traditions and to ritual syncretism and layering.[90] Exemplary studies such as the Turners' research on pilgrimage have not only opened up these topics to fuller anthropological discussion, they have raised exciting and threatening possibilities for ritualists both in the traditions they studied and in other traditions as well, because they are performed with such highly reflexive, largely aesthetic consciousness. They have enriched North American drama and challenged North American Catholicism, Protestantism, and perhaps even Judaism.

THE RITUAL STUDIES LAB

These days two popular stances toward ritual are evident—one that flees it as a useless, boring appendix to a postindustrial society and the other that pursues it with postmodern enthusiasm and romantic nostalgia across religious and cultural boundaries. Here we are concerned primarily with the latter. Ritual has become a countercultural fad, the object of rampant experientialism, that is, the belief that experience per se is authoritative. Once or twice a month I hear of some new workshop or retreat in which ritual is being offered as the latest [and most ancient] form of religious experience.

My own attitude toward the search for ritual experience is mixed. On the one hand, I have no use for weekend enlightenment and the workshop circuit. On the other, I am convinced that we are a ritually disabled people and that religious institutions and academic theories of ritual too often contribute to this disability. For this reason I direct the Ritual Studies Laboratory, which engages in cross-cultural, interreligious research on ritual. I am committed to experimenting with ritual in alternative contexts and to engaging in self-criticism at the same time. I am deeply sympathetic with those who attempt to ground their sense of ritual in human experience and are dissatisfied with bookish rites and participation without heart. But I have little patience with cultivated naïveté, and I often smell self-deception in the air that surrounds weekend initiations and vision quests. Ritual is so easy to exploit that I worry when people's search for it makes them needlessly vulnerable to manipulation by it. However, the academic's preoccupation with self-deception and manipulation easily leads to hiding behind theories out of fear of actual ritual experience. So, of course, I hope for the best of both worlds—a deepened capacity for ritual experience and a heightened ability to engage in ritual criticism.

The Ritual Studies Laboratory (RSL) was established in 1975 on the campus of Wilfrid Laurier University to work in the interstices between anthropology and liturgics—between analytical and normative approaches to the study of ritual. Most of the students who do research in it are in small, undergraduate credit courses; some are seminarians and graduate students. Occasionally, noncredit workshops have been given, but I generally avoid them because of the impossibility of follow-up, sustained critique, or adequate time to nurture attitudes.

Lectures in the lab are short; often they are printed and distributed. The readings and written assignments are lengthy. Discussions are usually confined to the ends of class periods. Much class time is spent either in silence or in using nonverbal means of communication. The spirit of silence is cultivated.

Like the Archaeology Lab, which has its quarters in the same building, the RSL is intimately linked with teaching. But unlike the Archeology Lab its purpose is not scientific—at least not in the narrow, North American sense. The purpose of the lab is to foster embodied, critical study of ritual. As such, it does not slot easily as either religious, academic, or dramatic, though our experiments draw on all three.

One assumption about ritual is that it is essentially religious and therefore beyond the reach of both academics and artists. From the point of view of artists, academics only think they can evaluate it. From the point of view of academics, artists only imagine they can create it. In the Ritual Studies Lab we reject this assumption. Our aim is both to construct and to analyze ritual processes. Since the RSL is fundamentally concerned with the construction and assessment of ritual, it resembles an art or dance studio as much as it does an archaeology laboratory. As in any studio course, one of the chief aims is practical. Students are expected to absorb attitudes and skills necessary to the construction of effective rites. And like a lab in any discipline, its aim is to test and evaluate various ways of engaging in ritual practice; this is its primary academic function. Analysis and hypothesis-testing are themselves academic rites, and our attempt to synthesize these with other kinds of ritual is not different in principle from the synthesizing of rites that always goes on in longstanding traditions.

In the lab we work on various kinds of ritual skills: music, chant, spatial design, bodily movement, object-making, and so on. We study different sorts of rites—initiations, marriages, funerals, graduations, divorces, birthing rites—and work with gestures, motifs, and other basic factors out of which they are constructed. We do not "do" rituals per se; we experiment with ritualization processes.

"Rites of Passage," one of the thirteen-week courses taught in the RSL,[91] is itself a simulated rite of passage. One might compare it with mock parliaments in political science or stock-market games in business and economics. It follows the three phases described by Arnold van Gennep's *Rites of Passage*: separation, transition, incorporation. The pattern is repeated in some fashion at every class meeting and then intensified during a weekend retreat called simply "Journey," during which a dying/rising motif becomes the content around which this threefold process is structured.

At the beginning of the course, participants are not sure what to expect. The usual academic contract is different from the one that must be negotiated here. A prerequisite is my permission, which is granted (or not) on the basis of an interview. Since the course is deliberately structured *not* to be an exercise in therapy, people who either want or need therapy are deterred. People who might have wandered into the course by accident are discouraged. Other agendas—learning to act, merely earning a credit, avoiding critical thinking—are redirected in the interview.

Initially, some participants fear that experimenting with ritual may objectify, and thereby undermine, their traditional beliefs and practices. Either they suspect this or they hope the lab will provide them with a religious substitute. Neither expectation is fulfilled.

Although we use ritual motifs that remind some participants of those in specific religions, we never borrow directly, nor do we enact whole rites taken from another culture. All symbols are deliberately modified if not invented. Criticism of the ritualized activities in which these symbols are embedded takes place, first of all, on the basis of either preexistent "interaction ritual" (Goffman 1967) or the declared and discovered intentions of participants. Later, in retrospect, the functions of ritualized activities for the group itself and for the larger society are analyzed.

We have found that much depends on the timing of analysis. If we separate the analysis of an event from the experience of it by a week, most participants eventually learn to hold two attitudes simultaneously: reverence and iconoclasm. Whatever we enact seriously we later invert. Whatever seems revelatory is later seen as fictive, and vice-versa. The effect is much like that of Hopi Kachina initiation (see Gill 1977): enchantment is held in constructive tension with disenchantment.

As Roy Wagner (1981) has shown, there is little question that we do, in fact, invent culture. What varies is the degree of self-awareness with which we do so. Religious studies and anthropology have both tended to identify as religious those elements of culture that we are least able, or least likely, to regard as inventable. To practitioners religious culture seems given (cf. Wagner, 104). In research at the Ritual Studies Laboratory we have been able to construct activities in which the given and the made-up are not experienced as mutually exclusive. Consequently, participants are less torn between their study of ritual and their practice of it.

Clannishness and occultism, if such impulses arise, are headed off by a steady diet of reading and reflection. We have found that not only can reflexivity and spontaneity coexist, so can unbelief and full ritual participation. A simple illustration is the person who does not believe in demons but who nevertheless can be frightened by a demon mask, or one who is not a believer but can stop nightmares by wearing a cross. It is relatively easy to achieve ritual effectiveness without belief in transcendent forces or divine beings and to do so in the atmosphere of critical reflection that is necessary if a ritual studies laboratory is really to be a laboratory.

Students are given a written statement describing the RSL, including its ethics of participation. They are not to come full of food or stimulants. No drug or alcohol use is to precede class. They are not to participate in activities that compromise their ethical or religious commitments. They are to keep lab staff informed of any illnesses or psychological difficulties. They are required to describe each session in writing, as if they were ethnographers in the field. And so on.

Each three-hour class consists of a set of activities designed to cultivate a sense for ritual. Each activity is preceded by brief instructions that lay out rules, describe parameters for improvisation. Usually the instructions do not specify any goal. These activities do not have genre tags such as "exercise," "ritual," "game," or "drama." Discussions of both genre and goal are usually held until the activities are over, the aim being to discover or infer what we have, in fact, done. The lack of explanation and sustained silence usually generate a sense of mystery—sometimes, feelings of anxiety. Students regularly say they find the course demanding physically, psychologically, and intellectually.

Since each session typically employs from two to five activities, only a sample can be described here. During the first session a blank white scroll is hung on the wall. Below it are a Japanese ink brush and ink. For the next three sessions students are given the opportunity to sign the scroll, indicating their commitment to stay in the class. Should they decide to drop the course, their only obligation is publicly to stroke their name off the roll. No explanation is necessary. Preceding the hanging of the scroll they hear a ten-minute lecture on rites of signing and the power of naming. Though not told to do so, some students choose a new name for the course. The result is that signing—ordinarily a light weight task (except in the case of large checks)—becomes heavy; deleting becomes even weightier. Students learn without being told, to observe and respond to the style and placement of handwriting. They are usually busy trying to infer personalities from formalized actions. Later, we discuss the importance of formalization and stylization to ritual.

During the first few sessions many ordinary activities receive special treatment: pouring tea, taking off shoes, greeting, saying good-bye, entering a room, walking, sitting down, breathing, and so on. The exotic is avoided in order to make the essential point that rituals are constructed out of the most mundane stuff imaginable. An attitude is deliberately cultivated. This attitude is attentive—though diffuse, not focused. Students are quite literally taught eye comportment. They are not to stare. They are to see with the eye of a fish—with circular, rather than focal, attention. They learn to respond bodily to what they see and hear as long as they can do so without violation of another. They learn to attend to the textures of the floor, the walls, the cushions, and to the smells of food and bodily odors all this without becoming sentimental about, or attached to, those things. They pause in the doorway, hands on the oak entrance, and chant—occasionally with considerable attentiveness, often with considerable hyperbole and humor—"separation, transition, incorporation." They develop a love-hate relation with van Gennep, whom they are, of course, reading.

The mood in class runs a wide gamut from quite solemn to rowdy and iconoclastic. Not only is this permitted, it is encouraged. Some of the sessions work on an inversion principle. What was sanctified by serious concentration and work in the beginning is turned upside and played with in the end. The movement from session one to session thirteen follows the same pattern. At first participants find this jolting and disconcerting. Eventually, they come to expect and enjoy it.

An example of a repeated activity is the "Bowing Paradigm," a set of simple movements involving bowing and prostration. The paradigm is an invention, though it reminds students of Buddhist, Muslim, and Christian monks they have seen bowing in films. Nothing in the set is said to symbolize anything, and nothing in it is borrowed directly from any of these traditions, though the similarities are deliberate. Eventually we discuss the associations that begin to collect around each of the movements or postures. Participants learn to distinguish evoked or associative meanings from imposed ones. They are encouraged to imagine freely as they do the paradigm and to record their associations and images. In this way we move toward a poetics of ritual.

Though I have emphasized the development of a ritual criticism in these essays, a poetics of ritual is also central to teaching courses in the lab. That ritualization depends not only on tradition but also on imagination is one of the main theses of the course. Some of the lectures reflect this concern for ritual poetics.

The most puzzling repeated activity for most students is the passing of a wooden egg around the circle. Its meaning is never explained, even when students inquire. Some do not even see it as an egg. This egg-passing is the most repeated action in the course. Each time it varies. The egg is dipped in water and passed. It is wrapped in cloth and passed. It is bound in gauze and passed. And so on. Because of the persistence of the action, students alternately despair at its meaninglessness and marvel at how meaningful it becomes. Some decide to look up eggs in symbol dictionaries; they do Jungian numbers on their classmates. Most eventually give up the attempt to decode the thing. Maybe decoding is not how these things work, one student says. By the end of the course the egg-passing is less like a cipher one decodes than a theme, a thread stitching together a patchwork of meanings. When this becomes a widespread perception, they learn about Lévi-Strauss's image, the bricolage, and discover the power of form over content.

Music figures heavily in the class agenda. Simple percussion instruments are used. No musical training or expertise is presupposed. Sounds are used to wake up the old house that contains the Lab and to attune individuals to perceive and follow the flocklike auditory and kinesthetic movement of the whole group. The sounds that emerge would not tempt anyone to record them, but the sense of contributing to some emergent whole is often a striking experience to students.

About two-thirds of the way through the course, people bring pieces of old clothing and build an effigy, affectionately named O.D. He/she sits silently in the corner after being built out of bailing wire, old ties, tattered underwear—bits of everyone's wardrobe. O.D. is the traditional name, but the class usually cannot resist amplifying it into something like Odee Melodee Barnswallow III. Unlike the music and paradigm, building Old Death is a one-time activity.

At this point the course begins to forsake repetitive actions for the sake of one-time acts, and class members sense that they are "finally going somewhere." But where?

The lab assistant and I begin to tease and tantalize the students. The atmosphere resembles Halloween or Christmas. Secrets are in the air. Students have known from the beginning that they must keep one special weekend free, so they surmise that the change of pace has something to do with Journey, about which they have heard vague rumors.

Journey occurs either in late November or in March, the dead of southern Ontario winter. A full, ethnographic-style account of it would require several hundred pages, so a summary will have to do. The overriding ethos is what one might call "subjunctive fear." This is the sort of fear that kids like to drum up in themselves by reading ghost stories.

Participants are blindfolded and taken in vans to an unspecified site. From Friday afternoon through Sunday afternoon they "meet their deaths."

They write wills, make death masks on their own faces, and hear stories about dying and rising deities. They fast and shiver in the cold. They huddle close to one another and wonder what is happening next.

Saturday night is the culmination as they sit around a fire making music. When Death arrives in a white mask, and Life, clothed in red, does battle with Death, they, of course, know they are watching their professor and lab assistant in costume. Nevertheless, many later confess their fright when it was "their time." When Death comes—as it must for each—the students' teeth sometimes chatter. When they are taken out alone and "buried" in a white sheet to the sound of a high-pitched flute, they sometimes cry or moan or remember things they had long forgotten.

When Death finishes with a person and Life takes over to lead him or her to the birth cave, they stumble in the deep snow and swear they hear someone else following behind. They squat or sit for two or three hours in the cave. Life gives them hot cider and new, blank-faced dolls, which they can name, keep, and en-face.

After all, these poor student souls have been through the great trial. Life leads them on a screaming chase after Death, whom they pummel, un mask, and drag back to the fireplace indoors. Afterward there is food and champagne as O.D. is fed to the fire.

The next morning is Sunday. The "cemetery"—built on Friday of sticks, stones, bones, and found junk—is dismantled. Kites and balloons are hoisted aloft. They get to see the cave in the daylight. The drive into town is followed by a huge breakfast of sausage, eggs, and pancakes. The last act of the weekend is a silent foot-washing back at the lab to remove the dust of the journey. Most of them are surprised by the sensuousness of the act.

This is the climax, but not the end, of the course. After any retreat there are reintegration problems. People are high for weeks, and their mates do not know what to make of them. Why can't it always be like this? Why can't the course go on forever? The remaining weeks are spent demystifying the experience. Everything is turned wrong side out. All the seams and glitches are pointed out. The entire schedule, which is several pages long and which indicates every planning detail, is passed out and analyzed. And finally, in whiteface, the whole thing is shamelessly mocked and inverted. It takes hours to clean up the Lab afterward, and the cleaning up reminds students of the initial housecleaning on the first day of class.

The first question scholars usually ask about the RSL is, Is it academic? This is the easy question; it has been debated in the University Senate. The answer is Yes, academic and more. In addition to the heavy reading and writing load, students are highly motivated by the course to do further study of ritual. The classes are always small, from six to fifteen, but the percentage who go on to graduate school to study ritual or who go into the performing and plastic arts to use skills developed in the course is higher than in other courses.

The next question is harder: What are these students being initiated *into*? My answer is always the same: They are being initiated into the tradition of this class and thereby the study of ritual. Of course, the process is not the same as being initiated into a religion. The class has a limited lifespan and it offers no ongoing community. Part of the implicit message of the course is that much ritualizing is predicated on the fact that all things, including traditions and courses, die.

After thirteen years the course itself is (or has) a miniature tradition of sorts. For instance, participants leave ritual objects for the next year's class. Stories and lore accumulate. Some of it is passed from student to student; some, through the lab assistant and me, to the next "generation" of students.

One concern is whether such a course raises unfillable expectations and whether it plays into the decadence of the late twentieth-century workshop-circuit spirituality. Students who take the course are sometimes tempted to try continuing the experience in other contexts in which they either feel exploited or feel that they are exploiting other peoples' traditions. No matter how "solid," "responsible," or "academic" such an experience, it still suffers from what the Protestants in the course call "the church camp syndrome." After the mountaintop everything else seems downhill.

Recently, several ex-lab students, and some others, organized themselves into a "ritual group." For some this group was merely an exercise in nostalgia attempting to re-create the experience that many of them remembered. For others it went beyond their experience in the lab. The predictable problems arose. Some wanted the group to become a therapy group. With no designated leader, no grades, no hierarchy, discipline was hard to maintain. People began to skip. Some shirked their responsibilities. There were ongoing debates: What is the group's real purpose—to study ritual, to be a community, to serve as a group of consultants for other people's rites, to have periodic celebrations? What motivates people to attend and participate when they are busy, tired, or on holiday? Which of the various ideologies will be determinative—feminist, artistic, therapeutic, scholarly? Which subgroup (e.g., ex-lab vs. non-lab students) should determine the direction of the group? Whereas in the Lab the infrastructure was built for the students, in this group they had to create it themselves. The process loses its mystery, and its demands sap the time the group would prefer to spend ritualizing. After a few months the group collapsed. It is hard to be optimistic about the longevity of ritual groups.

If students after the course find the usual ritual traditions boring, one has to ask how realistic a picture the RSL paints of the wide variety of rituals in the world's traditions. One danger in experimenting with ritual in a lab is that participants can begin to value experiment for its own sake. And the demand that ritual, like the market-at-large, provide something forever new and exciting could be destructive to ritual itself.

Another problem is that the design of a rite of passage depends on a great deal of mystification of authority. Even though this is opened up periodically to question and to overt iconoclasm in the end, it can easily create a false picture. Designing, executing, and evaluating a rite is not nearly as exciting as being led through it. Students who take subsequent courses either on the field study of ritual or on the construction of it find it hard to marshal the necessary energy and motivation for wading through the infinite list of details required to facilitate or study a rite. A rite of passage has a certain drama to it that is missing from more repetitive ritual forms such as worship and meditation. One cannot depend on Halloween and Christmas excitement in designing weddings and funerals. So the liminally heavy, rite-of-passage model has its limitations.

Criticism is not just a matter of immediate assessment but also of gaining cultural and historical perspective. Turner's and my experiments will no doubt one day seem dated, if they do not seem so already. The example of Turner is provocative, because it illustrates the permeability of the line between ritual enactment and theatrical performance, as well as the one between scholarly detachment and participatory engagement. This blurring of genres (Geertz 1980) does not occur in a vacuum. It is occurring in other places and in other ways. It is typical of parashamanism and postmodernism. Merely dismissing the Turners, Schechner, and others such as Colin Turnbull and Michael Harner as idiosyncratic or exceptional will not do, because one would still have to explain the growing penchant for ritualizing in the so-called counterculture, if not in the culture at large.

What psychoanalysts once regarded as obsessive-compulsive and anthropologists and theologians as merely private or idiosyncratic is becoming for some a serious religious option. On the edge of major ritual traditions, as well as in the margins between major social institutions, ritual experiment is generating a growing body of cross-cultural and inter-religious criticism and practice. In some instances these experiments take the form of rank, unprincipled eclecticism; in others, "tribalizing" modification of mainline traditions. One might want to argue that "self-generated ritual" (Hine 1981) is merely an instance of cultural decadence, a bourgeois pastime unworthy of serious attention. However one evaluates it, liturgists and anthropologists have largely neglected it because of their bias toward the traditional and the collective.

Not all contemporary ritual experiments are equally worth attending to, but they do convince one of the need for ritual criticism—something akin to literary criticism that takes as its central object of interpretation the ritual form itself and not just its ethical implications, theological justifications, or social ramifications.[92] These ritual prescriptive "texts" and descriptive "accounts" illustrate the need for ways to assess ritual as ritual. Whether one is considering a birthday celebration, civil ceremony, or ecclesiastical liturgy, our capacity for both imagining and assessing ritual processes and performances is weak.

6

ILLNESS, EMBODIMENT,

AND RITUAL CRITICISM*

. . . It was clear that the ritual was arrested and that no one quite knew what to do next.

. . . It seemed as if the ritual were tearing the society apart rather than integrating it, were disorganizing personalities rather than healing them . . . .
—Clifford Geertz (1973:156,163)

With this essay we begin the transition from case study to essay. Though based on participation and observation, this chapter is not the result of formal participant observation. Though consultative and prescriptive, it is not a case study focused on a single instance. The data are from several instances of informal observation and participation. So the presentation is more abstracted from particular times and places. No description is presented, and the actual observations are not detailed. The criticism is more deductive than in the previous chapters. Though in the case studies I followed the lead of empirical anthropology by approaching theory through fieldwork, I have no "romanticism of the particular."[93] It can be just as fruitful to begin with the general, that is, with a theory or philosophy. Here, on the basis of a philosophy of embodiment, I shall draw out some implications for the way we imagine illness and then make some specific recommendations regarding the ritual handling of illness in health care settings.

In controversies about health care the concepts "myth" and "ritual" have

*This chapter is based on "Ritual and Illness" published in 1984 in the *Canadian Journal of Community Mental Health* 3(1):55–65; it is reprinted here with the permission of the editors of that journal. The original article was written at the encouragement of two colleagues at Wilfrid Laurier University: Aarne Siirala, professor of psychology of religion, and Ed Bennett, professor of psychology and an editor of the *Canadian Journal of Community Mental Health*. Their request was that, on the basis of my understanding of the human body and ritual and in view of my clinical experience and training, I comment on the ritualistic dimensions of illness and make specific recommendations that might help inform decisions made by chaplaincy and staff in institutions like Kitchener-Waterloo Hospital in Kitchener, Ontario, Canada.

been used to criticize the medical establishment. Such usage illustrates how the idea of ritual, not just rites themselves, can become both political and symbolic. Ritual and myth are being bandied about with considerable flamboyance. For example, Ivan Illich in *Medical Nemesis* (1975) declares, "High technology medicine is the most solemn element in a ritual celebrating and reinforcing the myth that doctors struggle heroically against death" (17). Illich employs an extended religious vocabulary: the medical profession is a "priesthood"; scientific principles are its "theology"; technologists are its "acolytes"; physicians offer "salvation"; medicine promises "miracles"; TV programs about hospitals are "liturgies"; and medical "magic" reduces the patient to a voyeur (77,56,53).

Thomas Szasz (1975) argues that the answer to the drug problem lies in "demythologizing and deceremonializing our use and avoidance of drugs" (34). He considers "the psychiatric mythology concerning drug abuse an exact replica of the psychiatric mythology concerning self abuse (masturbation)" (50). Szasz goes even further than Illich to suggest that a medical and psychiatric "religion" exists alongside what he mistakenly calls "theological" (rather than "theistic") religion (97,110).

In these instances the rhetoric of ritual is being used to disempower the medical establishment. Such usage is a combination of genuine insight and polemical diatribe. Szasz and Illich are referred to in the literature as "labeling" theorists because of their wont to treat mental illness as a socially conferred label rather than as an objective state. These men who expose other people's labels use ritual as a label. To them ritual connotes habitual practices of health-care professionals insofar as they subordinate the health of patients to self-interested maintenance of the existing system. Earmarking the rituals of doctors is done by Illich and Szasz for the sake of breaking those rituals. Though from different premises Susan Sontag in *Illness as Metaphor* (1977) locates myths and metaphors associated with tuberculosis and cancer in order to discourage their use.

My objection to the usage of these writers is not that their attack on the medicalization of life is wrongheaded, that we need to protect myths and rituals from demythologizing and deritualizing, or that I disagree with their claim that health care is sometimes involved in *hubris* (Horrobin n.d.). Rather, it is that their understanding of ritual and religion is uncritical even though they put it to critical use. Implicitly following Durkheim, they consider ritual only a mirror and reinforcer of the status quo. Their view of ritual is unacceptable in the field of ritual studies, because they do not understand the critical and constructive capacities of ritual. Nor do they make distinctions between types of ritual. Their mistake lies, not in treating ritual as part of cultural illness (which it no doubt can be), but in their failure to see how necessary ritual can be to both diagnosing and recovering from illnesses, including the doctor-made ones that come under the heading "iatrogenesis."

It is essential to put the concept of ritual on a more solid theoretical base so it will be usable in medical and psychiatric discussions, not just in prophetic attacks on medical religion. By criticizing the uncritical use of the notion of ritual, it is possible to deepen rather than refute criticisms of certain hospital procedures. So my intention is not to deny but to sharpen the critique of health care by laying out some basic postulates of a philosophy of embodiment.

A PHILOSOPHY OF EMBODIMENT

Every culture devises simplified means for reducing its complexity to manageable proportions. We can think of these as "models" (Black 1962), "maps," or "mazeways" (Wallace 1970). Modeling and mapping take many forms: myths, rites, flow charts, lists, classification schemes, bureaucratization, and so on. At the root of all these are dominant, organizing metaphors.[94] Symbols of illness are interconnected by way of metaphoric processes which, in some cases, generate whole cultural systems. In one culture people "fight" cancer; in another, a "ghost" invades a bereaved person.

In ritual studies we try to understand the metaphors on the basis of which people act, especially those they repeatedly act out or elevate to the status of gesture. A metaphor is a drastic symbolic act. In a metaphor this is perceived as that: the bread is body, the heart is the person, the tumor is a child-substitute, and so on. A metaphor is drastic because it is not the sort of symbol that merely points or refers. And certainly it does not merely point or refer to some abstract idea. A metaphor *embodies* what it means. If one's means of symbolizing is one's own body rather than, say, a word, a picture, or an object, the possibilities for "becoming what one beholds" (to invoke William Blake) are much greater. Hence it is useful to regard ritualized symbols as metaphoric, because of the degree to which the symbolic vehicle and the thing symbolized become identified in metaphor.

It is a mistake to think metaphor is essentially verbal. Verbal metaphors are one kind, not the only kind. The most serious metaphors are of two sorts: those by which we condense our entire sense of the world and those that we enact despite ourselves, in other words, cosmic and somatic metaphors. An example of the former is the world-as-machine; of the latter, cancer-as-enemy. The two kinds of metaphor converge in a third example, understanding-as-seeing, which is both a worldview and a somatic experience.

Metaphors are identifications predicated[95] across strata. In the case of illness, the strata are somatic, psychosocial, and religious. And it is with these kinds of identifications that ritual studies concerns itself. Metaphors simultaneously predicate identifications and pose tensions. They are ways of attuning ourselves in the face of cultural and ecological dissonance. However, they do not merely placate; they incite. They "reach across" (*meta, phora*) and thereby unify; in the same moment they undermine. Metaphors are not tranquilizers. They "tensify" as surely as they connect. They expose conflict and set things in motion as surely as they identify and link up disparate states of being.

The body is no mere fact but both a value and a meaning. Good and Delvecchio (1981:175) say that "human illness is fundamentally semantic or meaningful and that all clinical practice is inherently interpretive or 'hermeneutic.'" As a bearer of meaning, the body is not merely a tool for obtaining knowledge or communicating; it *is* knowledge and communication (Polhemus 1978). The postulate of the centrality of the human body implies that meaning is embodied in overt action, posture, and gesture and that both culture and psyche can be "somatized" (Kleinman 1980:149) in the form of symptoms. Ultimately, culture and body are not opposites.[96] Bodies are enculturated. Cultures are embodied.

Symptoms, like any other bodily manifestation, are metaphors. They both are and are not identical with the person who manifests them. Symptoms are unconsciously "willed." Since they are not literally, that is, consciously willed, we have to put "willed" in quotation marks to indicate its metaphoric status.

The human body is a primary source of metaphors for imagining one's whole world. We inquire into the "heart" of the matter; our corporations have "heads," and so on. Because the body is so primary most cultures regard it as sacred. The body is a specially marked off preserve, a repository of ultimate value. The human body does not merely front for or point to the sacred; it is sacred, a locus of revelation and hierophany. Not only does skin "think" (Dossey 1982:217), skin "reveals." Jennings (1982b: 115) says, "Ritual knowledge is gained by and through the body. We might speak here of the 'incarnate' character of ritual knowledge or say that it is gained through 'embodiment.'" Consequently, bodily illness is defined by some theologians and psychologists as a crisis of soul, as well as of mind and community. During illness not only does the body's load of meaning become more evident, the body itself becomes a focus of activity and passivity. Knowing (or "revelation," if it is especially full or pivotal) is the outcome of a dialectic of action and passion, to use more religious language. "Knowledge" consists of facts we obtain by science, observation, and experiment, while "knowing" is a process of becoming attuned to the rhythms and structures of one's world. However much we may not like it, illness is necessary for knowing. Such a view runs counter to an analogy that is commonly assumed in Western thinking, namely, that action is to passion as health is to illness. This unfortunate analogy associates illness with passivity, especially its heightened form, passion. Passion in our minds is linked with suffering, which we try to avoid. But by avoiding suffering we also avoid knowing.

Because we humans are essentially embodied and our illnesses essential to self-knowing, our "deathstyle" and lifestyle are dialectically expressive of one another. By implication, one's style of getting ill is a conflation of one's mode of approaching death and one's habitual ways of get on with life. Put another way, illness and death not only threaten or end life, they also express it. If one's lifestyle is contradictory, one's illnesses and death will express that contradiction. Cultural contradictions manifest themselves in the form of bodily symptoms. Because illness brings up front dynamics that are ordinarily backstage, it is analogous to ritual. A ritual, like an illness, reveals the structural contradictions of a lifestyle or between a lifestyle and a culture.

Any action, including that of becoming ill, can be viewed in at least two ways: as a consequence, on the one hand, and as an expression, on the other. As consequence, a disease is the effect of preceding causes such as stress or micro-organisms. As expression, however, an illness is a condensation of a lifestyle with its attendant values and choices. An illness expresses one's style and values, as well as the double binds (Bateson 1972; 1979) in which individuals participate by virtue of their membership in a culture and ecosystem (Rappaport 1979). An illness is not just a bare fact or a mere consequence but a stylized transition and, as Twaddle (1981a; 1981b) and others have shown, an act of negotiation.

Arthur Kleinman (1980:205) has presented one of the strongest cases for focusing attention, not just on patients, healers, or families, but on the transactions among them. His attempts to locate symbolic reality (see 1980:22, fig. 1; 42, fig. 2) between personal and social space, as well as between the sick person and "clinical reality" accurately suggest where rituals must operate if their negotiating capacities are to be of any use.

Illness is not just another state, the opposite of health. Illness *is* also health somatized metaphorically. An illness is a state of health projected to its end—its goal and conclusion. Any mode of being healthy, if made normative for the totality of one's existence, implies a distinctive mode of being ill and of dying (see Gotthard Booth 1979). One's style of illness is one's lifestyle amplified to the point where its liabilities become embodied.

Illness, like ritual, is inextricably bound up with symbolization. However important the biological causes of disease and the community contexts of illness, they are not the whole story. The whole consists of more than a historical summation of chronologically ordered parts and more than systematically ordered flow charts that schematize power relations among hospitals, community health organizations, and government institutions. Illness is as surely the outcome of our images as of microbes and institutions (either of which can themselves become metaphors).[97] So a poetics of illness is as necessary as a pragmatics. Every disease theory has its controlling metaphors. In the biomedical model, disease is "challenge" (Pfifferling 1981:215); in the cultural models proposed by medical anthropologists and sociologists, illness is "meaning" or "negotiation."

RITUALIZATION AND ILLNESS

In view of this philosophy of embodiment, some implications regarding ritual and illness emerge. I suggest that (1) illness, or the "sickness career" (Twaddle 1981a), is itself a ritualized process; (2) that symptoms ought to be seen as ultimate gestures and the transitions back and forth between illness and health, as rites of passage; and (3) the distance between interaction rites in health centers, ecclesiastical rites in churches and synagogues, and domestic rites in homes is itself a source of illness.

Since many people, including scholars, are likely to identify ritual only with its religious form, it is important for both practical and theoretical purposes to distinguish at least three ritual levels based on the degree to which they are differentiated from ordinary action: ritualization (introduced in chap. 1), interaction ritual (Goffman 1967), and liturgy (Rappaport 1979).

We speak of illnesses as acute or chronic. We make a parallel distinction between occasional rites of passage and repeated seasonal rites. Rites of passage are "acute," occurring only once for individuals who pass through culturally defined developmental phases. Seasonal rites are "chronic," requiring that we do them over and over to replenish a resource or reenergize entropy-laden processes. Illness is a tacit ritual, which is to say, a ritualization process. The connection between ritual and illness is not that of mere analogy but that of metaphoric identification.

Stylization is what leads some doctors, ministers, therapists, and mental health workers to "read" symptoms as messages or treat illness as having a "voice" (Siirala 1981). Those stylizations to which we are subject by virtue of our sociobiological nature, I have designated "ritualization," and those to which we aspire by virtue of our spirituality I have labeled "liturgy" (Grimes 1982). Unfortunately, in our culture we sever these two modes of symbolic action or else expect liturgy to save us from ritualization. We do not readily consider clerically administered healing rites (e.g., anointing with oil, bedside prayer, and funerals) as *arising* from the more primary, less differentiated instances of ritualization, namely, falling ill or getting well. We wrongly think of liturgies as arising only from tradition and history, not from the body as well.

Ritualization is the least differentiated kind of ritual. It is the most likely to go unnoticed, because of its low degree of formalization. Ritualization is rooted in our own biorhythms and psychosomatic patterning.

Liturgy, on the other hand, is highly formalized and usually associated with ultimacy, transcendence, the sacred—in short, with people's aspirations. Whereas patients might wish they could escape ritualization, some aspire to the transcendence promised by liturgy and the playful freedom typical of celebration. Strictly speaking, liturgies do not aim at healing as such. To do so would be to lapse into magic, the manipulation of symbolic means to achieve material ends.[98] Since the mainstream of Western religion and culture polemically rejects magic, liturgically inspired healing rites performed by clergy are for the most part innocuous. They do not supplement, much less provide a viable alternative to, the tacit ritual elements, the interaction rites, of standard health care practitioners best illustrated in Goffman's *Stigma* (1963).

Even scholarly readers of Szasz and Illich or Goffman, Foucault, and Sontag are likely to think of the use of the term "ritual" as *mere* metaphor. Metaphor it no doubt is; "mere" it is not. It is a mistake to assume that "real" ritual is only what happens in churches and synagogues or, by extension, in clinics visited by chaplains or clergy who have come to offer prayers and, on rare occasion, anoint or chant. The rituals of which Szasz and Illich speak are not only "like" rituals, they are serious competitors with the liturgies of Judaism, Protestantism, and Catholicism. It is a methodological error to suppose that interaction ritual is merely ad hoc, powerless because of its low degree of formality. Actually, its low profile allows it to become pervasive. Its ultimacy is not less just because it has no ordained advocates. Ritualization is every bit as serious as liturgy. This fact becomes obvious if one examines, not just people's verbalized religious aspirations, but their habitual patterns of action.

Thinking of illness as a ritualized mode of behavior means that a sick person is not just a passive victim. We imagine falling ill as something that happens to us, like falling in love. And getting well, we fancy, is something doctors make us do. So we are caught between the Scylla and Charybdis of helpless passivity and arrogant activity. A view of illness and health as ritual processes bypasses this dualism. As a symbolic act, an illness is simultaneously an avoidance of action and an incipient action (Burke 1966). In illness ordinary, pragmatic functioning is minimized and symbolic functioning accentuated. To put it another way, *ritually considered, an illness is a heightened state of receptivity in which a patient calls not only for medical procedures such as injections but for another style of knowing, one that leads to embodiment and receptivity in a context not segregated from a person's community and ultimate values.* To regard illness as a ritual process does not preclude regarding it in other ways, say, as a reflection of genetic structures (d'Aquili et al. 1979) or ethnic background (Harwood 1981:1–36), but it does call attention to generic religiosity. I say "generic" because getting sick or getting well is not ritualized in the sense that attending synagogue worship is, but it is analogous to—in some cultures even identical with—undergoing a hierophany (a manifestation of the sacred). In other words, getting ill or well is *experienced* as a rite of separation or incorporation, not into a denomination, but into a fundamentally different state of being.

PROPOSALS REGARDING RITUAL
IN HEALTH CARE INSTITUTIONS

Disease is a physiological matter; illness is its psychosocial concomitant (Foster and Anderson 1978:40). Whereas disease has to do with a bodily transition, illness is a transition between mental states and between social institutions. When one's temperature rises past 98.6 degrees F., that indicates that a person has a disease. When people are admitted to hospitals, that means they are ill. Disease is literal; illness is symbolic, although, as Kleinman (1980) warns, we must beware of too strict a division between disease and illness (356) or too facile an assumption that symbols are what make a rite effective in healing (226). If patients are diseased, they will be so diagnosed only if they display symptoms, a ritualized process. On the other hand, if they play-act the metaphors of illness, they run the risk of evoking a disease. Though we can distinguish them, we can never ultimately separate physiological disease and symbolic illness. They are systemically related; a change in one usually precipitates variation in the other. Metaphors are not merely decorative or literary embellishment.

They are constitutive, along with psychobiological co-variants. If we express and evoke disease by taking on the postures and gestures of illness, we regain health by embodying other metaphors. Contrary to Sontag, Illich, and Szasz, I do not believe we escape metaphors, myths, and rituals; we only change them.

In North America we have institutionalized a segmented view of ourselves by paying doctors to care for our bodies, psychiatrists our emotions, clergy our souls, educators our minds, and artists our imaginations. Older, tripartite "doctrines of man," as they once were called, have given way to a complex, bureaucratized model of the self. This self requires "servicing" and just as we have to know enough about auto mechanics to figure out whether the car goes to the muffler or radiator shop, so we need to know enough medicine to decide whether a swelling abdomen means we should haul the body to an internist or to an obstetrician. In such a culture, knowing how to make transitions between institutions is essential to survival, and in most cultures ritual is the very essence of making such transitions.

As was obvious in our study of contemporary Catholic liturgies, religious institutions such as churches and synagogues are no longer genuine meta-institutions, that is, ones that provide connective tissue between cultural segments or encompass the full range of peoples' lives. We have assumed that every state of being requires a corresponding institution. Now we even have separate institutions for holistic health—a contradiction in terms. A religious institution, like a holistic health one, is now simply one among others.

Ordinarily, we suppose people design institutions to fit diseases: offices with comfortable chairs or couches for psychoanalysis; well-lit, easy-to-clean floors in operating rooms. But what if diseases design themselves to fit our institutions—if surgeons have scalpels and we unwittingly comply by growing them an epidemic of neoplastic tissue? This notion is not as far-fetched as one might think. If the field of ritual studies teaches any clear lesson, it is that the human body and psyche grow to fit the metaphors-become-institutions of its culture. A scalpel is not just a tool; it is also a metaphor ("He's a 'sharp' student"). Metaphors do not passively reflect culture; they actively, even aggressively, shape it. Our bodies are not just "in" culture; they are "of" it. We do not only invent metaphors; they invent us. So, we should ask, What sorts of illnesses do hospitals, doctors' offices, clinics, community health organizations favor?

Of course, not every disease fits what our health systems have to offer. I am speaking about trends of illness, not every individual illness. Medical anthropologists have shown how culturally dependent both disease and disease-perception are. The same is true of health-care and its perception. Becoming ill in our culture is a rite of submission. Not that patients want to please doctors, but that unconsciously we identify (that key to metaphor again) with those who do us violence. Not only was it true of, say, Jews who identified with their oppressors in concentration camps (see Ruben-stein 1966), it is true of our relationships with those who do us the "good violence" (Girard 1972) of surgery and therapy. Like it or not, the health-care worker is experienced as a ritual "headman" and praised and con-demned accordingly. Our health care institutions seldom know what to do with this symbolic status other than exploit or deny it.

Health institutions provide services. Even though theorists speak of "delivering" health services, these institutions do not literally produce "goods." In this respect its institutions resemble religious ones. Religious ones cannot "deliver" salvation, enlightenment, or wisdom any more than health can be delivered. What service-oriented institutions "market" are symbolic goods. Symbolic goods are real, but they are neither products nor deliverable. Yet if we are dissonantly related to those symbolic goods, we become ill. If a culture's health services only distribute or consume meta-phors, *using* them as advertising fodder without *following* and *attending* to them as objects of meditation, those services themselves become agents of contamination. What we saw among archaeologists (chap. 3) we find among health-care workers: the manipulation and use of objects without the sense of identification that comes from attending to them. The danger is that health institutions will dismember the whole "story" and substitute a series of "procedures" and "steps" in its place. If community health is a "service" only in this sense, in the long run it probably does people a disservice.

The problem is not merely that health workers and clergy do not work as a team. If a team administers health and soul care seriatim, little more is accomplished than is achieved when two faculty call it "team teaching" when all they do is take turns. Nothing is helped if cleric and doctor visit patients, each assuming he or she is ministering to a separate sphere; substituting stratified for seriatim care accomplishes little. Those who aspire to heal others must embody health. This does not mean they have to be well scrubbed or *display* sanity. It means they cannot just "deliver" health care. No matter how good their goods, it is the style of delivery that is one of the primary sources of illness and health. Embodying health care rather than delivering it is a more effective style.

So far, I have argued that whenever we fall ill, we do so metaphorically and psychobiologically. I have intimated that we get well in the same way (see Simonton 1975; cf. Scarf 1980). I have suggested that we need a form of health care not presently provided, one that is explicitly ritualistic and able to bridge the chasm between domestic, religious, medical, and psychiatric institutions. On rare occasions clerical visits have served this function, but clerical rounds have increasingly taken the form of counseling rather than ritual. The result has been "thin" ritual (ritual as routine) rather than symbolically "thick," or healing, ritual.

Some ways of beginning to change this situation are these:

1. Chaplains and clergy ought to receive training in nonverbal communication and ritual construction, since training in counseling and the conduct of worship is by itself clearly insufficient to deal with illness and healing.
2. Professional health-care workers, as part of their training, ought to observe and work with folk and religious healers who practice in the same society but on the basis of other models. This is an effective way to ensure a critical perspective on the assumptions embedded in their own health-care system.
3. Religious institutions and health-care centers should consider establishing what one might call "nests" or "sanctuaries" (in the archaic sense of the term)—places in which the ill and their families can dwell for the sole purpose of meditating on images of illness and health.
4. Ritologists need to work with health-care workers and clergy to design simple domestic healing rites that do not require the presence of professionals.
5. The training of clergy in liturgics should include anthropological and cross-cultural perspectives in order to understand better both healing rites and the interface between tacit and explicit ritual.
6. Training in pastoral psychology needs to be rooted firmly in ritual studies so "talking cures" can be supplemented with gestural, iconic, and spatial work.[99]

The third point above requires elaboration. What we need is a milieu in which patients can be brought into bodily contact with a "nest" of the sacra (objects, gestures, postures, and spaces) of their culture.[100] Such contact could facilitate the visualization, even tactilization, of images of health. Our particular cultural pathology lies in thinking we can attend to medicine, psychiatry, and spirituality seriatim (first the doctor or therapist, then the priest). It is the "then" that counterritualizes the illness. We shall never construct a whole by stitching together parts, any more than Dr. Franken-stein did.

A nest, if I may press the metaphor, should contain in symbolic form both treasures and sacra. In such a nest a patient ought to be surrounded with the sacra, images of health and wholeness, concretions of extolled values. But it should contain repressed "treasures" as well. A culture keeps its treasures psychosomatically locked up (see Hillman 1972), as if in a dragon-guarded cave. The whiteness of a nurse's uniform, the cadences of a priest's prayer, and the authority to write prescriptions—all symbolize cultural aspirations such as purity, transcendence, and competence, but they are insufficient to heal (no matter what they "cure"), because they make metaphorically present only the "top" of the culture, not the "bottom" as well. Just as the post-Vatican II church (see chap. 2) has cleaned up itself iconically, becoming streamlined and linear, so hospitals hide refuse, symbolic and literal. It is no accident that Ken Feit, Welfare State International, and other ritual-makers sacralize refuse, making it the very stuff of celebration.

Illness is a gestural way of searching for the bottom, the ground of things. As such, it requires that the lairs be opened, carefully, but nevertheless opened. Ritually, an illness requires not only its opposite, cure or idealization of health, but reflections of illness as well. So the nest of symbols made for a patient should include repressed or rejected images—not just the whiteness of purity but the blackness of night, not just the orderliness of numbers and charts but the babel of names, not only the smell of disinfectant but the odor of earth, not just the solemnity of professionals but the antics of clowns.

I am not merely turning phrases; I am referring to specific ritual practices. Nests, environments rich in symbols capable of incubating the process of passage between illness and health, are essential in many cultures. As I understand the community health movement, it arises from a critique of the overinstitutionalizing of illness and a recognition that health is not just a quality of mind or body but of community. My contention is that it is also a quality of action. Just as extended isolation of ill people from their communities can undermine medical and psychiatric care, so sterilizing their environment, making it bereft of gestural and iconic metaphors, literalizes and further sickens a patient. The implication this has for both hospitals and the community mental health is that health care-workers need training—bodily, not just theoretical—in the methods for constructing environments in which symptomatic symbolization can be "read" rather than "cured." At present neither religious nor health institutions successfully do this. Health care workers need to participate in and adapt, not just observe, techniques from cultures more symbolically literate than our own. What is most urgently needed is actual experience with modes of symbolic action that are not characterized by a split between active-interventionist and passive-consumptionist ideologies. The alternative is a posture best described as "active receptivity," a Taoist idea with parallels in other traditions. We need to develop ways of bypassing many of the dualisms that feed illness: activity/passivity, illness/health, and politics/play. The community mental health movement is in a good position to cultivate attitudes and techniques that disable these crippling dualisms unless it clings uncritically to an activist ideology that considers ritual as lacking in utility because of its indirection—its way of "overcoming from underneath," as the Taoists say.[101]

7

NARRATIVE AND RITUAL CRITICISM*

Narrative is the fundamental scheme for linking individual human actions and
events into interrelated aspects of an understandable composite.
—Donald E. Polkinghorne (1988:13)

In developing the idea of ritual criticism I have adapted and transformed
models found in other disciplines, notably anthropology, performance
studies, and liturgiology. Since the emphasis has been so squarely on
actions, little has been said about language and literature studies, which
claim criticism as one of its tasks. Recently, narrative has become an
important topic in both religious studies and literature. Insofar as narrative
theory changes, the criticism of texts changes. Those texts most often
linked theoretically with ritual are mythic ones. Many scholars still treat
myth and ritual as a pair (see, e.g., Doty 1986), and some still read secular
literature for its mythic and ritualistic resonances (e.g., Grimes 1989;
Hardin 1983). What happens when a criticism nurtured on the field study
of ritual encounters theories of narrative derived from the study of mythic
and literary texts?

Narrative theology (see Goldberg 1982) is in its formative stages.
Whether it becomes a useful method or dies as a passing theological fad
depends in large measure on our ability to coordinate and criticize the
rapidly proliferating ways of writing it. Doing so may be difficult, since the
terms "narrative" and "story" are exercising an almost incantatory sway
over the field of religious studies.

One can identify several clusters of writers, books, and articles that do
not quite constitute schools of thought, subfields, or formal methodolo-
gies, yet all of them concentrate on narrative and its relation to religion.
Among the prominent ones are: (1) *a sacred biography group*—largely
historians of religion working on the lives of founders, saints, and reform-

---

*This chapter is a revision of "Of Words the Speaker, Of Deeds the Doer" originally
published in 1986 in the *Journal of Religion* 66(1):1–17. Portions from that article are
reprinted here with the permission of the University of Chicago Press.

ers and utilizing the vocabulary of the history and phenomenology of religion to interpret these narratives (see Reynolds and Capps 1976); (2) *a faith development group*—religious educators and psychologists of religion assessing biographical progression through six stages of religious development based on Piaget and Kohlberg (see Fowler et al. 1980);(3) *a psychobiography group*—psychologists of religion applying Erikson's life-cycle theory to biographies and autobiographies of religious individuals (see Capps et al. 1977); (4) *a character and community group*—theological ethicists who use narratives, especially biographical ones, to guide character-building, social criticism, and decision-making (see Hauerwas 1973, 1976, 1977, 1981; McClendon 1974; and Novak 1971); (5) *a Biblical narrative group*—Biblical scholars using a variety of methods to understand biblical narrative and its relation to nonbiblical narrative (see Frei 1974, and Crossan 1975), and (6) *a myth and ritual group*—literary critics, classicists, and some ancient Near Eastern specialists working on both ancient and modern narratives with a view to explicating their connections to ritual (see Kirk 1970; Ackerman 1975; Hardin 1983).

Such a list indicates how difficult it is to say precisely what narrative theology is and who does it. It also suggests that the term "theology" is too narrow to describe the kind of attention being paid to narrative's place in religion. My concern here is with neither the precision nor the narrowness of the terms but with the relations between narrative and ritual, or more broadly, language and action. I do not conceive them dualistically, but neither do I think language-based models and metaphors are all-sufficient. I resist the tendency to construe the whole of religion and selfhood "as language" or more specifically "as narrative."

In the current discussions of narrative, theologians claim with apparent ease that the self is narratively constructed. Stephen Crites (1971:291) is typical in wanting us to believe that "the formal quality of experience through time is inherently narrative." Boldly, some narrative theologians are making a second leap, namely, to the assumption that ethics is the natural concomitant of storytelling. Michael Novak (1971:46) asserts, "All action is the living out of a story in a cosmos." The sort of action he has in mind is ethical, "the history of acts of will, the history of choices made" (45). A third theme of narrative theologians is that some special affinity exists between time and narrative. Crites's statement illustrates this. A fourth feature of much theology and narrative discussion is the largely unquestioned belief that storytelling is good, because it fosters "the continuing advance of consciousness through reflection" (Winquist 1978:11).

From a point of view within ritual studies I want to question all four propositions and show (1) that it makes just as good sense to claim that the self is performatively constituted, (2) that storytelling is as akin to ritual enactment as it is to ethical behavior, (3) that time has no more privileged status than space, and (4) that narratively inspired reflection is as much a problem as it is a virtue. In short, these items, around which a consensus seems to be growing among narrative theologians, are preferences not necessities.

TO NARRATE IS HUMAN, IF NOT DIVINE

One would hardly bother to question the claim that human experience is inherently narrative if all anyone meant by it was the truism, "People tell stories." But theologians seem to be claiming more. They want to convince us that narrating is not simply an optional activity, something we can choose to do or not. Rather, it makes us who we are: selves or human beings. Consequently, it has, for them, a privileged status. In trying to assess such a view, it helps to understand what the story theorists are arguing against. Stories instead of what? The answer seems to be: stories instead of principles, reasons, or authority. Keen (1970:2) does not want to speak with the voice of theology or philosophy, which is to say, with "authority," so he tells us stories in the first person instead. Novak (1971:63,65,68) appeals to story (note the metaphysically generalized singular) rather than principles, because the former is more "productive," "flexible," and "concrete." Winquist (1978:2), who finds in stories a legitimate way to debunk the "pretensions of consciousness" and "claims of absolute knowledge and objectivity," claims that without stories we are left in the throes of mere immediacy unable to link our present to our past and future. He comes dangerously close to making storytelling a criterion for deciding what is or is not authentically human by making statements like "Storytelling is part of the becoming of the human spirit" and "Mythology increases being" (9). Regardless of its content, a story seems to him to be a positive value, never a liability.

The drift of the narrative theologians has been to imply that one is human or religious by virtue of some association with "story" (the idea) or stories (the specific narratives told). The nature of this association is often left vague. Occasionally, we are told what it is we must do to be saved: have a story, tell it, act on it, or reflect on it—any or all of these. Shortly after Keen's story book was published, he felt it necessary to write a do-it-yourself volume called *Telling Your Story: A Guide to Who You Are and Who You Can Be* (Keen and Fox 1973). Some theologians, Richard Rubenstein (1974), for instance, under the impact of the "God made man because he loves stories" ethos, wrote their own theological autobiographies. One may love stories but find the new autobiographical self-consciousness in religious studies susceptible to self-deception. Despite this danger confession has become in some circles the necessary ritual prelude to scholarly reflection: "In his book on Erikson, Robert Coles tells us that it is dangerous not to follow Erikson's example of daring to be autobiographical when dealing with the thoughts of others. Heeding this counsel, I shall start by saying something of the history of my encounters with Erikson's work" (Lindbeck 1977:7).

How have we arrived at the point where autobiographical narrating is such a necessity? Two reasons given for the current "love of stories" and for equating narration with selfhood or humanity (if not divinity) are: (1) the Bible is a story, so theology should either be storytelling or, if theologians insist on writing systematic theologies, they ought not lose touch with the narrative sources of theology; (2) everybody tells stories, but not everyone writes systematic theology, so storytelling must be pan-human and therefore a fair standard for judging who is truly human.

I shall simply point out the obvious and then leave the first point to the biblical scholars. The Bible includes poetry, legislation, genealogy, aphorism, poetry, dream accounts and other genres that are not narrative in quality. Construing the sixty-six books as a story is already a highly interpretive, culture-bound act, one that hardly warrants the implication: to narrate is divine.

I am more concerned about the ethnocentrism that lies behind the second claim. One good example throws the "narrative self" into a culturally relative light. When Renato Rosaldo (1976) tried to elicit from Old Tukbaw the story of his life, the anthropologist became stalled: Tukbaw had no idea what a story was. Rosaldo had assumed that "every man has his life story within him" (121) but was forced to concede that he did not believe "members of [Tukbaw's] culture were accustomed to telling their life stories in any form . . ."(122). Rosaldo does not argue that the Ilongots have no stories, only that the self is not the object or result of them. But, according to the story theorists and theologians, narrative is supposed to lead to selfhood—for all people not just Christians. What shall we say of the Ilongots who have no biographies or autobiographies? Or of the early Romans, who, as Kluckhohn (1965:94) points out, got along well without myth? Shall we say they lacked selfhood or humanity? I doubt it. A more probable answer is that their selfhood is constituted in other ways, by ritual, for instance, or according to "principles."

It would be pointless to claim that ritual, rather than narrative, constitutes our humanity. And it would be an exaggeration to insist that all religious narratives, myths, for example, "need" ritual enactment. Kluckhohn has shown that there is no necessary connection between mythic narrative and ritual enactment. The one does not always reflect or accompany the other. Nevertheless, they do so with sufficient frequency that one wonders why it so seldom occurs to narrative theologians to ask whether ritual enactment can function as effectively as narration as a means of "homecoming" (Keen 1970:chap. 1; Winquist 1972: chap. 1). Paul Ramsey (1979:139) intones in weighty Latin: "*Lex orandi lex credendi lex bene operandi*" (As we pray so we believe and do). A paraphrase in more recent rhetoric, might be, "As we enact ritually, so we narrate theologically and act ethically." Ramsey says the order ought to be reversible and that all three activities should be on a par with one another. But as a matter of practice many theologians follow a twofold, nonreversible order: from telling to choosing; or else a circular one: from telling to choosing back to telling the story of the choosing. Liturgy and ritual are either left out of this loop altogether, construed as variables dependent on ethics, or used as mere illustrations of narrative.

It is not enough to say that there should be parity among ethics, ritual, and myth. Every religion or culture has its own ways of organizing, emphasizing, and subordinating the three. They do not go together automatically, nor do they always do so harmoniously. A mythic narrative may contradict a ritual enactment, and a ritual image may undermine a narrative one. There is no good reason for assuming that narrative is more foundational, more human, or more conducive to selfhood. Some stories, in fact, undermine selfhood and lead to inhumanity (see, e.g., Hauerwas 1977:82–98). But there is good reason to suspect that the sort of humanity constructed by narratively emphatic religions is quite different from that sort undergirded by ritually emphatic ones.

Mary Wakeman (n.d.) has raised a serious question about narrative theology. She wonders whether the insistence that selfhood is constituted by a specifically narrative way of organizing images is a patriarchal legacy (cf. Hillman 1975:142). To my knowledge, her challenge remains unanswered. John Dixon, Jr., (1979:182,226) has leveled another charge, namely, that theology (even of the type based on narrative rather than systematic structures) without enactment and dramatic processes has exhausted itself. Who is to say, Dixon wants to know, that the narrated image is more human or more theologically fundamental than visual or performative ones? Dixon's view is at least more pluralistic than that of the narrative theologians. He says, "Art, ritual, myth are the spiritual situation because they are the essentials of the world the imagination has constructed around the paradoxical situation of being human" (1983:21). He counters the verbal-textual bias still dominant in academic theology.

Certainly, viewing one's life "as story" or action "as text" (Ricoeur 1973) has its place. The Toronto Towneley cycle (chap. 4) was a marvelous wedding of ritual, drama, and storytelling. But "story" and other language-based metaphors have their problems too, as Geertz (1980:175ff.) has illustrated. My argument is simply that they are metaphors and, as such, can, but do not necessarily, constitute the self or define what is authentically human. Performance-based metaphors (the world as stage, interaction as ritual, social conflict as drama) have wider applicability because they do not imply that storytelling or worse, literacy, is a condition of human selfhood. A performatively grounded hermeneutic also exposes the ritual avoidance that is still deep in the heart of post-Protestant theology. We are still afraid that if enactment were to take its place alongside narration, we would have to perform, that is, do good works or do something other than write and speak in order to be religious.

FROM STORY TO ETHICS

A well-worn track is being cut from narrative to ethics. Crites (1971: 311) argues, "Among those for whom the story is alive there is a revival of ethical authority otherwise almost effaced in our society." The theologians' itinerary seems to be from the Bible to narrative to ethics, or from biblical narrative to ethics, or from narrative back to the Bible then to ethics. In any case, ethics seems to be the Rome to which all roads lead. A story's test is whether it leads to right action, and by "action" narrative theologians like McClendon and Hauerwas mean the sort that occurs in community and political life, not in dramatic performance or ritual enactment. The sort of character that interests them is moral character, not the kind of character one finds wearing masks or feathers. What would happen if the road from narrative to ethics passed through ritual? Probably the ethicists and theologians would not object as long as the narrative were biblical and the ritual liturgical. But what if the narrative were *Watership Down*, to mention an example brilliantly interpreted by Hauerwas (1981:chap. 1), and the rituals were experimental initiation rites like those described by Roberts (1982) or Starhawk (1979)?

What is bothersome about the narrative-ethics syndrome is that it seems to be an attempt to control stories even though Hauerwas (1981:11), for example, says that "Christian social ethics can only be done from the perspective of those who do not seek to control . . . but who are content to live 'out of control.'" McClendon's (1974:89–90) rhetoric is revealing. Consider these two sentences: "Now let us consider the suggestion that a key to these biographies is the *dominant* or *controlling* images . . . ," and "Moreover, I believe that the living out of life under the *governance* of such a vision [i.e., a set of controlling images] is the best way to conceive of 'religious experience'" (italics added).

Missing from the narrative-to-ethics way to doing theology is the possibility of acting in what some are calling the "subjunctive" mode. We are hurried along from reading and telling stories to ethics, the realm of "imperatives." Immediately we are made responsible for what we read, as if narratives were poised, waiting to guide our lives. What if controlling and guiding are not the only things stories do?

Narratives, however much they may inspire or inhibit social action, also call for subjunctive, as-if (Vaihinger's term, 1935) responses—at least as an interlude before we enter the arena of the social world where ethical decision making and character formation count. Ritual could provide such a liminal zone. Ritually, one can die, drink blood, or be crucified with Christ, not with immunity, of course, but at least without the same legal and physiological repercussions that such an act would provoke in non-ritualized zones.

Rituals as such are no better, freer, or more human than ethics as such. Rituals can prevent embodiment as surely as they can facilitate it. In my estimation Ramsey's "Liturgy and Ethics" (1979) is a good example of the ways in which ethics and ritual can be made mutually to inhibit one another. But because ritual actions can be cordoned off from the nonritual world by virtue of their symbolic nature, they can allow for fuller exploration of unconscious motives than the image-to-action models usually allow. If a narrative inspires, say, the act of smashing objects or other persons, the ethically minded would want to prevent it, but the ritually minded might propose a potlatch rite instead. In other words, narratives are capable of evoking not just moral or immoral actions but amoral ones insofar as ritual, rather than ethical, framing of those actions is cultivated. Ritual can contain rich dramatic possibilities that allow us trial runs and explorations not possible in the ethically framed world. Too often the problem with religious ethics is that the only laboratory for experiment is the mind of a theologian or a forum for debate. There are huge gaps, as Kierkegaard was fond of reminding us (since he fell into them so frequently), between narration and action.

We should ask ourselves precisely how, having read the life of some religious hero such as Dag Hammarskjöld or Martin Luther King, Jr. (two of McClendon's examples), we embody the images that supposedly guide us. The process is neither automatic nor natural. It is cultural and dramatic, and we lack an ethic sufficiently sophisticated to deal with either stage drama (see Burns 1972) or social drama (see Turner 1974a, 1980). Without a ritual-dramatic stage between the narrative experience and the ethical judgment we are extremely subject to self-deception (one of Hauerwas's emphases) concerning the degree to which we have embodied our ethics. Without a keenly developed ritual-dramatic sense, our narratives are at best intellectual ideals and at worst sources of heteronomously imposed, introjected images.

Moral behavior is learned by its ritual suspension, inversion, or exaggeration as surely as it is learned by its enforcement. The symbolic anthropologists have demonstrated this convincingly (see, e.g., Babcock 1978). So ritual-drama rooted in play, which can be quite serious, can serve as a useful hinge between speaking and doing. For too long we have elevated the "word event" to the point where it has become a magical act, a leap from text to deed, and have flattered ourselves into believing that all our words (theological, narrative, homiletical, and otherwise) are "performative utterances" (Austin's term, 1962). They are not. Some of them, given the right conditions, might develop performative force. But narratives are not necessarily incipient actions; they can be, and often are, as Kenneth Burke (1969:235ff.) suggests, substitutes for action. Most of our utterances lack sufficient body and drama to arc all the way across the gap, thus connecting text and event.

In her dated but still provocative work on Greek religion, Jane Harrison (1927) defines myth simply as "the thing said" (*to legomenon*) and ritual as "the thing done" (*to dromenon*). She derives the distinction from a statement made by old Phoenix to Achilles, "Thy father . . . sent me to thee to teach thee to be both of words the speaker and of deeds the doer" (328). What sort of deeds? Don't all our fathers want us, men and women alike, to be "men of our word"? The fathers will refuse, won't they, to be satisfied if we try squeezing by with mere words? They might permit us to be "men of few words," that is, doers of deeds with little need to talk about them. But it is best, isn't it, if our words and our actions are consistent?

By expecting consistency, the fathers hope our words will go with our deeds rather than contradict (*contra dicere*, "to speak against") them. The reason Achilles' father must send his son a teacher is not because Achilles is short on oratory or action. The reason is to teach the young man to do deeds and speak words that go together. But what if they do not? Suppose language and action become dissonant rather than consonant, then what?

Must we deem them unethical? How do we know they are not tacitly ritualistic or dramatic?

A place to practice living with dissonance between things said and things done is ritual. Making consistency, narrative or logical, the only ground of virtue is a mistake. For one thing, doing so is likely to make us hate, and therefore deny, our inconsistencies. And inconsistencies denied, rather than embodied in some subjunctive way, become "somatized" (Kleinman 1980:149), which means they take the form of symptoms.

NARRATION, ENACTMENT, AND REFLECTION

Some anthropologists, like theologians, have begun to study the "passing over" from speaking narratively to performing ritually. Barbara Myerhoff and Deena Metzger (1980), for example, treat journal writing as a rite of passage laden with liminal possibilities. Whether they are speaking metaphorically is difficult to determine however. Surprisingly, they too try to argue that the self is constructed narratively, specifically, in journal writing. Furthermore, they believe that the reflexive aspect of this activity is what leads to self-construction, and they consider this reflexivity the function common to both rites of passage and narrative.

This view is a clue, perhaps, to the reason narrative theologians avoid ritual or want to make it the handmaiden of narrative. Winquist (1978:103) puts the matter plainly: "Ritual can replace thought as an interpretive modality. It can never be fully satisfactory because the denial of reflective consciousness masks a dimension of selfhood."

I doubt that ritual denies reflective consciousness any more than narrative does; some rituals do and some do not. Assuming that they do as a matter of principle is a remnant of nineteenth-century speculation about the naïveté and immediacy of primitive participation in rites. A good example that illustrates how reflexive a ritual can be is the Hopi Kachina cult initiation described by Sam Gill (1977). This rite, on ritual grounds, is as self-conscious and self-critical as any narratively or systematically organized theology.[102]

Even so, we must ask whether reflexivity is really what makes us human and therefore, narrative and ritual valuable. Reflexivity seems to be a dominant theme of the 1970s and 1980s, especially in literary criticism, theology, symbolic anthropology, and ritual studies, so I am suspicious of it when it begins to sound like a criterion or virtue.

Schechner (1980:12–13) identifies narcissism as one of four foundations of the postmodern era (discussed more fully in chap. 10). Hutcheon (1980:1) lists other, less prejudicial, synonyms: self-reflective, auto-referential, and meta-fictional, for instance. There are variants of reflexivity, but my point is simply that as a cultural theme and preoccupation it may define an era without being the essence of either humanity, narrative, or ritual. That it can be one among many functions I do not deny. So even though reflexivity is an activity human beings engage in, they do so in many ways, and neither literature nor performance nor theology has a monopoly on it.

Reflexivity, whether performative or narrative, signals a crisis. Whether reflection causes or expresses the crisis, I do not pretend to know. Perhaps both. Kierkegaard, more than any other theologian of the modern era, embodied and understood, but could not therefore escape, the paralysis of hyper-reflection. Whereas he knew that at some point one had to escape the hermeneutical circling with a leap, postmodern theology has become increasingly snarled in it. Theological narcissism turns theology into a "self-consuming artifact," if I may borrow Stanley Fish's (1972) term. Theology ought to have many objects, not just one, and certainly not just language or itself.

Winquist, whom I take to be one of the more perceptive narrative (now deconstructionist) theologians, was invited to participate with Victor Turner, Eugene d'Aquili, and others in a symposium on ritual in human adaptation, the papers for which were published in 1983 in the journal *Zygon* (18[3]). Winquist's paper scarcely addresses the issue of ritual's function and instead uses Turner's theory of social drama to analyze the social location of theology. His conclusion is that theology is "a victim of secularization" and now exists in a liminal zone, having breached its connection with public life.

But all Winquist can suggest as redress is that "Theology cannot cease to be itself" (1983:297). By "self" he seems to mean its dwelling in language and its disengagement from the body. Even if I were to agree that theology is largely a verbal enterprise, I would refuse to follow Winquist's practice of it insofar as he makes texts its primary or only object. His "deconstruction" of theology makes a virtue of something I consider a serious deficiency. Theology's subject matter is religious practice, something Winquist avoids (see 295) or is ambivalent about (see 298). Theology, as he illustrates it in this article, is not a "speech act" (296) at all but a speech that is ambivalent about action. And the ambivalence, one suspects, is a function of excessive emphasis on reflexivity—to such a degree that "theological reflection" becomes a synonym for theology.

Paul Ricoeur (1967:19,347ff.) has provided us with what he regards as "an excellent maxim": "Myth gives rise to thought." No doubt it can. One might also ask whether it gives rise to action. Winquist is not unaware of the dilemma, but I fear he wants to make the dilemma the answer. He says, "The scene of the origination of thinking is the scene of a wound," and "The repression of the economics of force through semantic substitution of a textual world is an erasure of the body in its environment. There is only a trace of the body in the body of the text because it is always other than the text" (1983:303).

I could hardly agree more. But one can only be disappointed when Winquist, having made an incisive critique, ends by endorsing disembodied theology, which takes the form of "a theater of memory" and an "intellectual liturgy" (1983:307). Theology, instead of being reflection upon (or after) enactment, has itself become ritualized, and, far from subverting patterns of discourse in prophetic fashion as Winquist hopes, it becomes simply self-serving and worse, immobilized, trapped in language, unable to leap. Ricoeur's sympathetic "reenactment" is always in quotation marks, indicating that one acts out myths only in a disembodied imagination; the re-enactment is sedentary.

Theodore Jennings (1982b) comes much closer both to bridging the theology-ritual gap and to cutting the knot of theological narcissism that many of us hoped the narrative emphasis in theology would challenge. He argues that ritual itself is a legitimate means of knowing; it is "minded," not mindless, action (124). Specifically, it is an "incarnate" means of knowing. Not only the object of theological reflection but a ground of it, ritual is as essential to theology as narrative is. Much of what Jennings says would probably seem obvious to Orthodox theologians, perhaps even to some Catholic ones, so one might inquire whether the problem of rightly conceiving the relation of narration to enactment is a post-Protestant one. Post-Protestants are those of us who have exhausted our polemical stance toward ritual but are unable simply to return home as penitent "separated brethren" or go elsewhere posing as "natives." Post-Protestants are those who suspect that our participation in ritual must be ludic and subjunctive, just as our naïveté toward myth must be of the "second," chastened kind.

TIME—THE HOME OF NARRATIVE?

According to some theologians, narrative has its "home" in time. Crites (1971) makes the baldest claims for this special kinship:

Narrative alone can contain the full temporality of experience in a unity of form [303]. Consciousness grasps its objects in an inherently temporal way, and that temporality is retained in the unity of its experience as a whole [298]. Without memory, in fact, experience would have no coherence at all [298].

The New York Review of Books ran the story of "Jimmy R." as told by his neurologist, Oliver Sacks (1984:14–19). Jimmy, who is about fifty-seven by now, has no memory for the period from 1945 to the present. His memories prior to that time are crystal-clear, but now he forgets everything as soon as it happens. The disease is labeled, but hardly explained, by the tag "Korsakov's syndrome." Dr. Sacks never finds a cure, so this story, simply and elegantly written, seems destined to go nowhere.

Then one day Sacks asks the sisters in the hospital if they think Jimmy has a soul. Like the narrative theologians, Sacks suspects memory, temporality, and narrative constitute selfhood. The sisters are outraged. "Watch him in chapel and judge for yourself," they advise.

What the neurologist sees is worth quoting at length:

> . . . I was moved, profoundly moved and impressed, because I saw here an intensity and steadiness of attention and concentration that I had never seen before in him or conceived him capable of. I watched him kneel and take the Sacrament on his tongue, and could not doubt the fullness and totality of Communion, the perfect alignment of his spirit with the spirit of the Mass. Fully, intensely, quietly, in the quietude of absolute concentration and attention, he entered and partook of the Holy Communion. He was wholly held, absorbed, by a feeling. There was no forgetting, no Korsakov's then, nor did it seem possible or imaginable that there should be; for he was no longer at the mercy of a faulty and fallible mechanism—that of meaningless sequences and memory traces—but was absorbed in an act, an act of his whole being, which carried feeling and meaning in an organic continuity and unity, a continuity and unity so seamless it could not permit any break.
>
> The sisters were right—he did find his soul here . . .
>
> I have known Jim now for nine years—and neuropsychologically, he has not changed in the least. He still has the severest, most devastating Korsakov's, cannot remember isolated items for more than a few seconds, and has a dense amnesia going back to 1945. But humanly, spiritually, he is at times a different man altogether . . . rich in all the Kierkegaardian categories—the aesthetic, the moral, the religious, the dramatic.

The Mass does not cure Jimmy of his illness, but his way of participating in it convinces his neurologist of the presence of soul (call it "selfhood" or "humanity") despite the absence of a sense of time and narrative in his life. Whereas diary-keeping failed with Jimmy, because he could not recognize earlier entries, taking part in the Mass "holds" him. Sacks's interpretation of this fact is that Jimmy is disoriented in "spatial" time but organized in "intentional" time. By "spatial time" he means what theologians sometimes call *chronos*, time as an abstract sequence of uniformly divided units.

Sacks' view does not answer the question, Why was Jimmy so "intentional" during the Mass but not in writing the diary? So I would frame the interpretation another way. Jimmy can locate himself best in situations characterized by non-narrative intentionality. I am tempted to say in "spatialized" or ritualized reality, meaning by "space" here, not "formally abstract," but "having tactile qualities and literal extension."

My temptation is to say that if the narrative theologians are correct in maintaining that narrative resides in time, then why not make a clean division of labor and give space to ritual? As a crude generalization (of the same order as the distinction between verbal, visual, and performative arts), this half-serious proposal has some limited use. We might say that what Jimmy lacks in temporal (therefore, narrative) competence he makes up with spatial (therefore, ritualistic) competence. Like his neurologist, many of us may initially feel that Jimmy's lack is one that raises questions about the presence of his soul, if not his humanity. But we ought not forget how often religious people speak about "timelessness" as if the word connoted a desirable state of mystical consciousness. I am not for a minute suggesting that mystical unity and Korsakov's syndrome are identical but am arguing that temporality is not necessarily a virtue. Nor is it the sole possession of narrative. What the parceling out of time to narrative, and space to ritual, does is lead readers and storytellers to repress the spatial qualities of narrative and ritualists to overlook the time-laden features of ritual.

Lonnie Kliever (1977) has written a telling critique of theologians and narrative theorists who neglect spatiality because of their preoccupation with time. He suggests that what they are avoiding in so doing is either "mystical or polytheistic religious sensibilities" (552). If Kliever is right and Wakeman correct in her suspicion that preoccupation with narrative is patriarchal, then narrative theology begins to look like a function of patriarchal monotheism. This is not necessarily bad, but it does begin to make narrative theology seem the child of a specific interest group or tradition and less like an offspring of interdisciplinary reflection.

"Proxemics" (Hall 1966:1), the study of human spatial organization, is relatively recent as a discipline. I find it revealing that, in order to gain recognition and legitimacy for the field, Edward T. Hall, one of its primary exponents, had to resort to language-based metaphors, for instance, "Space Speaks" (a chapter title). He also had to refer to space as *The Hidden Dimension* (1966).

Kliever shows how ignored and "invisible" space is to modern religious thought. He summarizes the situation this way:

> The full measure of this ignorance of human spatiality can also be seen in the almost Manichean stance toward space in contemporary theology and philosophy. Here man is portrayed as time-binding and time-bound, but not space-disposing and space-disposed. The landscapes of individuals and groups are temporal configurations of inwardness and history. Spatial configurations—*terrene, polis, domicile, corpus*—are seen as external and extrinsic to being and value. Indeed, cosmos and corpus are little more than the theaters within which the dramas of life are played out and played through [Kliever 1977:530].

Kliever argues that de-spatialization—and I would add, its results: hyper-temporalization and narrative preoccupation—are outgrowths of the Enlightenment's spirit/matter dualism. Most theologians, narrative and systematic, are on principle opposed to this dualism, but we find ourselves lapsing into it anyway. If we are serious about overcoming it, we must (1) learn to perceive narrating in relation to enacting, (2) not sever temporality from spatiality, and (3) discern the spatial and ritual possibilities of narrative.

Movement in this direction is already implicit in the work of some narrative theologians and philosophers. Despite the title and argument of John S. Dunne's *Time and Myth* (1973), the recurrent, dominating metaphors of his book—"journey" and "crossing over"—are spatial. Winquist (1978:4) implies the ritualization of narrative itself by stating that "the ability to tell a story is more important than the story which is told." By focusing on the act of storytelling rather than Story or specific stories, like most narrative theologians, he verges on a theory of religion as performance.

Paul Ricoeur opens his article, "Narrative Time" (1980:169), with the usual equation, "Indeed, I take temporality to be that structure of existence that reaches language in narrativity and narrativity to be the language structure that has temporality as its ultimate referent." And he makes the inflated claim that I have already criticized because it implicitly writes off both Jimmy R. and the Ilongots: ". . . Narrative does more than just establish humanity . . ." (178).

What could be more?

Halfway through this article Ricoeur makes a fascinating turn. Having just characterized the temporal dialectic of narrative as irreversible and linear (1980:178–179), he begins to speak of a narrative dimension that is "more deeply temporal." The spatial metaphor, "deep," is a clue that something strange is about to happen.

Shortly thereafter Ricoeur begins discussing retelling and repetition—thus we have arrived on the edge of ritual. Like many theological treatments of narrative, Ricoeur's fails to distinguish between reading (or hearing) and rereading (or hearing again). When we hear again, we are less likely to be sitting on the edge of our seats, less likely to be tipped forward into some eschatological future.

A phenomenology of "narrative repetition" (Ricoeur's term 1980:183) would take us much more decisively to the bridge between myth and ritual. Ricoeur's article—at first clichéd, then provocative, is, in the last analysis, disappointing. Having arrived at "the logical abolition of time" (184), instead of pointing the way to a new conception of space-time relativity, he proposes an "existential deepening" of time, a view he characterizes as "'timeless'—but not a-temporal" (185).

Ricoeur (1980:187), referring to Hannah Arendt's way of distinguishing work, labor, and action, says:

> Action deserves its name when, beyond the concern for submitting nature to man or for leaving behind some monuments witnessing to our activity, it aims only at being recollected in stories whose function it is to provide an identity to the doer, an identity that is merely a narrative identity.

Alas, we are back where the narrative theologians began, with Elie Wiesel and the all-sufficiency of narrative, and, to boot, we have managed to reduce action to what is worth the telling.

I am certainly not beyond quipping, Arendt-style, in my religion and narrative course that the only actions worth doing are those that make good stories, but I would not want to turn my quip into a principle, lest I undergird further the ritual illiteracy of our day.

FROM STORY TO RITUAL

Elie Wiesel (1966) uses a delightful, thought provoking story in opening *Gates of the Forest*. This little tale, full of Hasidic wisdom, is mentioned or quoted in almost every work I know on narrative theology. It tells of four generations of religious men, each of whom knows less than the preceding one. In the procession of generation gaps much is lost: first meditation, then knowing how to light a fire, then prayer. All that is left in the end for

Rabbi Israel of Rizhyn is story. "And it was sufficient. God made man because he loves stories."

Of God's delight there is no doubt. But being a few generations after, and a few cultures removed from, the said rabbi, modern Moroccan Jews in Israel meet in *Zohar* societies, Abraham Stahl (1979) tells us. And they do not even know the language, much less "the story" of the *Zohar*. Nevertheless, reading it aloud is essential. What is necessary is the act of reading. God, these pious men say, delights in babble as a parent does with a child. The act of reading, not the act of narration or narrative comprehension, is what produces spiritual effect. "Sometimes only the rabbi reads while others are passive, and even yawn or doze off. But it is not rare to find people reading their portion with great fervor, charging the meeting with emotion" (117). Stahl quotes a taxi driver, "These really are books! When you hold them in your hands, you tremble from their very holiness. It is terrifying" (117).

Our narrative theologies must also be ritual theologies if we are to understand the taxi driver.

Story in Wiesel's story is a remnant of the rite of fire-lighting, and storytelling could be leading us back to ritualizing again. If we tell stories often enough or if we forget the tongues appropriate to their telling or if we repeat the word "narrative" with sufficient fervor and babble, we rekindle the flames. Don't we?

8

Dʀᴀᴍᴀ ᴀɴᴅ Rɪᴛᴜᴀʟ Cʀɪᴛɪᴄɪꜱᴍ*

. . . No ritual can be properly interpreted because our own values and sense of "fact" are implicated in a quite different system of belief. Even the religious "belief" of those who participate in such a ritual may simply be a rationalization of the ritual itself, the origin of which has been forgotten.

—Peter Ackroyd (1984:48), summarizing T. S.
Eliot's view of ritual when he was a student

Neither the opening chapter nor the final one constitutes a formal, explicit theory. Although a conception of ritual informs the criticism engaged in so far, the generalizations offered are more nearly a politics or hermeneutics of ritual than a theory of it. However, in these two penultimate essays we move closer to theory as such by exploring the works of two theorists for their critical implications.

Here I shall play two texts off one another. Though both concern the same event, neither is derived from the other. The first is a historical case study approached anthropologically and published in 1974 by Victor Turner. It brings his theory of social drama to bear on the confrontation between Archbishop Thomas Becket and King Henry II of England in 1170 C.E. The second is a ritual drama published by T. S. Eliot in 1935 as part of a commemoration of Becket's martyrdom. The genres and intentions of the two texts differ considerably. Nevertheless, reading each in the light of the other leads to a mutual critique by revealing the dominant metaphors that organize Turner's and Eliot's treatment of the same historic event.

TURNER'S THEORY OF SOCIAL DRAMA

"Social drama" is Turner's term for any conflict-laden social interaction. He identifies four phases: (1) breach, (2) crisis, (3) redress, (4) reintegration. Although he acknowledges the possibility of models other than this

---

*An earlier version of this chapter was published in 1985 in *Anthropologica*, New Series 27(1–2):79–99. This version is published with the permission of the editors.

agonistic one (1980:151), he himself tends to treat all social conflict in terms of it. He says he arrived at it by observation of social interaction among the Ndembu of Zambia and subsequent recognition of the same pattern elsewhere. He did not, he insists (153), derive it from Aristotle's description of tragedy on the stage and then impose it on social interactions. Consequently, his dramatistic method is anthropological rather than aesthetic in origin. Despite his recognition that aesthetic drama (which he calls "cultural performance") and social drama are dialectically related, he often assigns priority to social drama. In his "genealogy of genres" social drama is the "grandparent," while stage drama is the "child." The "parent" between generations is ritual. Thus social drama is the basis of social and judiciary processes, which, in turn, become the bases of cultural performances.

It is difficult to determine whether Turner imagines the movement from one level to another as historical, causal-developmental, theoretical-methodological, or phenomenological-typological. He seems to vacillate among the possibilities. In any case, the "genealogy" becomes dialectical insofar as cultural performances such as narrative and drama, functioning as paradigms, provoke further social dramas, thus completing the circle. Put simply, stories can "emplot" (1980:153) lives. When they do, they reach below the level of consciousness and lay "fiduciary hold" (154) on a person or group. Such persons[103] seem possessed. Their actions seem driven by scenarios exercising cognitive, emotive, and conative force.

Of special importance is redress, the third phase of social drama. According to Turner, it evokes rituals and other cultural performances and gives rise to reflexivity. If we are to think of cultural performances as derivative of social ones, it is not to social drama in general but to this phase in particular that we must look for their origin. Redress occurs when judicial proceedings and religious ritual provide symbolic feedback during a crisis. Law, whose ritual dimensions Turner designates "ceremony" or "secular ritual" (1989:156,161), *indicates*, while religious (or liminal) ritual *transforms*. Ceremony reflects the normative, structured, social realities, while ritual (in the narrower sense of the term) dissolves order and casts things into a "subjunctive" mode. And this subjunctivity, says Turner, is the "mother of indicativity" (164). Chart 8.1 (p. 176) amplifies the four phases.

Reflexivity, which Turner thinks can heal a breach in a social fabric by enacting it, is derived from rituals of both the juridical and the religious sort. In turn, this reflexivity is the kind of self-awareness that can lead to an aesthetic frame of mind and thus produce drama and various sorts of

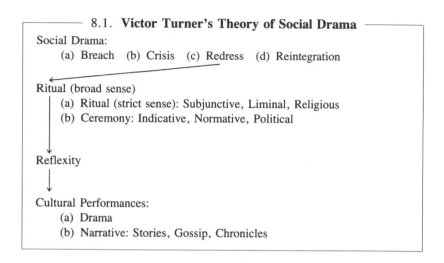

8.1. **Victor Turner's Theory of Social Drama**

Social Drama:
    (a) Breach   (b) Crisis   (c) Redress   (d) Reintegration

Ritual (broad sense)
    (a) Ritual (strict sense): Subjunctive, Liminal, Religious
    (b) Ceremony: Indicative, Normative, Political

Reflexity

Cultural Performances:
    (a) Drama
    (b) Narrative: Stories, Gossip, Chronicles

narrative: chronicle, story, and gossip. Turner's discussion is more ambiguous than my diagram makes the progression seem, because he is not explicit in saying whether he thinks of dramas as a form of narrative. Another caution about this flow chart is that ritual does not *produce* reflexivity so much as it *is* reflexivity in somatic and performative mode.

Turner's model for understanding ritual consists of the phases of a rite of passage as schematized by van Gennep: separation, transition, incorporation (see chart 8.2). As is well known by now, Turner emphasizes the middle or "liminal" phase, regarding it as a powerful source of transformation and innovation in culture. Since he himself posits a parallel between the phases of a rite of passage and those of a social drama, one wonders which is really the model for which.

Does Turner perceive social dramas in terms of rites of passage or a rite of passage in terms of social dramas? Or do such striking homologies between ritual experience and social experience occur as the result of some underlying, third factor? Turner neither raises nor answers the question. Nevertheless, it is clear why redress is so emphasized: if ritual transition is going to be, it follows that its counterpart will also. To recapitulate my piecing together of Turner's argument thus far: (1) redress is the ritual hinge of social drama; (2) the model for ritual is the rite of passage; (3) the hinge of a rite of passage is its liminal phase; (4) liminality in ritual *is* a cultural mode of reflexivity; (5) an increase in ritual reflexivity helps heal a social breach, and gives rise to aesthetic narrative and drama.

Turner (1980:161) claims that ritual has a dramatic structure, a plot.

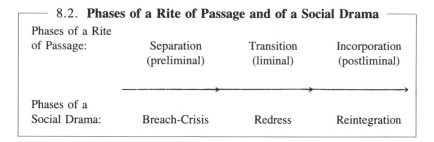

8.2. **Phases of a Rite of Passage and of a Social Drama**

Phases of a Rite of Passage:	Separation (preliminal)	Transition (liminal)	Incorporation (postliminal)
Phases of a Social Drama:	Breach-Crisis	Redress	Reintegration

Sequencing in a ritual is irreversible. In maintaining this, he challenges ritual theorists such as Eliade who treat ritual in terms of circular imagery. For Turner, ritual does not "return"; it goes somewhere. It has a "point," namely, to transform. He is willing to imagine ceremony as circular, but ritual in the "pure" sense (his term: [1980:163]) is linear.

By now it is obvious that Turner thinks of social conflict, ritual enactment, and stage drama as "dramatic," by which he means linear, conflict-laden, and time bound. Whether the source of his dramatism is one or the other or all three is impossible to tell. But clearly, he sees "drama" everywhere, which inclines one to treat it as part of his method.

Turner uses the term "narrative" to refer to (1) the chronological connections between events; (2) indigenous words, stories, and gossip about those events; and (3) an anthropologist's account of the same events. Symbols are what connect the different levels of narrative (1980:145). Turner is especially careful to warn against the "cognitive ethnocentrism" of failing to recognize that an anthropologist's narrative is emic and culture-bound from the point of view of those indigenous to the culture being studied. An "anthropology of experience," he insists, must always strive to know "men and women alive" (143–144) before it tries to account for their action nomothetically. The nearest one can come to actual experience is to discover what events mean to these men and women. For a definition of meaning he relies on Dilthey and thus defines it as what "enables us to conceive of an intrinsic affinity between the successive events of life," that is, memory's ability to negotiate a fit between past and present (156). Obviously, such a definition of meaning commits its proponent to a method that is historical and time-conscious. An implication of it, I believe, is that meaningful reflexivity is also retrospective and inescapably historical.

TURNER'S INTERPRETATION OF BECKET'S SOCIAL DRAMA

Thomas Becket (1118–1170 c.e.) had held minor clerical and civil offices until he became friends with King Henry II of England. In time,

Henry ensured that Thomas was elevated to the office of archbishop of Canterbury; the king probably thought he could thereby control both church and state. Eventually, a bitter conflict arose between the two men. Becket had his own mind. He insisted on the autonomy of ecclesiastical office and soon found himself in defiance of his king. Responding to harsh words spoken by Henry, a group of knights forced their way into Canterbury Cathedral and in 1170 slew the archbishop. Three years later, accompanied by Henry's public penance and support, Becket was canonized as a martyr and saint. His veneration continues today with the shrine at Canterbury as its center.

Turner's analysis of Becket (1974a:chap. 2) focuses specifically on the Council of Northampton, which preceded his martyrdom by six years. One might have expected Turner to concentrate on the "ultimate drama" (1974a: 79) at Canterbury. Instead, he chooses the earlier one at Northampton because (1) he believes this to be the initial breach of a social drama, and (2) there is suggestive historical evidence that it was during this week-long council that Becket began to enact a "root paradigm," that of the martyr entering upon the *via crucis*.

Turner does *not* organize the historical data chronologically or present it in terms of the four phases: breach, crisis, redress, reintegration. In fact, his scheme falls into the background. Having noted that King Henry tries to *begin* at the redressive stage, Turner remarks, ". . . Breach soon becomes crisis and crisis grew so severe that available, formal means of redress proved inadequate, throwing back the situation into deeper crisis . . ." (1974a:79). One can infer from this statement that Turner's theoretical insistence on the linear, temporal nature of social drama and ritual is not, in practice, as strict as it sometimes sounds. The phases, as he alludes to them here, seem to be repeatable, and they do not necessarily follow a single, chronological order. They are less a rigid scenario or plot structure and more akin to "layers" of consciousness or of action. Yet Turner was deeply resistant to cyclical models (see, e.g., 1980:154), because he associated them with the timeless, abstract structures produced by synchronic methods (see 1971:349–353). Like Evans-Pritchard he felt that anthropology ought to be closely linked to history and its diachronic methods. "Social dramas," he says, "represent . . . the time axes of fields" (1971:363). Nevertheless, when he speaks of social dramas as "possessing a regularly recurring 'processional form' or 'diachronic profile'" (1971: 351), one can hardly resist pointing out that terms like "recurring," "form," and "profile" connote structures abstracted from their time-bound historical contexts.

Turner (1974a:63) says his study of Icelandic sagas (1971) led him to the study of Becket. In both cases he introduces the social-dramatistic scheme but abbreviates his actual use of it (see, e.g., 1971:369 and 1974a:79) to a page or so. Both analyses are split between discussion of theoretical terms (e.g., "arena," "field," "paradigms," "root metaphors") and chronicling of historical contexts. The specifically anthropological contribution of his reading of the Icelandic sagas concentrates on kinship; and the treatment of Becket, on the martyrdom paradigm. In both cases Turner seems to have to let go of his model of social drama in order to follow the actual course of events. The result is a less than perfect integration of narrating and theorizing, both of which are in themselves provocative. I suspect that the technical terms of his theory serve as a repository for the "timeless," structural side of his interpretation, while the chronicling and narrating carry the processual side. If forced by data to choose, he typically narrates [104] Occasionally, the storyteller overcomes the anthropologist, for example, consider his tone and personal involvement in the following passage:

> This was Thomas's low point, the rock bottom of his life, Black Monday. Picture the gloom and desperation of the scene. There was Thomas, sick on his pallet in St. Andrew's monastery outside North ampton town, having been debarred by royal pressure from taking up the more comfortable quarters to which his rank entitled him—but in a strange way foreshadowing his exile among Cistercian monks in Pontigny and his attempt to emulate the humility of the ideal monk. The king was all cold cruelty, masked in moral law and accusation. The weather was dank and dull, as I have often known it myself in the Northampton area in autumn (Turner 1974a:84).

Turner's central thesis about Becket is that he is controlled by an "archetypal" paradigm (1974a:92), which Turner speaks of as being "in people's heads" (96). The curious thing about his terminology is how static and timeless "archetypal" sounds and how intellectualistic "people's heads" rings. Such connotations go against the grain of his own insistence that symbols are dynamic and emotion-laden. In any case, his point in introducing the notion of an archetypal paradigm is to suggest that the series of events beginning at Northampton is not best treated as if it were a series of political or moral decisions (69) but, rather, as if it were a "fate," "genetic code," or "rite" (72). The evidence that Becket himself was unconsciously driven by, if not consciously aspiring to, a model is his having deliberately chosen to violate the liturgical calendar by saying, out of season, the Mass of St. Stephen the martyr. It begins, "Princes sat and spoke against me: and the wicked persecuted me..." (Psalm 118). Turner does not appear to sense any contradiction between treating the paradigm as having a "fiduciary hold" (64) on Becket and suggesting that he "stage manages" (66) the whole affair. His general point is that in the throes of crisis people act from preconscious roots, and those roots stylize and dramatize actions.

ELIOT'S RITUAL DRAMA

In order to gain a perspective on Turner's interpretation of Becket, I want to examine T. S. Eliot's *Murder in the Cathedral* (1935; quotations from 1963 edition). Were it not for Turner's "incursive nomadism" (his term), it might seem like an odd mixing of genres to compare a case study and a play: neither the forms nor the authors' intentions are quite parallel. But I maintain that just as there is storytelling and drama in Turner's analysis, so there is a theory of action—ritual and dramatic—in Eliot's play. Although both Turner and Eliot were Catholic—the one Roman, the other Anglo— we should not consider their differences to be an indigenous squabble over meaning, since Turner writes as an anthropologist and Eliot as a Christian poet. So I am prone to view Eliot's play as the more emic view and Turner's as the more etic one.

In *Murder in the Cathedral* Eliot is not at great pains to tell a story. Since it was written to be performed at the Canterbury Festival of 1935 on the very grounds where King Henry II had incited the slaying of Archbishop Thomas Becket, Eliot could assume that most of his audience knew the story of the historical events that the play dramatizes. His aim is to propose a proper interpretation, something he once thought impossible, as the epigraph suggests. Eliot did not produce art for its own sake. That the play was written for the sake of the occasion of martyrdom it commemorates makes it ritual drama. In ritual drama the actions are no surprise. People know what is coming, so interest does not depend on being kept in suspense until the end. As the concluding *kyrie* illustrates, the primary actions of such a performance are its making symbolically present the political-ecclesiastical event of December 1170 C.E., its drawing down the mercy of God, and its evoking the intercessions of Blessed Thomas. For one kind of audience member these actions must have been liturgical; for another kind, entertainment. But this plurality of intentions is probably no different from that obtaining in most ritual dramas. The fact that the 1935 event was both ritual and drama invites this intermingling of frames and motives.

Eliot's script opens with a chorus of poor women from Canterbury. In the seasonal limbo between harvest and new year they wait. This theme of waiting dominates their song. "For us, the poor," they say, "there is no action, / But only to wait and to witness" (1963:13). Their action of walking to the cathedral precincts is but the "presage of an act" (11). Their feet and eyes have been "forced" by this incipient foreboding of action. They fear Thomas's action will disrupt their cycle of "living and partly living."

An activist ideology might regard all waiting as impotent passivity. A Marxist version would take it as evidence of peasant religion's functioning as an opiate. But Eliot has something different in mind, namely, the waiting of martyrs and saints. Even if the waiting of the peasant women were parasitic—the circling of vultures ready to suck Becket's blood and pick his bones—there is another kind of inaction that demands to be understood differently.

Passive inaction is an opiate. Receptive inaction is not. Ritual proper, as Eliot poetically dramatizes it, is of the receptive sort; Turner would have called it "transformative." Receptive inaction waits for that more inclusive action, destiny, which is in the hands of God. When the Second Priest complains about the "foolish, immodest and babbling women," Thomas replies:

They know and do not know, what it is to act or suffer.
They know and do not know, that action is suffering
And suffering action. Neither does the agent suffer
Nor the patient act. But both are fixed
In an eternal action, and eternal patience
To which all must consent that it may be willed
And which all must suffer that they may will it,
That the pattern may subsist, for the pattern is the action
And the suffering, that the wheel may turn and still
Be forever still [1963:21–22].

Eternal action, especially when symbolized by the image of a turning wheel, sounds very much like the "action which is repose" or "overcoming from underneath" of Buddhist thought. But Eliot, says Grover Smith (1956:190), was interested in Aristotle at the time he wrote the play. Eliot's view of action is in keeping with both Christian mysticism and Catholic theologies of martyrdom and sainthood, to which Aristotle, as appropriated by Thomas Aquinas, contributed significantly.

Ritual action of the liturgical sort is not supposed to be ordered in some arbitrary fashion. Rather, liturgists intend it to accord with ultimate principles of order: God, and the cosmos as an expression of his *logos*. Not only is liturgical action patterned, it is supposed to replicate a greater, nonarbitrary pattern, the one that "subsists" and is "forever still." Actually, the notion of replication does not go far enough; it is too Platonic for Eliot's Aristotelian Thomism. The same passage I quoted above, in which Thomas patronizes the women, gets quoted back to him by one of the Tempters (1963:40–41). It is almost verbatim except for the omission of one line: "For the pattern is the action / And the suffering." What the Tempter does not know that Thomas knows is that the pattern is not somewhere else in eternity; it is here in the "sordid particulars." The action does not simply imitate a pattern; it *is* the pattern. Put another way, a ritual gesture does not imitate the *logos* so much as incarnate it.

Although Thomas is higher on the ladder of ecclesiastical hierarchy than either the priests or the women of the chorus, he both knows and does not know what action and passion (suffering) are. As "agents" people move and act. As "patients" they suffer and are still. In this they do not differ from the wheel of the cosmos, which at its circumference turns and at its center is forever still. The difference between the actions of performers and the movements of the wheel is that ritual actors seem unable, except in special moments like martyrdom or meditation, to do both at once. Instead, they oscillate back and forth between activity and passivity, between taking cosmic law into their own hands and resigning from responsibility for the direction of their own feet. The knights in the play typify the first possibility and the chorus of women, the second.

I have said there are no surprises in ritual drama. But in social drama there are. The audience spectating on a ritual drama may know what is going to happen in a play about Becket, but Becket, caught in a ritualized event, does not know what is going to happen to him, even if he suspects the knights will kill him when he enters the cathedral. He "knows and does not know." What he does not know is presented to him by the Tempters, who "do not wait upon ceremony" (1963:23).

In deciding on a course of action, Becket is tempted to do a number of things. But, he says, ". . . The substance of our first act / Will be shadows, and the strife with shadows" (1963:23). Among the shadowy deeds that tempt him are: (1) to forget the past and return to his easy friendship with the king; (2) to give up his ecclesiastical office and again be chancellor under the king (then, to use this office with intelligent self-interest to obtain justice); and (3) to form alliances with the English barons. Thomas says he expected these temptations, but the Fourth Tempter, who "precedes expectation," presents a surprise. The other Tempters identify themselves at least by function. This fourth, however, has no name. The temptation he offers, as he quotes Thomas back to himself, is twofold and specifically ritualistic. It is to exercise the power of the keys in excommunicating the king (37) and to seek the way of martyrdom (39). This is the temptation "to do the right deed for the wrong reason" (44). It is to turn a religious act into a political one, thereby making the greater cause, which Thomas ought to serve, serve him instead.

Thomas views this temptation as emerging from his "soul's sickness" (1963:40). In its face he can neither act nor suffer action without damnation. He is doubly bound. Yet in the end, the action-passion of becoming a martyr is precisely what makes his gesture efficacious and revelatory. The deed arising from the depths of his temptation becomes the ground of the ritual of dying in faith. Untransposed, of course, the deed would destroy him, but done for the right reason, it would sustain him. "Right" does not mean "good." Nor does "reason" mean "rationally justifiable." Thomas is wiser than this: "Sin grows with doing good" (45), he says. The action of the heights can tempt as surely as any action of the depths. What Thomas must find is the action that is both. This kind of action can arise only at the still point. It is an action with no name.

Structurally, the prose interlude is the still point of the play. Its homiletical prose contrasts sharply with the dramatic poetry of the first and second parts that it separates. The sermon is preached on Christmas morning—by Christian reckoning, the hinge of time. In his homily Archbishop Becket points to the paradox involved in re-enacting Christ's passion and death in the Mass while at the same time celebrating his birth:

> For who in the World will both mourn and rejoice at once and for the same reason? For either joy will be overborne by mourning, or mourning will be cast out by joy; so it is only in these our Christian mysteries that we can rejoice and mourn at once for the same reason [1963:48].

By comparing the death of martyrs to that of Christ, the sermon suggests that the only valid reason for an action such as allowing one's own death is the will of God. This amounts to implying that such a deed is unmotivated, at least in any psychosocial sense. The right sort of action is one God himself performs through a person. Here we approach the liturgical motive proper. Perhaps we should call it a nonmotive. There are other motives—personal, political, and social—but from a martyr's point of view they are secondary to the problem of overcoming attachment to any motive whatsoever, including unconscious ones. Thomas's struggle is to find a motive for action that is neither willful activism nor resigned passivity. His dying as martyr is at once a ritual, ethical, political, psychological, and theological conundrum. Ritually, martyrdom is formal self-sacrifice in the context

of a historical tradition of such gestures. Ethically and politically, it is a
choice pressured on all sides by group interests and capable of substantially
altering the balance of power. Psychologically, it is a contest between a self
and its shadows, a struggle of self against the desire for revenge. Theologically, martyrdom presents the difficulty of aligning temporal deeds with
eternal ones and of orienting the cycles of this world to the movement of
the great cosmic wheel.

The chorus's song, which opens part II, emphasizes spatial and temporal
orientation: Where are the signs of spring? Is the wind stored up in the
East? East and spring are the directional and seasonal symbols that orient
the event taking place in Canterbury. "Between Christmas and Easter what
work shall be done?" the chorus queries. ". . . The time is short / But
waiting is long" (1963:54). The playwright's task is to orient the action that
everyone—audience, chorus, and characters—knows is going to happen.
Not the outcome, only the orientation, of the action is in question. When
questions of orientation displace those of outcome, ritual begins to overshadow drama.

The slaying occurs on December 29. Between Christmas and this date
the feasts of St. Stephen the Martyr, St. John the Apostle, and the slain
Holy Innocents have been celebrated, almost as if establishing Thomas's
lineage. But all of time—that of natural and liturgical season, as well as
that of eternity—is now coagulated by virtue of the action-passion about to
transpire on Thursday:

> What day is the day that we know that we hope or fear for?
> Every day is the day we should fear from or hope from.
>   One moment
> Weighs like another. Only in retrospection, selection,
> We say, that was the day. The critical moment.
> That is always now, and here. Even now, in sordid particulars
> The eternal design may appear [1963:57].

By carrying in banners of the martyrs, the priests orient the deed in
ecclesiastical history. The knights arrive and, by rhetorically rehearsing
Thomas's actions (such as his having once anathematized the king and fled
to France for seven years), they orient his martyrdom in secular political
history. As always, the chorus orients the action cosmologically and
cyclically; it both knows already, and still does not quite know, what is
going to happen. What the knights know by decision and counsel with the
king, the women know by premonition, in their veins, brains, and guts
(1963:68). Even though they do not commit the deed, by complicity they

consent and must beg Thomas's forgiveness. The chorus forgets easily—
"humankind cannot bear very much reality" (69)—but its feet always
remember.

Spatial orientation follows the temporal. The priests, in an effort to save
their archbishop's life, drag him into the cathedral and bar the door. He will
die in a sacred place. Thomas shouts at them to open the door; a sanctuary
is not a fortress. They try to convince him that the knights have become
beasts and the door has always been barred against animals, but Thomas
accuses them of arguing by results. In doing this deed, he believes that
only form and motive, not end, must be considered. He must become a
"patient" who suffers action rather than an agent who commits it, and he
must assent to it, not simply be its victim.

When Thomas is killed, the action ramifies. Ritually, it becomes a
transaction in which the saint offers his blood to pay for Christ's death just
as Christ had sacrificed his blood to buy Thomas's life (1963:75). Eventually, the event will have the effect of a sacrificial cleansing. But presently, for the chorus, it is a polluting action, because its orientation is
eternal rather than cyclical:

These acts marked a limit to our suffering.
Every horror had its definition.
Every sorrow had a kind of end:
In life there is not time to grieve long.
But this, this is out of life, this is out of time,
An instant eternity of evil and wrong.
We are soiled by a filth that we cannot clear, united to supernatural vermin,
It is not we alone, it is not the house, it is not the city that is defiled,
But the world that is wholly foul [1963:77–78].

The drama among the characters ends here, but that between characters
and audience intensifies. The knights turn directly to the audience, asking
it to judge between them and Thomas. Arguing in rhetorical prose that they
are fair-minded Englishmen, men of action rather than word, they argue
their case like modern, liberal lawyers. They claim they deserve our applause. Even if they are guilty, they say, the audience is too. The passivity
of the audience is considered complicity similar to that of the chorus. The
Fourth Knight, like the Fourth Tempter, presents the most convincing case.
He seizes on the ambiguous aspects of Thomas's actions, demanding to
know who *really* killed the archbishop (1963:83). His answer to his own
rhetorical question is that Thomas's action constitutes suicide rather than
martyrdom; the archbishop deliberately set out to provoke his own death. If

this is true, Thomas's action is not patience or passion at all, but disguised aggression.

The case is left unsettled and the verdict unrendered as the priests take over and form a bridge to the final chorus. The third priest berates the knights, who have already exited, accusing them of trying to justify their actions by weaving fictions that unravel during the very moment they weave them. They will never succeed, even by losing themselves in "filthy rites" and "libidinous courts" (1963:85).

The chorus has the last word, but its language and petitions are priestly and accompanied by a *Te Deum* sung in Latin in the background. The concluding notes are of confession, petition, and thanksgiving. Whatever the nature of Thomas's final motive—whether it was suicidal or sacrificial—the concluding action and widest frame of the play is liturgical. The ending is not happy, moving from confession of sin to thanksgiving and praise. Its movement is just the reverse, so one is led to read it as ironic. We know very well that the chorus, waxing archaic and priestly in its last chant, will surely do the same thing again. Always there will be the need for "mercies of blood" (1963:81); the cycle must go on, the wheel must turn again.

COMPARING A RITUAL DRAMA WITH A SOCIAL DRAMA

Even though Eliot's work is a ritual drama focused on an ultimate moment in Becket's life and Turner's a social dramatistic analysis, focused on an initial phase in it, they are by no means incommensurate, as chart 8.3 illustrates.

Drama is the continuum between Eliot and Turner though they make quite different uses of it. Turner's dramatistic theory of action leads him first to locate drama in social interaction and then to find this analogized or reflected on the stage; whereas Eliot, even though he is a poet, does not locate the primary drama on the stage. A more "Platonic" playwright might have done so. As a Christian dramatist he has located it in history, specifically in the events that link Jesus's crucifixion to Becket's death and both in turn to the commemorative festival of 1935. Turner has erected an etic, political frame around events that devotees would frame religiously, while Eliot has cast a religious frame around an event regarded by historians as political. Both men do, however, retain elements of the religious-political dialectic. In both treatments the dialectic is deliberate, though each work sometimes seems to lapse into its own opposite genre—Turner's interpretation into hagiographic storytelling, Eliot's Becket into Aristotelian theorizing about action. The outcome is that Eliot's drama, classic though it has

8.3. Comparison of Turner and Eliot

Turner	Eliot
1. "Ritual Paradigms and Political Action: Thomas Becket at the Council of Northampton," a social-dramatistic analysis	1. *Murder in the Cathedral*, a ritual drama
2. Analysis is focused on breach, an initial phase	2. Dramatization concentrated on redress, a concluding moment
3. Primary drama is in phase of social interaction	3. Primary drama is in the eras of Christian history
4. An etic political frame for handling an emic religious event	4. An emic religious frame for handling an etic event
5. Lapses into hagiographic storytelling	5. Lapses into Aristotelian theorizing
6. Too little analysis?	6. Too little narrative?
7. Social drama threatening to become ritually fixed	7. Sacrificial rite threatening to become dramatically polluted
8. Political motivation as the principle of explaining the event	8. Political motivation as protagonist's temptation
9. Becket both "stage manages" and is the "fiduciary hold" of a paradigm (i.e., his martyrdom is both manipulative and unconscious)	9. Becket "knows and does not know" (i.e., he neither unconsciously chooses nor deliberately avoids martyrdom)
10. Paradigms are in actors' heads	10. "Eternal design" is in the sordid particulars
11. Paradigms emplot actions, which, in turn, form patterns	11. The pattern *is* the action
12. Dominant metaphors: temporal, linear, processual (e.g., "flow")	12. Dominant metaphors: spatial, circular, static (e.g., the "forever still" center)

become, is not strong on narrative. Similarly, Turner's treatment contains too much narration and too little analysis for anthropologists with nomothetic goals in mind.

Turner's treatment, by its emphasis on the paradigm that has hold of Becket, makes the events of the social drama appear to be like a rite. And

Eliot, despite the sparse attention he pays to either characterization or plot, manages to dramatize a sacrificial rite with his poetry. For all that might be said about the kinship, or even identity, of ritual and drama on a theoretical level, in actual performance one or the other may dominate. Even though Turner is analyzing a social drama, usually characterized by flow, an archetypal paradigm threatens to fix the action into a rite or fate. The opposite is true in Eliot. His Becket is in danger of undermining the efficacy of martyrdom if he yields to dramatically instigated acts. What for Turner is a principle of explanation is for Eliot's Becket a temptation, namely, to do the right thing for a wrong, that is, political, reason.

Turner and Eliot both depict a motivational struggle in Becket. But Turner's characterization has Becket vacillate between manipulative stage managing and unconscious compulsion. Turner's "fiduciary hold," since it is "beneath conscious prehension" (1974a:64) is not a synonym for faith. In contrast, Eliot's Becket, who knows and does not know, is hardly unconscious. Instead he struggles to reject not only stage managing but even benevolent political action. He aims at—though we do not know if he achieves—faithful action, which is neither mere resignation nor willful coercion.

The paradigms that compel Becket are located metaphorically by Turner "in actors' heads." Eliot places the "eternal design" in the "sordid particulars." Even though Eliot's conception might seem to remove such a design from the possibility of criticism, its roots in culture and politics are never denied, so, in fact, eternity is no less (or more) accessible than the insides of actors' heads. Eliot's Aristotelian insistence that the pattern *is* the action means that one cannot avoid doing cultural criticism at the same time one thinks theologically. The difference between Turner and Eliot on this point is probably that Eliot would be less willing than Turner to subject theological standards to cultural criticism. On the other hand, Turner is more prone to see the connection between paradigm and action as automatic, as unmediated by highly self-conscious ethical reflection. He locates reflexivity in the time after, not before or during, a crisis.

In the final analysis many of the differences between our dramatist and our anthropologist are results of their dominant metaphors. Turner appeals to temporal, linear, or processual ones, "flow," for example, and thus conceives action as phasic. Eliot uses spatial, circular, or static ones, for example, the center that is "forever still." He treats actions as if they were layers or rings.

My comparison could go on, but by now its basic parameters are drawn and it is obvious that I am not content merely to "apply" Turner's theory to

Eliot's play, thus casting it in the role of "data." Nor am I willing to admit that the differences in form and social function of dramatic and scholarly work warrant our compartmentalizing them. If we allow the play to question the theory, and not merely apply the theory to the play, we are forced to ask Turner whether it is adequate (1) to consider either narrative or social drama as only linear and (2) to claim that all rituals have a dramatic plot. Eliot's play helps us notice the static, circular side of Turner's interpretation. The play, dramatic though it is, makes minimum use of plot, thus calling into question Turner's treating all rites as if they were narratively structured.

Allowing Turner's theory and case study to question Eliot, we must ask (1) whether it is really so clear that Becket was even conscious of the intricacies of martyrological theology. Could he not have been unwittingly compelled by *images*? And (2) to what extent is martyrdom only a retrospective view—one sufficiently removed from the original events generating it that the desire to canonize a saint can outlive the desire to account for the event politically?

Reading or seeing the play makes one keenly aware that the only access to the social drama Turner analyzes is through data strongly marked by earlier ritual drama. In other words, one may take the ritual drama to be hermeneutically primary even though the social drama was historically primary. The paradigm that Turner locates historically in actors' heads can just as well be located in the Mass, in yearly Canterbury festivals, or even in Turner's head. Where one locates it is important but by no means obvious. There is no reason why the paradigm cannot arise in two heads—Becket's, and, because he is British and Catholic, Turner's. But it is not so easy to locate the martyrdom model both in the "depths" (1980:163) and on the "surface," which is where we would locate it metaphorically if we believe Becket may have been stage managing.

Another problem emerging from the comparison is whether stage drama is a reflection of social drama or vice-versa. Can we on principle assign priority to one or the other? Where does the drama occur—between Becket and Henry, between Turner and Becket, between Eliot and Turner? Perhaps there are several overlapping dramas: (1) within Becket's head, (2) between Becket and Henry, (3) between Turner and Becket, and—if we are to be fully reflexive—(4) between Turner's and Eliot's readings of the affair.

If we take Eliot's reading seriously, we cannot simply consider the social and political forces surrounding Becket but must consider (1) his motivation struggle as well as (2) the exegesis of the event offered by pilgrims, performers, and clergy at Canterbury. Theologies of martyrdom and ecclesiastical assessments of Becket's act are partly "indigenous exegesis" (Turner's term) and partly competing anthropological theory. On one level the emic and etic accounts of Becket's actions are in conflict. What Eliot specifies as Becket's motive is overridden not just by Turner's social-dramatism theory but by *any* theory that argues from results or assumes the priority of stage-managed martyrdom. To put it bluntly, Eliot's Becket is, among other things, implicitly challenging the omnicompetence of any social-psychological way of accounting for action. And, I maintain, he is not merely hiding behind dogma to do it. He is presenting an argument. What Thomas presents in his Christmas sermon is not the announcement of some infallible revelation but an argument for taking seriously reflection and theological attitudes and not just the results or phases of a process. He, or Eliot through him, challenges any view of action that either makes it the result of personal decision and will power or construes it more passively as the product of reified social forces. In another work Turner himself criticizes those who reify culture and make it a causal agent (see 1980:144). Considered as a motive for action, "culture" is no less mystical than Eliot's "eternal design."

The process of juxtaposing a case study of the Becket social drama with a ritual drama of that same event may seem to confuse two orders of conceptualization. For some this procedure constitutes a transgression of a sacred boundary. Whether or not theorists would like to keep the two spheres, explanation and belief, separate, they as a matter of historical and social fact are sometimes experienced as competing and clashing.

9

Infelicitous Performances and Ritual Criticism*

No enchantment against Jacob,
No divination against Israel [Numbers 23:23].

The magicians tried by their secret arts to bring forth gnats, but they could not [Exodus 8:18].

But for Cain and his offering he [God] had no regard [Genesis 4:5].

Now he [Jacob] has taken away my blessing [Genesis 27:36].

And [Nadab & Abihu] offered unholy fire before the Lord, such as he had not commanded them. And fire came forth from the presence of the Lord and devoured them [Leviticus 10:2].

I hate, I despise your feasts, and I take no delight in your solemn assemblies [Amos 6:21].

Do not lay your hand on the lad [Isaac] or do anything to him [Genesis 22:12].

The practice of ritual criticism presupposes the possibility of ritual failure, which is seldom taken account of in theories of ritual. Engaging in ritual criticism presupposes that rites can exploit, denigrate, or simply not do what people claim they do. Consider the biblical passages above. Clearly, rites do not always go smoothly in the ancient Hebraic world any more than they do in modern synagogues, hospitals, or courtrooms. Often they seem to be more trouble than they are worth.

Amos's God has little use for solemn assemblies. Nadab and Abihu are killed for performing an unauthorized rite. Esau loses the benefits of the blessing rite to his brother Jacob. Cain's offering is disregarded for some

---

*Portions of this chapter, which are reprinted here with the permission of Scholars Press, were originally published in 1988 as "Infelicitous Performances and Ritual Criticism" in *Semeia* 41:103–122; the whole issue is on speech-act theory in religious and biblical studies. Both the chapter and the article grew out of a presentation in 1984 called "Infelicitous Performances, or, How Rituals Fail" to a joint meeting of the American Academy of Religion and the Society of Biblical Literature.

unspecified reason. The Egyptian magicians' magic cannot match that of Moses and Aaron. Balak cannot get Balaam's oracle to tell him what he wants to hear. And if Abraham's ritual sacrifice of his son had been successful, it would have failed.

Curiously, little has been done in a theoretical way to take account of ritually related trouble, but speech-act theory has some promising features that might enable us to begin rectifying this gap in ritual studies. Speech-act theory, which developed out of philosophical linguistic analysis, is usually applied only to verbal phenomena. Here we shall extend its application to ritual, a performative phenomenon.

Specifically, I want to explore the applicability of J. L. Austin's typology of "infelicitous" (his term) performances to both biblical and nonbiblical examples of troublesome ritual. The reasons for putting speech-act theory to this use are simple: some of the examples used by Austin are ritualistic, and ritual contexts, more than any other, make use of what he calls "performative utterance," that is, speech insofar as it accomplishes tasks rather than merely describing them. Speech-act theory has proved generally useful in understanding the relations between "things said" and "things done" (to paraphrase Jane Harrison), but I want to explore one specific dimension of the theory.

Austin's typology is applicable not only to things said in ritual contexts but also to things done in them, especially if the things done seem to go awry. There is no necessary reason why one has to apply speech-act theory to failed rites as opposed to successful ones, but applying it to "happy" (Austin's term) instances has been done; applying it to unhappy ones has not.

Ritual is not a single kind of action. Rather, it is a convergence of several kinds we normally think of as distinct. It is an "impure" genre. Like opera, which includes other genres—for example, singing, drama, and sometimes even dancing—a ritual may include all these and more. Accordingly, applying speech-act theory to ritual is unlikely to explain every sort of action that can transpire in a rite. Initially, one might expect it to be of use only in understanding the verbal aspects of it, particularly those facets of ritual language that do rather than merely refer.

All speech acts are not ritual acts, and not all ritual acts include speech acts. Therefore we would suppose speech-act theory would be of little use in rites characterized mainly by silence or movement. Ritual is a more complex cultural form than speech, because it can include all the variants of speech, but speech cannot include all the varieties of ritual.

Just as what we label with the single term "ritual" is a complex phenomenon requiring multiple methods to understand it, so there are numerous ways a rite can succeed or fail. A fertility rite may not make crops grow. Nevertheless, it can succeed socially while it fails empirically. Worship can lapse into civil ceremony and thus serve a vested political interest, thereby failing ethically. Meanwhile, it can succeed in providing symbols that nourish or comfort individuals. A wedding may legally bind a couple but fail to generate a festive air. In short, different kinds of ritual fail in different ways. And a rite need not fail on every level or from every point of view for it to be worth our while to consider the question of ritual infelicity.

Since rites are often multiphased as well as multileveled, and since symbols have a fan of overlapping meanings as well as several kinds of meaning, one can seldom demonstrate that a rite has failed in all phases and on all levels. Of the many varieties of human behavior, ritual is probably the most difficult to evaluate. And when we do evaluate it, justifying our assessments is notoriously difficult. Consequently, quarrels over ritual are often settled by violence or counterritualization—not by discussion, argument, or vote-taking. Furthermore, criteria for considering a ritual as successful or failed may be inescapably religiocentric or ethnocentric.

Despite these difficulties and caveats, people still engage in ritual criticism. As religious traditions and cultures clash and converge, and individuals engage in overt and covert syncretism, criticism becomes increasingly necessary—if not for participants themselves, then for us who study ritual behavior.

Religious studies generally and ritual studies in particular typically ignore rites that do not do what they are purported to do. Although participants probably experience the failure of ritual as often as they do the success of it, people who study rites pay little attention to the dynamics of ritual infelicity. Questions such as the following remain not only unanswered but scarcely even considered: Does it make sense to consider rituals "happy," "true," or "successful," hence, "unhappy," "false," or "failed"? By what criteria do participants judge rites? Why is there such resistance to ritual criticism? Are there any cross-culturally valid ways to assess a rite? Are there specifically ritualistic, as opposed to moral, criteria? What do we mean when we say a ritual "works"? Is "working" a criterion equally applicable to every kind of ritual?

Understandably, anthropologists usually avoid making explicit, written judgments about the failure or success of the rites they observe and record. Liturgists are supposed to do so because of the normative, religious nature of their work, but as we have seen in chapter 2, they have difficulty in doing so. Liturgists do not typically pose their criticisms so as to make them open to cross-cultural assessment, nor are they always explicit about their grounds for engaging in ritual criticism in the first place.

To open the discussion of some of these questions I shall first summarize some of the research of speech-act theorist J. L. Austin and then inquire how his theories have been used to understand ritual. Finally, I shall reformulate and illustrate his criteria in order to make them more useful in ritual studies.

RITUAL INFELICITY IN SPEECH-ACT THEORY

Austin's *How to Do Things with Words* (1965) was originally delivered as the William James Lectures at Harvard in 1955. In it Austin introduces the idea of "performative utterance," which has become the foundation of modern speech-act theory, whose leading contemporary proponent is John Searle. His *Speech Acts* (1969) and *Expression and Meaning* (1979) elaborate and refine Austin's original research.

Austin's stated intention is to describe the way words do things, as opposed merely to describing or expressing them. He employs a set of classifications that (1) enable us to distinguish words that say something ("constatives") from those that do something ("performatives"), and (2) help us judge when performatives are "happy," on the one hand, or "infelicitous," on the other.

Here we are concerned with types of "infelicitous performance" and the light they shed on ritual failure. I do not believe this approach stretches Austin's terminology. He recognized that it had implications for ritual (see, e.g., 1965:17, 20, 24, 36, 76, 84–85), but does not develop them. In the most explicit passage he says, ". . . Infelicity is an ill to which all acts are heir which have the general character of ritual or ceremonial, all conventional acts . . ." (18–19).

Which infelicities are likely to occur in which types of ritual Austin never says. Nor does he consider any kind of act other than that of uttering words. So we are left to infer and imagine how to proceed from the kind he treats. He proposes two large categories of infelicity: "misfires" and "abuses." When a ritual misfires, its formula is not effective; the act is "purported but void." An example of a misfire would be a wedding performed by someone unauthorized to do it, say, the choirmaster rather than the priest. When a rite is abused, it is "professed but hollow." An abuse would be saying "I do" while secretly resolving not to do.

It is clear from Austin's analysis that recognizing ritual misfires requires attention to the total situation of the speech act, not just to the words alone. Assessment requires a consideration of the tradition and social context. I would add that recognizing ritual abuses requires that attention be paid to the psychology of the ritualist, especially insofar as one can infer such psychology from tones of voice, grammatical moods, and gestures.

Some performatives are easy to recognize, because they include explicit grammatical cues such as the first-person singular or certain adverbs: "I bid you welcome" or "I hereby name you the Queen Mary." But the line between explicit and implicit performatives is not always so clear. "I am sorry" can be the description of a feeling or the enactment of an apology, and pipe smoking can be either a habitual activity or a sacred gesture.

In John Searle's refinement of Austin's research, a great deal of effort is spent reformulating the taxonomy of illocutionary acts (see Searle 1979: chap. 1) and almost none on the infelicities. Searle (1969.chap. 5) argues that predication ("saying") is also an act, thus softening Austin's contrast between constatives and performatives. In addition, Searle (1969:136ff.) identifies the "speech act fallacy" that results from trying to overextend speech-act theory. But "defective" (see 1969:54) performatives receive little attention from him. So the main contribution of speech-act theory to a theory of ritual failure still consists of Austin's taxonomy, which he himself took to be provisional and incomplete.

SPEECH-ACT THEORY IN THE STUDY OF RITUAL

Speech-act theory has not been used often in religious studies generally, nor in the study of ritual specifically. Even though it assumes the primacy of language, a value I questioned in chapter 7, it serves as an effective bridge between linguistic and performative theories. So it may be useful to summarize what has been done so far.

Although not explicitly based on Austin's theories, anthropologist S. J. Tambiah's article, "The Magical Power of Words" (1968), is sometimes referred to in discussions of ritual and language. Tambiah argues that ritual is not action (as opposed to language) but, rather, a way of connecting action and language. He notes the wide, cross-cultural occurrence of three ways of accounting for the power of language: that it is from the gods, that is from human beings, and that it is indigenous to words themselves. In an extended re-analysis of the data on Trobriand magic (first presented by Malinowski), he goes to great lengths to demonstrate that magical utterances are not mumbo-jumbo or mere emotional release. Instead he tries to show that they are a metaphoric means of constructing blueprints or self-fulfilling prophecies. His summary of the argument is worth quoting:

Thus it is possible to argue that all ritual, whatever the idiom, is addressed to the human participants and uses a technique which attempts to re-structure and integrate the minds and emotions of the actors. The technique combines verbal and non-verbal behavior and exploits their special properties. Language is an artificial construct and its strength is that its form owes nothing to external reality: it thus enjoys the power to invoke images and comparisons, refer to time past and future and relate events which cannot be represented in action. Non-verbal action on the other hand excels in what words cannot easily do—it can codify and analogically by imitating real events, reproduce technical acts and express multiple implications simultaneously. Words excel in expressive enlargement, physical actions in realistic presentation.

It is a truer tribute to the savage mind to say that, rather than being confused by verbal fallacies or acting in defiance of known physical laws, it ingeniously conjoins the expressive and metaphorical properties of language with the operational and empirical properties of technical activity. It is this which gives magical operations a "realistic" coloring and allows them to achieve their expressiveness through verbal substitution and transfer combined with an instrumental technique that imitates practical action [Tambiah 1978:202].

Because Tambiah concentrates on showing how ritual language works, he does not entertain questions about its failure. On the contrary, he thinks Malinowski misinterpreted his own data insofar as he regarded Trobriand magic as "prosaic pedantry" (Tambiah 1968:192). The failure, he shows, was the anthropologist's not the magicians'.

Ruth Finnegan's "How to Do Things with Words: Performative Utterances Among the Limba of Sierra Leone" (1969) appeared a year later than Tambiah's article and in the same anthropological journal. Her claim, which she amply supports with both linguistic and behavioral data, is that for the Limba performative utterances have broader currency than they do in English. She shows that accepting gifts, announcing, pleading, greeting, and saying good-bye are highly valued; they are not just polite expressions but substantive social acts. Among the Limba failure to perform them at the proper time or in the correct way has serious social consequences. But beyond this gross point of omission Finnegan does not analyze the dynamics of such failure.

Benjamin Ray in "'Performative Utterances' in African Rituals" (1973), shows that ritual language in Dinka and Dogon ceremonies does not merely symbolize and express meanings. Rather, the Dinka and Dogon accomplish ends by virtue of "the authority involved in the act of uttering the words" (28). Ray accepts Finnegan's data as supportive of his own find-ings, but he is sharply critical of Tambiah. He charges Tambiah with implying that the efficacy of magical words lies only in the overt actions accompanying them (25). This interpretation violates ritualists' own beliefs that their words directly affect the objects toward which they are directed (see 28). Ray contends that ritual language is not metaphoric or symbolic at all but, rather, performative in Austin's sense of the word.

What Ray actually succeeds in demonstrating is only that the expres-sive/instrumental dichotomy, as applied to the Dinka and Dogon under-standing of ritual, violates the practitioners' own views of it. He shows that speech-act theory is homologous with Dinka and Dogon views on the matter—a thesis resembling Finnegan's regarding Limba usage. Ray does not really demonstrate that or how their utterances achieve their effect. If he had, he might have been forced to deal with some instances of their ineffectiveness—with infelicitous as well as happy instances.

Another effort in religious studies to use speech-act theory is Hugh White's "A Theory of the Surface Structure of Biblical Narrative" (1979). White contends that the Bible's heavy use of direct, first-person discourse to convey the divine voice makes it "performative" rather than "classical." The classical mode, as he defines it, encloses discourse in a third-person narrative framework. Like Ray and Finnegan, White basically wants to show how a particular tradition of usage illustrates Austin's description. But once again it is beyond the scope of his treatment to consider in-felicitous instances. All of the examples are "happy."

The only extended treatment of the failure of ritual language in terms of Austin's theory appears to be Fenn's book length examination of conflicts between the requirements of courtroom utterances and those of the liturgy. In *Liturgies and Trials* (1982) he examines three court cases: "In the Matter of Maria Cueto," "In the Matter of Karen Ann Quinlan," and Daniel Berrigan's "The Trial of the Catonsville Nine." In each court case he shows how religious utterances are reduced in court to mere opinions. The liturgy, he argues, is the only context that comes near to being "the closed linguis-tic garden of paradise" (xv). The arena within which religious utterances have actual performative force, he shows, has become quite small in North American culture. What is a felicitous utterance in an ecclesiastical social context is infelicitous in the courts. Fenn demonstrates how context-dependent the failure of ritual language is.

Prophetic and kerygmatic speech, one might suppose, are two of the most performatively oriented types of biblical language. Both Fenn and White seem to imply as much. What Fenn (1982:173) claims, however, is that religious institutions, by attempting to establish permanently the meanings of these kinds of religious speech, unwittingly secularize them, making them precarious and transient. By "secularizing" he means "the identifying of ambiguous and open-ended terms with referents and meanings that are so specific as to become outmoded and irrelevant in other contexts and at later times and occasions" (172).

Prophetic and kerygmatic speech acts are disallowed in the courtroom; only a specialized form of testimony is permitted even from religious authorities who, in other contexts, have the authority to utter things performatively. By controlling ritual proceedings, courts further contribute to the secularization of speech initiated by religious groups. The outcome is often ritual conflict and failure. And "when ritual fails, individuals and groups break the usual roles for testimony and speak for themselves outside the context of their institutional roles" (Fenn 1982:141). Loss of legitimacy and loss of illocutionary force accompany one another. In such a crisis symbols no longer evoke what they represent. What was once a performative utterance now only expresses a pious wish.

A good example of this kind of failure—though not one offered by Fenn—is Charles Winquist's (1983:296) assumption that theology is a speech act. If he intends this as a description of theological practice, one would have to question his claim. Theology, unlike prophetic and kerygmatic speech, has seldom been performative. If he intends it merely as an expression of hope, one might be enabled to agree.

Curiously, Fenn's pioneering treatment makes no use of Austin's typology of infelicities even though he makes good use of Austin's conception of illocutionary force and acknowledges (1982:124ff.) heavy dependence on speech-act theory. Why do Fenn, White, Ray, Finnegan, and even Searle not make use of the typology of infelicities? Are there unconscious apologetic motives? Clearly not in the case of Fenn; probably not in the case of Searle. Why do these scholars depict religious speech only when it is happy? Do they think Austin's typology is either wrong or too restricted for use in religious contexts? Not one of them criticizes Austin's discussion of ritual failure.

Let us give them the benefit of the doubt and assume that they examined Austin's positive thesis as a prelude to considering his negative one at a later time. Let us assume that they have presented a convincing case that biblical, Dinka, Dogon, and Limba speech make considerable use of illocutionary constructions. The next step is inquiring into the dynamics of the loss of illocutionary force.

TYPES OF INFELICITOUS PERFORMANCE

Not all of Austin's examples depend solely on language-related features. His taxonomy turns out to be much broader than his declared intentions of developing a theory of utterance; it includes instances in which failure stems from some problem with attitude or action. In fact, examined carefully, only "breaches" necessarily involve words. In all the other categories failure could occur without the involvement of language at all, even though Austin often gives examples that are language-oriented. His categories are more general than one might initially suppose. Furthermore, we might surmise from the amount of space he devotes to infelicities that he expected them to occur as frequently as he did happy performatives.

Austin identifies two major types: (1) "misfires" and (2) "abuses". I shall describe the various subtypes and provide actual ritual examples to illustrate their usefulness beyond the arena of language.

(1.11)* "Nonplays" are procedures that do not exist, therefore the actions are disallowed. Strictly speaking, there would be no examples for this category (which may be one reason Austin never found a term for it that satisfied him). However, his intention seems to be that of defining a category of rites that someone, say, a ritual authority, believes to be nonexistent or illegitimate. I use the term to include invented or recently borrowed rites that are disconnected from the structures that might legitimate them. Austin says that nonplays lack "an accepted conventional procedure" (1962:14). Such a procedure does not fall within the boundaries of legitimacy or the domain of efficacy. For instance, recall that, when William O. Roberts, Jr. (1982:11), designed initiation rites for the youth of First Church of Christ in Middletown, Connecticut, a denominational executive responded, "In Christianity we confirm faith. We do not initiate people." In his view Christian initiation is a nonplay.

(1.12) If a rite fails by "misapplication," it is a legitimate rite but the persons and circumstances involved in it are inappropriate. An example alluded to earlier is the funeral in 1954 of a ten-year-old Javanese boy named Paidjan. Clifford Geertz's (1973:153ff.) sensitive description and probing analysis show how the *slametan* (a communal feast) of the funeral became arrested because of social and political circumstances—because of what he deems "an incongruity due to the persistence in an urban environment of a religious symbol system adjusted to peasant social structure"

---

*These numbers refer to the divisions outlined in illustration 9.1, p. 204–5.

(169). One might wish to add to this category procedures that fail because they are ill-timed, such as harvest celebrations (e.g., Thanksgiving) that occur two months later than the actual harvest or weddings that are undergone too soon or too late.

(*1.21*) "Flaws" are ritual procedures that employ incorrect, vague, or inexplicit formulas, including, I would add, nonverbal or gestural formulas. Indigenous attempts to account for the failure of magical rites often appeal to some such notion. If a ritual is considered merely flawed, participants may easily be convinced to repeat it. Obviously, ritualists themselves are not eager to keep records of their mistakes, so even though flawed enactments may be rife, recorded examples are rare. An interesting one is reported by Morris E. Opler (1969:92–93). Look-Around-Water, a Mescalero Apache, believed that a protective rite failed, allowing him to be struck by two bullets, because he had been singing a deer song instead of the one that properly belonged to him. As soon as he changed his song he was healed.

(*1.22*) "Hitches" are misexecutions in which the procedures are incomplete. One of Austin's (1962:37) fictional examples is the official who declared, "I hereby open this library," only to discover that the key had broken off in the lock. A more poignant instance is the case of Lulu (recounted in Leacock 1975:200ff.), a forty-year-old Afro-Brazilian woman who for twenty years was unable to have a trance experience even though she repeatedly showed the usual signs of incipient possession.

(*2.1*) "Insincerities" are a type of "abuse"—an act "professed but hollow." Ritual insincerity amounts to saying—I would add, doing—things without the requisite feelings, thoughts, or intentions. Lévi-Strauss (1967: 169ff.) retells the story (first told by Franz Boas) of Quesalid, a Canadian Kwakiutl who did not believe in shamanism. He learned it in order to expose it. Later, he continued to practice this "false supernatural" without believing in it, because people believed in him, and because he knew of techniques even more false than his own.

(*2.2*) "Breaches" are failures to follow through; they are abrogations of ceremonially made promises. Since "breaches" includes breaking promises and failure to abide by contracts, it is one of the more familiar types of infelicity. Sometimes rites fail to bind. One can avoid the conclusion that the fault is the rite's by claiming that persons, not ceremonies, fail—that rites are "victims," not agents. A widely publicized breach was former U.S. President Richard Nixon's violation of his oath of office by his involvement in Watergate. No longer "protecting and defending," he was guilty of undermining and attacking—at least this seemed to be the public verdict.

Here Austin's typology ends, yet there remain other examples that cannot be handled by his scheme, so further additions to the typology are necessary:

(2.3) "Glosses" are procedures that hide or ignore contradictions or major problems. Glossing over conflict is a function that rites proverbially (in anthropological theory) do well. In fact, some scholars argue that this is its primary function. However, rituals may also fail because a gloss is too thin and people see through it, or because it is too thick and is recognizable only by its repercussions in the psyche or social structure. I once attended a wedding in which the bride was pregnant, followed a few months later by a child-blessing in which this same new wife participated with a black eye from her husband. Both ceremonies were "applied" in the same manner (and about as successfully) as her eye make-up. They "glossed" rather than "bridged" the chasms. It is not uncommon for participants to believe that one's wedding day should be perfect—ideal and unmarred by any recognition of difficulties.

(2.4) In a "flop" all the procedures may be done correctly but the rite fails to resonate. It does not generate the proper tone, ethos, or atmosphere. In some rites mood is less important than precise execution of procedures; this might be true of a healing rite or baptism. But in a fiesta or a birthday party, having a good time and being festive is a primary aim. At a retirement ceremony for a colleague things went without hitch or flaw (in Austin's sense of these terms), but the praise was so exaggerated and the jokes so strained that the farewell went flat; it flopped.

(3) Austin thinks of illocutionary acts almost solely in the context of interpersonal relations and legal procedures. Consequently, he omits consideration of the performative utterances that would be most obvious to scholars in religious studies and anthropology, namely, magic. Hence we need a new, major category, "ineffectuality."

Ineffectualities are procedures that fail to bring about intended observable changes. Ineffectualities are more serious than flaws, because the latter are partial. In the case of the former a rite may be properly performed, but it does not produce the goods. (For instance, Maria Sabina (cited in Halifax 1979:213), a Mazatec shaman, was unable to heal seventeen-year-old Pefecto José García and concluded her chant, "Dangerous things are being done, tragedies are being worked out. We are left only perplexed, we mamas. Who can stand all these things? It's the same; it's the same here. Really this thing is big." The chant may have prepared those present for grief and loss; it was not a "flop." But it was, in her view, ineffectual inasmuch as the boy died.

(*4*) To label an act a ritual "violation" reflects a moral judgment. Violations may be effective, but they are demeaning. From some points of view they are judged to be deficient. Rites such as initiations that deliberately maim or inadvertently degrade are difficult analytically as well as morally. Clitoridectomies are a case in point. Recently, some anthropologists, particularly women, have attacked them regardless of their indigenous support. Judging actions to be moral violations may be culturally relative, but this does not relieve us of moral responsibility. An example about which there seems to be obvious warrant for debate is the Aztec ceremony (see Vaillant 1962:205) in honor of Huehueteotl, the fire god. In it priests danced with prisoners bound to their backs and then, one by one, dumped them into the flames. Before death could relieve the pain, the priests dragged the captives out with hooks and cut out their still beating hearts. This example, along with burnings at the stake, head-hunting, and human sacrifices, challenges the easy cultural relativism of broad-minded academics.

(*5*) Ritual "contagion" occurs when a rite spills over its own boundaries. It may be effective, but it is uncontained. In *Violence and the Sacred* René Girard (1972:31ff.) has offered the most provocative analysis of this sort of infelicity. However, he typically emphasizes the way in which rituals contain the social contagion of violence rather than the way in which rituals themselves can contaminate. Maya Deren (1970:254ff.; 322n.8), a filmmaker, tells how the Voodoo rite she went to Haiti to study broke its bounds. It is rare for a non-Haitian to be possessed, but Deren was, producing considerable complications for her recording project. From one point of view this occurrence shows the power of the rite. From another, it is a problem, if not evidence of some sort of failure.

"Rituals of conflict" (Norbeck 1967:226) often spread as if they were a contagious disease. From the point of view of rebels and proponents of social change this is as it should be. From the point of view of the established elite, contamination is tantamount to failure.

(*6*) In instances of ritual "opacity" a ceremony or some element in it is experienced as meaningless; the act is unrecognizable or uninterpretable. Either it fails to communicate or it communicates such conflicting messages that someone—either participant or observer—fails to grasp its sense. There are short-lived varieties of opacity, but there are long-range ones too. Most rites probably contain some opaque symbols, and most religions, some opaque rites, but the situation becomes problematic if opacity is widespread. Opacity may incite one to curiosity, but when rife or sustained, it can damage a rite. Perhaps the most common example of opacity is the use of a sacred language (Latin, Hebrew, or Sanskrit, for instance) to such a degree that it ceases to create mystery and begins to obfuscate. How much opacity participants can tolerate seems to differ widely from culture to culture.

When tourists witness the Pueblo corn dance at Santo Domingo Pueblo, New Mexico, it is opaque to most of them; hence their concentration on the rhythm of the drums, the weather, or the color of costumes. The opacity may protect the rite from meddling, but it sometimes results in the spectators' inadvertently interrupting a sacred performance by an inappropriate response. In this case opacity is the result of being an outsider.

In the following case, recounted by Apuleius (1962:248–249) ritual opacity is deliberate, the result of priestly mystification:

> Thereupon the old man took me by the hand and led me towards the spacious temple. . . . He produced from the secret recesses of the shrine certain books written in unknown characters. The meaning of these characters was concealed, at times by the concentrated expression of hieroglypically painted animals, at times by wreathed and twisted letters with tails that twirled like wheels . . . so that it was altogether impossible for any peeping profane to comprehend.

(7) Ritual "defeat" is more common than might be supposed, because ritual competition and conquest are widespread. In a ritual defeat one ritual performance invalidates another. The eighteenth chapter of 1 Kings, for instance, tells of a contest between Elijah and Baal's prophets. The story is told from the point of view of the victors, so they are the ones who conclude that the opposing rite (and its attendant deity) are failures. Often a ritual defeat is followed by ritual "theft," that is, the plundering of a conquered ritual system for its symbolic wealth.

That ritualists explicitly compete in magical battles is obvious enough. What scholars sometimes fail to notice is how rites may be thrown implicitly into competitive "market" situations. Fenn's (1982) analysis seems to imply that liturgy is sometimes defeated by courtroom ceremony. On occasion rites from the same system inadvertently become competitors, for example, a Sunday worship service and its televised counterpart.

(8) In cases of ritual "omission" the rite does not fail; rather, one fails to perform it. Ruth Finnegan (1969:545) says that if a Limba husband can complain against his wife, "You haven't greeted me," it is a serious breach

of decorum. Like "flaws," omissions are a favorite way for participants to account for trouble. If one fails to make prayerful requests, offer the expected sacrifice, or give due thanks, then it is easy to claim that such omissions account for subsequent suffering or disaster. Omissions are the opposite of "nonplays." In the former there is no accepted procedure; in the latter there is a procedure but it is left undone.

(9) Outsiders are more likely than insiders to commit "misframes." When we misframe a rite, we misconstrue its genre. The result is akin to missing the point of a joke or taking irony literally. Perhaps we understand it on some level—it is not "opaque" to us—but on some other we miss the point. If one does not understand the shit devil rites described by Jeanne Cannizzo (1983:124–141), one might assume that boys who stumble, defecate, and wear ragged clothes were mentally ill instead of engaging in ritual caricature. It is not always easy to tell whether we are witnessing drama, symptoms, or ritual. It is a common error to misconstrue magic as drama or vice-versa. Since frames can shift or multiply in the course of a single cultural performance (e.g., a dramatic pageant within, or subsequent to, a civil ceremony), even participants can misframe the activities in which they participate. Sometimes this is an advantage, allowing ritualists to believe they share a common definition of the situation. In other instances, however, the misframing is disastrous or funny. Erving Goffman's *Frame Analysis* (1974:324) is replete with examples, such as the story of a thousand enraged Mexican farmers who drive their priest out of town because he will not celebrate Mass at a tree that, after lying five years dead on its side, is found upright after a thunderstorm. They frame the event as "miracle"; he does not.

To summarize, the complete typology, consisting of Austin's categories (without quotation marks) as well as my own (in quotation marks), is as follows:

9.1. **Types of Infelicitous Performance**
1. Misfire (act purported but void)
    1.1. Misinvocation (act disallowed)
        1.11. Nonplay (lack of accepted conventional procedure)
        1.12. Misapplication (inappropriate persons or circumstances)
    1.2. Misexecutions (act vitiated)
        1.21. Flaw (incorrect, vague, or inexplicit formula)
        1.22. Hitch (incomplete procedure)

9.1 Continued

2. Abuse (act professed but hollow)
   - 2.1. Insincerity (lack of requisite feelings, thoughts, or intentions)
   - 2.2. Breach (failure to follow through)
   - 2.3. "Gloss" (procedures used to cover up problems)
   - 2.4. "Flop" (failure to produce appropriate mood or atmosphere)

3. "Ineffectuality" (act fails to precipitate anticipated empirical change)

4. "Violation" (act effective but demeaning)

5. "Contagion" (act leaps beyond proper boundaries)

6. "Opacity" (act unrecognizable or unintelligible)

7. "Defeat" (act discredits or invalidates acts of others)

8. "Omission" (act not performed)

9. "Misframe" (genre of act misconstrued)

RITUAL INFELICITY IN THE HEBREW BIBLE

As anyone who has ever tried to apply and test some theory or scheme knows, all sorts of unanticipated problems appear as soon as one faces a specific tradition with that theory. When we engage in extended case studies rather than selecting examples, the lack of fit between theory and data begins to show. I am no biblical scholar and have neither the space nor the training to pursue a case study here, but it might be helpful at least to suggest lines along which a study of performative infelicity in the Hebrew Bible might proceed. Some of the more interesting examples are suggested by the epigraphs.

Beginning with biblical texts is basically, but not entirely, an inductive procedure. I have, after all, picked texts that appear to be relevant to the typology. For instance, the tale of the confrontation of Moses and Aaron with the Egyptian magicians seems to be, among others things, a story about magical combat. Comparative religion and symbolic anthropology are replete with similar stories about sorcerers and magicians who pit their rites against one another. This feature of the account appears to be a straightforward illustration of ritual "defeat" (#7).*

By itself this sort of labeling does not tell us very much; the work of interpretation has hardly begun when one categorizes the action. It begins to get interesting, however, when we inquire why these same magicians are

---

*Such references are to illustration 9.1.

said to have been successful in an earlier phase of competition. Like Moses and Aaron they too succeed in bringing frogs upon the land of Egypt by use of their secret arts (Exodus 8:7). It heightens suspense to have the magicians seem like real competition and then have them defeated. It may be that a symbolic, possibly ritualistic, issue is at stake when the magicians are successful in bringing frogs (amphibians associated with water) but fail with gnats (creatures of the air associated in the text with dust). Whether or not my speculations bear any fruit, the point is simply that categorizing the conflict as ritual defeat, a species of performative infelicity, precipitates an avenue of inquiry not entirely typical of biblical scholarship.

Consider a second biblical example, that of Cain's offering (Genesis 4). Popular interpretations of the story fill in the silence of the text by assuming that God rejects the offering because Cain hides some secret sin such as arrogance or that he is insincere. Such an interpretation implies a classification of the problem as "insincerity" (#2.1), "lack of requisite feelings, thoughts, or intentions."

Modern scholarship, on the other hand, often reads the story as personifying a conflict between two ways of life: agricultural (symbolized by Cain and his vegetable / fruit offering) and nomadic (symbolized by Abel and his offering of livestock). Whereas the popular view treats Cain's failure as a form of "abuse" (#2), an act professed but hollow, the scholarly one treats it as a "misinvocation" (#1.1) of some sort; "the act is disallowed." Following speech-act theory we would have to inquire whether it is disallowed because there is no accepted conventional procedure for such an offering or whether the persons or circumstances are inappropriate. If the latter, then we would have to ask, Inappropriate in what respects?

A third instance is Abraham's near sacrifice of Isaac, popularly regarded as a "test" but considered by some scholars as reflecting a cultural transition from child sacrifice to a more sublimated, more ethically sophisticated, rite in which an animal is substituted for a person. In the language of speech-act theory we would say this is a "misapplication" (#1.12), because it involves an inappropriate object: a human rather than an animal.

But from the point of view of Isaac, we might imagine, it is better regarded as an instance of ritual "violation" (#4)—or near violation, since the act was not completed. From the point of view of a child-sacrificing culture (if there ever was one), Abraham's failure to follow through would have constituted a "breach" (#2.2). But modern Jews and Christians might well question whether any sort of infelicity or failure has occurred at all. The story, they might insist, is about a successful ritual revision or a successful attempt to resist a temptation to use ritual to satisfy an infanticidal obsession. What this third example illustrates is that the typology does not answer questions so much as precipitate them by providing a vocabulary.

A final example is the short folktale of Nadab and Abihu, the sons of Aaron (Leviticus 10). In one sense it parallels the Cain and Abel story: God is not happy with an offering. But instead of refusing it, he destroys the brothers with fire because they offered "unholy fire." The pun notwithstanding, the act is a "misfire" (#1), but of what sort? The only way to be precise is to know more about what constituted unholiness for the ancient Hebrews. Does the problem lie in intentions? In procedures? Or should we circumvent these alternatives altogether and classify the action according to its results? If the latter, we need a new category, say, "backfires," which we could make an independent category or a subcategory of "contagion" (#5), which is what occurs when a performance leaps beyond proper boundaries.

FURTHER RESEARCH ON RITUAL INFELICITY

I have raised far more questions than I have answered— deliberately so. The aim has not been to "apply" a theory of speech acts to biblical "data." Rather, it has been to experiment with the theory, both extending its scope and exposing its limits, as well as teasing a few texts with some new questions. The typology is incomplete, although I have shown how one might begin to expand beyond Austin's original aims and to build on his vocabulary. The categories need much more testing by application to specific rites. For the moment, the most one can expect of them is that they call attention to what is often ignored, namely, infelicitous performances, and that they provide a tentative glossary for beginning to assess them.

An obvious limitation of the typology is that it does not solve the problem of point of view. Who—participant or observer—is to decide whether procedures fail, and if they do, what sort of infelicity has been committed?

The typology does not fully explore how kinds of infelicity transpire in relation to one another. For instance, one may "gloss" a rite, deliberately making it "opaque," thereby laying the grounds for a ritual "defeat." Something like this happened when Spanish conquistadors taught Native people of the new world to venerate crosses without fully conveying their meaning. Later, the conquerors used this devotion as a means of discouraging rebellion among the conquered and of obtaining formal, ceremonial submission.

An unanswered question is this: What are the motives and mechanisms for evading the judgment that a rite does not work? What is it about ritual itself that seems so regularly to discourage critical thinking?

One also might want to inquire whether the terms are ethnocentric. Austin's British, understated "infelicitous" / "happy" and my overstated, North American "failure" / "success" might suggest that ritual criticism is inextricably bound up with national or even temperamental sensibilities.

Another problem is that the typology does not systematically separate "failure in" and "failure of " rituals. In some types the problem lies with the ritualists, in others with the rite itself, and in still others with the relation between the rite and surrounding religiocultural processes.

Finally, there are undoubtedly other types and examples. What shall we call the rite that is so rigid that it cannot change? How shall we name those ceremonies that are so weak dramatically, conceptually, or socially that they simply have no effect? And what of annulments, for example, of weddings? As the types and examples proliferate, we must, of course, begin to examine the logic of sub- and super-ordination of the categories. Are there "levels" of failure?

Among these issues the point-of-view problem and the failure-in / failure-of distinction are in my estimation the most important and troublesome, so a few additional comments may be necessary, if only to encourage further reflection and research.

Put simply, there is no resolving the point of view problem if one imagines there is some universal, meta-ritualistic criterion which, like a meter stick, can be used to measure every rite cross-culturally. Even the exemplary meter stick lacks currency not only in the New Guinea bush but in the United States. I have deliberately refrained from referring to the categories as "criteria." They constitute a typology, an organized (perhaps in the future, systematized) phenomenology. Their worth consists of their ability to point to troublesome dynamics and to provide a vocabulary for recognitions, debate, and discussion. They are useless as some kind of performative canon with which to prove failure or rebuke ritualists. Ritualists have so little difficulty evading ritual criticism that a set of a-cultural criteria would be of little practical use to anybody who is not already convinced that a problem exists.

Since rites, especially religious ones, function as paradigms, they themselves are sometimes the ideal by which the ordinary is judged. Rites, like myths and dreams, resist criticism or, if you prefer, people resist having their rites, myths, and dreams subjected to criticism. The right to engage in it all is probably either bought with membership and participation or directly dependent upon the richness of one's observations and interpretations. Ritual criticism is but one phase—and not a privileged one either—of the hermeneutics of ritual. So if we are to speak of criteria at all, they are definitional not moral. Their weight comes from their ability to articulate, not their ability to prove or coerce. Consider, for instance "violations," those ritual acts that demean. Demeaning may be defined as in bounds for an initiation rite. If one chooses to resist this definition, he or she will probably have the most success by appealing to one part of the rite as a basis for criticizing some other part. In the Abraham-Isaac story ritual infanticide is prevented not by a bare moral interdiction but by a ritual substitute. The most effective ritual criticism is probably that which transpires on the basis of the ritual systems itself, not on some heteronomous rule.

This brings us to the failure-in / failure-of distinction. Infelicity is often taken by participants to be the result of a failure in some detail of performance. They will blame themselves before impugning the rite and will criticize some part of it before challenging the whole of it. It is a mistake always to blame persons rather than rituals—a tactic that prevents ritual criticism. Using a literary critical analogy, we might say that in such instances functional infelicity is translated into formal infelicity. Formally, a rite is a self-contained system; functionally, it achieves something in the environment or does something to or for participants.

However, I do not think a merely formal or morphological treatment of ritual failure will suffice, but neither will one that considers failure in purely functional, sociological terms. I doubt that one can ever judge a rite as failed or flawed in any absolute way. It is always flawed from person or group X's point of view or in relation to goal Y. If we learn to make such discriminations, we may become less susceptible to the wholesale waves of ritophobia and ritophilia that periodically sweep Western cultures. Analyzing ritual failure involves more than defining terms, supplying examples, or applying labels. But learning to do so is a first step toward a useful ritual criticism.

10

THE SCHOLARLY CONTEXTS AND

PRACTICES OF RITUAL CRITICISM*

Interdisciplinarity consists in creating a new object that belongs to no one.
—Roland Barthes (1984:97–103)

All knowledge, taken at the moment of its constitution, is polemical knowledge.
—Gaston Bachelard (1950:14)

Narcissus' tragedy then is that he is not narcissistic enough, or rather that he does not reflect long enough to effect a transformation. He is reflective, but he is not reflexive—that is, he is conscious of himself as an other, but he is not conscious of being self-conscious of himself as an other and hence not able to detach himself from, understand, survive, or even laugh at this initial experience of alienation.
—Barbara Babcock (1980:2)

One might expect a chapter on the scholarly contexts and practices of ritual criticism to have come at the beginning, not the end. Here, after a series of case studies and the essays one could wish for a unified, comprehensive theory of ritual. I have none to offer, because I have explored several types of ritual, tried out varying critical strategies, observed ritual only on a single continent, and focused on one phase of the ritual process. But lack of a unified theory does not mean lack of intellectual context or lack of principles. Now it is time to make these explicit by putting both the case studies and essays in their scholarly setting.[105]

Ritual criticism is not a field, much less a discipline. There are no models for it, so one must begin forging them from bits and pieces found elsewhere. One must look for analogous practices. Obvious places to search are aesthetics generally (including literary criticism, theater criticism, and art criticism) and liturgiology (the theological criticism of the rites of one's own tradition).[106] Any serious attempt to formulate an ethic

---

*This chapter is based on a paper, "On Ritual Criticism," presented in 1986 to the Ritual Studies Group of the American Academy of Religion and on an article, originally published as "Ritual Criticism and Reflexivity in Fieldwork," in the *Journal of Ritual Studies* 2(2):217–239. The latter is used with permission.

for engaging in ritual criticism must be interdisciplinary and take seriously the conflicts and convergences among the humanities, social sciences, and theology.

The phrase "ritual criticism" is not a familiar one. Many will hear it as analogous to "literary criticism."[107] Criticism is a notion nurtured specifically in the humanities, but it has been appropriated in both the social sciences and theology. Ritual criticism is a practice thoroughly entangled with norms, judgments, and evaluation. But whether it is an artistic or a scientific practice is a matter of debate.

Literary scholars debate whether literary critics ought to exercise normative judgments, especially if they are made for the sake of a literature-consuming public, but, as far as I know, their differences do not lead them to reject the critical task altogether, as is sometimes the case in other fields. Criticism in literature has a longer history than in either religious studies or anthropology. A classic volume on literary criticism, with much to say about ritual, is Northrop Frye's *Anatomy of Criticism* (1968). In this book criticism assumes the form of an "anatomy," a laying out of parts in order to classify them and relate them to genres, literary slots, or categories. The book's usefulness to ritual criticism is limited, however, because ultimately it reduces ritual to repetitive patterns in literary works. Frye's theory does not enable one to take note of the ways literature implicates extra-literary moral and ritual behavior. However, Siebers' *The Ethics of Criticism* (1988) and Merod's *The Political Responsibility of the Critic* (1987) are clear evidence that more recent literary criticism is no longer necessarily confined to texts alone and that it is seriously interested in the relations among readers, texts, and the larger society.

Two of the most reliable, recent guides to the state of literary criticism— Wayne Booth's (1979) *Critical Understanding* and Frank Lentricchia's (1980) *After the New Criticism*—illustrate well the morass of misunderstanding that is possible among critics who think they must disprove other critics' perspectives before they can proceed. There are so many options that histories of literary criticism have become essential. A meta-criticism (a criticism of criticism) has become necessary in order to classify schools of criticism, so one should be extremely careful when using literary criticism as a model.

The most obvious difficulty with appropriating a literary critical model for ritual criticism is the dependence of the former upon language. Though most rites utilize language, not all of them do. And among those that do, many aspects of those rites are nonverbal. Whether or not these nonverbal dimensions ought to be regarded metaphorically as language is a debatable question that I took up in chapter 8. By now it is obvious that I oppose this strategy. But there are mediating positions. Kenneth Burke has argued that language is symbolic "action," and J. L. Austin has called attention to the ways words "perform." As much as I agree with both men, I believe it is essential to notice ways in which ritual action differs from writing poems and making pronouncements. Thus I am wary of too literary an approach to ritual criticism.[108]

Perhaps a more obvious place to look for clues to the proper formulation of a workable ritual criticism is theater. Here at least one finds texts and scripts related to overt bodily action. The most provocative theoretical research in this field is that of Richard Schechner, particularly his *Essays in Performance Theory* (1977) and his *Between Theater and Anthropology* (1985). Because his research is directly relevant, I shall comment on it in more detail. Even though Schechner emphasizes the similarities among drama, popular entertainment, and ritual, he does not ignore the essential differences, which he plots on a continuum running from efficacy to entertainment (1977:75ff.). The basic opposition, he insists, is not between ritual and theater but between efficacy and entertainment. Both ritualistic and theatrical activity have effect and entertain, but ritual emphasizes efficacy, and theater emphasizes entertainment. Schechner's own theatrical values are such that he would reject a purely entertainment oriented theater.

When a performance is efficacious, Schechner calls it a "transformance," because its work is to transform. Girls become women; boys, men; and trance, revelation. One identity, situation, or role is remade into another. Although this sort of transformation is traditionally attributed to ritual, theater has its own sort: destructive behavior is displayed and thus rendered nondestructive; people are made into characters. So Schechner's theory implies that efficaciousness is an essential criterion for criticism. Though there may be others, one has to ask of rites of passage, for example: Are the girls successfully transformed into women? Are two singles really wed into a couple?

Schechner does not think of ritual and drama as enemies. They become so only in specific cultures where aesthetic theater develops or ritual is shorn of its entertaining functions. As we saw in chapter 2, embracing the performative qualities of ritual is difficult for the post-Vatican II church. Performance is a "braided structure" of efficacy and entertainment, but sometimes the braid is loose and sometimes tight. When it is tight, performance flourishes. In Schechner's thumbnail historical sketch this tightening occurs in the theaters of fifth-century Athens, late medieval to Renaissance Europe, and in contemporary Euroamerican societies. Of the latter he says, "Efficacy lies at the ideological heart of all aspects of this new theatre" (1977:77). He says nothing about efficacy in liturgical performance. In all three historical periods there is noticeable ritualization. Schechner's own theatrical productions have tried to overcome what he regards as the senile, ineffectual aesthetic of Western theater. His reason for arguing that Japanese Noh, Indian Kathakali, Balinese Ketchak, and medieval European morality plays offer the best models for the future of theater (66) is that they balance modes of transformation. Not mere shows, they are "showings of doings."[109]

Another discipline in which important research on criticism is going on is anthropology. It has the advantage of taking social and historical contexts seriously, whereas aesthetic criticism tends to ignore them. Also, the discipline of anthropology has been committed to overcoming the parochial biases one sometimes finds in theology. At an earlier time anthropology was considered only a scientific, and thus analytical or explanatory, discipline.[110] Recently, however, some anthropologists are speaking of anthropology as a critical discipline.

Though there is a large anthropological literature on ritual, there is no explicit, systematic research on the topic of ritual criticism. However, a great deal is either implied or said in an offhand way about it in anthropological writing. Among the most useful works on the critical dimensions of anthropology are Marcus and Fischer's *Anthropology as Cultural Critique* (1986), Clifford and Marcus's *Writing Culture* (1986), and Clifford Geertz's *Works and Lives: The Anthropologist as Author* (1988). These show increasing awareness of the literary dimensions of the ethnographic enterprise and also of the critical nature of writing about cultures other than one's own.

The so-called new, or meta-, ethnography is highly reflexive. By this I mean that it is self-conscious about its own processes, a theme that connects it with countercultural and postmodern concerns. The outcome in written ethnographies is the appearance (or reappearance) of the ethnographer as a character in his or her own account. No longer the omnipotent hand that paints the natives as if he or she were not present among them, the new ethnographer appears there in the photographs alongside the natives. No longer mere objects of an all-seeing camera's eye, these natives are less "informants" than consultants or collaborators.

To some this shift of attention seems narcissistic—the crass introduction of autobiography into ethnography. No doubt, in its worst examples this is the case. But in its best ones something else is going on. In these instances criticism is assuming the form of self-examination and self-criticism.[111]

What becomes evident in reflexive ethnographies are the ways field-workers bear the values of dominating cultures, the ways author-ethno-graphers "construct" the very people they study. The ritual that gets criticized, then, is less that of indigenous people and more that of doing fieldwork. In new ethnographies fieldwork functions as the initiation rite it tacitly is. The importance of anthropological study for ritual criticism lies in its historic commitment to understanding the politics of all intercultural activities, including research itself.

Theology is another field with strong commitments of the assessment of ritual. To their own detriment the humanities and social sciences studiously ignore theological disciplines, while the latter are busy reading, evaluating, and appropriating the former. Anthropological perspectives have deeply penetrated the heart of Christian theological reflection on ritual, otherwise known as liturgiology or liturgical theology.[112] The writings of Victor Turner, Clifford Geertz, and Mary Douglas are widely read by liturgical theologians.[113]

Unlike anthropologists, liturgiologists are not shy about making value judgments or covert in their assessments of rites. What they often lack, however, is cross-cultural perspective. What humanists and social scientists have to learn from them is how to sustain a long, literate tradition of ongoing criticism and consequent practice. The critical dimension of liturgics constellated in the late nineteenth century largely as a result of historical research on liturgical texts. Putting liturgical innovations in historical context began to relativize the liturgy itself.[114] Symbolic meanings no longer appeared timeless. Their meanings were seen as changing in relation to cultural and political contexts. Now it is not uncommon for liturgiologists to be articulate about the imperial politics of liturgical controversies and conciliar decisions and compromises.[115] Furthermore, liturgical theologians are beginning to engage in field study. Though insiders, they assume the postures of observers, pit texts against performances, and speculate about operational and unconscious meanings that differ from intended or explicitly stated meanings.[116] So the idea that a theological understanding of ritual is only in-house and thus incapable of examining its own presuppositions is clearly false.

Mary Collins recently wrote an essay, "Critical Ritual Studies: Examining an Intersection of Theology and Culture" (in her *Worship: Renewal to Practice*).[117] On the basis of field study she provides data illustrating how the rites for the profession of vows by women religious preceded, and thus implicitly criticized, systematic theological reinterpretation. Her fieldwork illustrates the fallacy of assuming that systematic theologians in seminaries are more critical than practitioners in the field. Her findings reverse the usual assumption that priests and women religious are mere technicians of the sacred, while the theologians are the critical minds. She concludes:

> To state the basic position of this paper succinctly, ritual studies are worth pursuing by researchers interested in the interplay between theology and culture precisely because ritual acts constitute a distinctive kind of religious and cultural expression, one which is corporate in its manifestations and bodily and nondiscursive in its presentation of content. These very characteristics make ritual inaccessible to ordinary theological methods, which work with texts [1987:97].

Just as utilization of historical methods in the late nineteenth and early twentieth centuries turned liturgiology into a critical discipline, so the contemporary shift of attention to nontextual, nonverbal aspects of ritual is an implicit critique of liturgy and liturgical theology. This shift has called attention to the local qualities of liturgy, which has the effect of tempering claims about its universality. It also has stirred a great deal of interest in enculturation, the process whereby rites are rendered indigenous and local.[118] No longer can liturgical theologians assume that symbols have meanings detached from relations of power and domination. Theologians have long understood that ritual is programmatic, or paradigmatic, and that critical judgment, therefore, must be exercised in the selection of rites and their constituent symbols. But now, as representatives of so-called world religions, they must face the fact that their own traditions are also "multinational religions." Like corporations, religious institutions ritualize local interests and bill them as if they were universal ones.

Religious studies is not identical with theology. Insofar as ritual studies is carried out within the field of religious studies, it often mediates between the analytical methods of anthropology and the prescriptive ones of theology. In practice, religiologists emphasize phenomenological, hermeneutical, and historical approaches to religious phenomena. The usual way of describing the differences between religious studies and theology is to say that religious studies is teaching *about* religion while theology is the teaching *of* religion. Fearing they might be accused of being covert theologians, religiologists have generally avoided evaluative methods. Typically, religious studies has left fieldwork to anthropologists and evaluation to theologians. As a result its study of ritual has been impoverished and in need of more sustained contact with critics in the humanities, theology, and the social sciences.

Religiologists have tried to avoid what one might call "religiocentrism," making judgments about one religious tradition from the point of view of a privileged other tradition. How is it possible, we have asked ourselves, to criticize ritual disinterestedly? Is not any act of assessing a rite necessarily centered in the religiosity (or lack of it) of one's own culture? Biblical criticism, which once seemed so scientific, now appears in historical retrospect to be rooted in the specificity of late nineteenth- and early twentieth-century Euroamerican societies. And if biblical criticism, having borrowed its objectivity from various kinds of literary and historical criticism, now has to admit to being an agent of enculturation rather than a universal science, how can we expect ritual criticism to fare any better? I do not argue that we can, because there is no such thing as disinterested criticism. For this reason we must systematically attend to the politics of critique.

However clean in theory is the distinction between teaching *about* religion and the teaching *of* religion, in practice it is less so. No discipline is without values and judgments. All scholarly activity, like all religious activity, is local and therefore enculturated. All teaching about religion is religiocentric, which is to say, biased by cultural perspectives and religious presuppositions. From the point of view of certain Native American traditions, for example, even the commitment to the objective, comparative study of religious traditions is a violation, a blatant expression of dominant White ideology (see Layton 1989:2ff.).

In religious studies, which claims both theology and social science as kin, the usual way off the horns of the dilemma of religiocentrism is to resort to phenomenology, a peculiar kind of description, or, more accurately, a rhetoric used for description. At best a phenomenology of ritual is preliminary, and at worst, psychologically projective and ethically evasive. Religious studies cannot not assume a posture of neutrality between normative and explanatory disciplines or for that matter between religious traditions and cultures, because the assumed universality of phenomenological characterizations is in fact local, culture-bound ideology. Avoiding criticism will not get us off the hook. We cannot hide behind phenomenologies (presentations of "things as they appear" without judgments concerning their ontological status), because descriptions of people's practices are tacitly critical. They function as critiques when, for instance, they are experienced by ritualists as exposures of sacred activities. Since we cannot refrain from criticism, our only choice is to engage in it overtly so as to invite countercriticism.

One of the most important works on criticism to emerge from religious studies is Giles Gunn's *The Culture of Criticism and the Criticism of Culture* (1987). Primarily conversant with research in American studies,

Gunn has little to say explicitly about ritual. Still, he has considerable insight into both the culture-bound nature of any critical undertaking and the essentially ethical nature of criticism. An important difference between cultural criticism as he defines it and ritual criticism as I characterize it is that of scope. Cultural criticism takes as its focus what ritual criticism construes as context, namely, the entire ethos of a people. Though Gunn is quite aware of the need for cross-cultural perspectives, his history of cultural criticism construes it as the outcome of American history specifically. And when he says "American," he really means United States, not Canadian and not Latin American. When he links cultural criticism to humanism, the kinds of human beings his text assumes are largely Euro-North American, educated males. Such is the limitation of his work. The strength of his account is that it recognizes the liabilities of having all critics fit this privileged profile. In his deeply moral view the possibility of cultural criticism must be predicated on a primary respect for the other and for ethnic, economic, and political differences. At least in intention, his cultural criticism is every bit as cross cultural as any anthropologist's ritu alized journey to a far place in order to return home with a more sharply critical eye.

Gunn's hypothetical cultural critic is not eager to import divine transcendence into criticism, is shy of appropriating other people's lifeways, is self-critical, and yet wants to reconnect criticism and practice. He has had enough of merely academic, purely theoretical criticism, hence his commitment to pragmatism.

There is a growing consensus in religious studies that the criticism of ritual ought to mediate between practice and theory and that theorizing about ritual ought to be rooted in field study. Even ancient ritual texts are best interpreted in the light of methods developed out of actual observation of contemporary rites. In religious studies the priority of field study is not so clearly established as in anthropology, but there has long been a practice of anchoring theories of religion in the history of specific religions. The recent emphasis on fieldwork in ritual studies extends and deepens this commitment to the particularities of local practice.[119]

Besides Gunn, Ruel Tyson is the other religiologist whose work has direct relevance to this sketch of the scholarly context of ritual criticism. Engaged in joint fieldwork with anthropologist James Peacock, he comments:

If the practice precedes the theory of it and if the explication of methods presupposes a history of application, then field work should precede theories of culture, including the relation between religious action and other cultural forms; and practical criticism should precede theoretical criticism [Tyson 1975:12].

Tyson refers to himself as a "practical critic," by which he means one who richly describes and interprets specific cultural performances.[120] Perhaps one is not stretching his intention too far by suggesting that the practical critic is one who criticizes practice. If this extension of his definition is acceptable, the proposals I make here obviously fall under the same heading.[121]

AN EXAMPLE OF RITUAL CRITICISM

Because a scholar's conception and sense of ritual is so radically embedded in its cultural and intellectual matrices, the practice of ritual criticism itself ought not be immune to criticism. Further, the canons of postmodernism, one of the cultural contexts in which I initially set ritual criticism, demands a reflexive loop. So it is essential to examine the eye that observes the enactments—to turn criticism back on itself. Accordingly, what follows is a representation of my own criticism in process followed by a critique of it. The extract below was written by me to be delivered orally in a response to a performance of *Bharata Natyam*, classical Indian dance. Subsequently, the remarks themselves will be subjected to critique.[122]

On other occasions I have been asked to respond to a *Bharata Natyam* performance. The responses were of differing sorts: bodily in a workshop, informally in discussions with a theorist and critic, and now, formally "from the point of view of ritual studies." Not invited as an expert on either dance or Indian religions, I come as a student of ritual. On another, earlier occasion organizers, dancers, audience, and I queried each other, Is *Bharata Natyam* ritual or drama? Usually we concluded with a both-and answer of some sort. How to define what was transpiring in front of us was a major question, not just for me but for performers and audience.

It is not easy to say what *Bharata Natyam* is. Usually, it is described as a classical performance style from India, one that combines dance, drama, storytelling, and ritual. Publicity refers to such an event as a "classical Indian dance." To the Western ear the phrase creates certain expectations. "Classical" suggests "quasi-canonical." This is not entirely inappropriate, because Bharata's codification of the Natya Shastra, on which *Bharata Natyam* is partly based, is sometimes referred to as "the fifth Veda." "Fifth Gospel" would be a loose analogue. Of the classical we do not expect radical innovation or obvious experimentation but fidelity to a finely honed tradition. However, like classical ballet dancers, *Bharata Natyam* performers can exercise considerable creativity by recombining elements within the tradition, and practitioners differ in their sense of obligation to the purity of the tradition.

For Western audiences the classical is likely to be consumed "with taste." "Classical" connotes "not folk" and is for "the cultured." We do not, for example, speak of classical Pueblo or Shaker dance; clearly certain class and ethnic values are encoded in the designation. We are likely to construe the classic as purer and more static than it really is.

To the Westernized ear "Indian" may at first mean only "not American," "not European." By virtue of its otherness, Indian dance can be dismissed as "theirs, not ours." It can be liberally and tolerantly appreciated, venerated just because it is different, or romanticized as exotic. Because it is other than North American, we inevitably search for similarities and analogues. We are unable to see it with an Asian eye; this inability is both a liability and an opportunity. Purists—and they are as numerous among buffs as among practitioners—might insist that classical Indian dance is "archetypally" Indian or that the iconography of its gestures, postures, and rhythmic patterns should be traditional, as opposed to imported or made up. But the complexity of modern Indian, as well as North American, society and history militates against purism. In the previous *Bharata Natyam* performances that I have witnessed both the Indianizing of the North American eye and the Westernizing of classical Indian dance were transpiring. The cultural dynamics of such cross-fertilizing are not unique. Tourists in Arizona, for example, regularly fail to recognize that twentieth century rock music and nineteenth-century pan-tribal circle dancing are now as Navajo as traditional "sings" (see Martin 1979).

Ritual studies, at least as I view it, begins with the act of describing the performance events themselves rather than with standards "above," parallels "beside," or heritages "behind" what is seen. And such a description has to include in it the frames of reference of those involved in the event, not just the primary actors. And this includes the audience. The interpreter of ritual is obligated to say as much about the *seeing* of the performer's dance, as about the seeing of her *dance*, or the seeing of *her* dance. One's seeing and hearing are almost as ritualized as an actor's performance, and the study of ritual must attend the ritual of spectating as well as the ritual of dancing.

This performance event has transpired in a nonsacred time slot. By being situated in the postdinner hour of 8 o'clock and not, say, at 11:00 A.M. on Sunday, sundown on Friday, or 9 A.M. on Monday the event is dissociated from worship and work and associated with entertainment.

This event functions as both interlude and finale in relation to events that surrounded it. As interlude it helps us relax and recover from the major "acts," the usual sequence of academic discussion and lecture. As finale, it suggests that intellectualizing exists for the sake of the object of study—in this case, performance. Following the performance with a discussion between a moderator and a discussant, however, re-frames it as "subject matter" or "data," thus implicitly confessing our ignorance of it while symbolizing our intention to understand it. We are supposed to enjoy it as entertainment, appreciate it as culture, and understand it as subject matter—all this in a focused American two hours, not a diffuse, Indian afternoon.

Spatial framing of classical Indian dances in North America tend to be simple. Wooden floors are essential for the drumming actions of the dancer's feet. Beyond this requirement settings and physical properties have been minimal in all the cases I have observed including this one. One such event was held in the basement of a church; another in an auditorium.[123]

In the performance we have just witnessed action clearly dominated scenery. The set did not "act" except, according to a few audience members, to detract. The flowers, candles, incense, and small pictures provided by the performers were relegated to the background and defined as devotional rather than dramatic accompaniment to the dance itself.

This is the second occasion on which I have seen performers who were North American women trained by Indian teachers. And their self-understanding of their roles differs from that of conventional North American theater actors. Although they played their roles in subjunctive mode, "as if " they were real, this dramatic self-consciousness did not stop them from denying that they were merely acting. One of the performers said she incarnated the deities she danced; the other spoke of it as an act of devotion.

Both wore traditional Indian costumes, the main function of which was not to convey office or character but to create beauty and generate an atmosphere. The costumes were neither official uniforms nor theatrical, character-specific costume. In the West this way of using costume is probably more characteristic of oral storytelling than of ritual or drama. In storytelling, dress is often neutral, since a single teller may have to tell about, and act out in a limited way, several characters.

Bodily training is essential in classical Indian dance. Neither performer denied the body; both affirmed it. And both insisted that, done properly, bodily training and spiritual training were the same thing.

One of the most Westernized features of these two performances was the tendency toward autobiography. Both dancers and audience showed explicit interest in performers' autobiographies. Many audience members were looking for autobiographical traces between the cracks of the formalized structure of the dance. The dancers spoke of their own lives and spiritual journeys. Audiences wanted to know how each woman came to do what she was doing and what it meant to her personally. Audience members implied that they venerated dance forms for their capacity to express performers' personality and values. Inquirers, with very little questioning, took the performers' feelings about their own performances to constitute the meanings of those performances. In ritual criticism one ought not ignore ritualists' comments but interpret them in the light of gestures, social situation, and historical context.

But what about the actual art form itself? Diagrammatically representing the form, style, and movement patterns of a dance is notoriously difficult. The earliest dance notation records (as opposed to descriptions) are from fifteenth-century Catalonia, and the major systems presently in use, for example, Labanotation, date back only to the turn of the century. These technical ways of describing movements are not intelligible to untrained audiences. So it is best to attempt a brief, nontechnical description of characteristic gestures and postures.

As audience, we can respond to the geometric and kinesthetic qualities of classical Indian dance without ever knowing whether or what they signify. In this sense, and only in this sense, is a dance "universal." Classical Indian dance is not universally intelligible—probably no art form is—even in India. Even there, the dance sometimes survives for viewers by virtue of formal qualities, which do not mean anything, at least not in the same way some of the *mudras* (hand gestures) do.

Seen formally, *Bharata Natyam* is not basically aerial, though it can include occasional spins and leaps. The distinctive bent knees form a triangular base that grounds the flowing upper limbs. The style is less flight-oriented than ballet, which in its early history sometimes used wires to lend birdlike qualities to dancers. We are shown most postures frontally; seldom are profiles or back sides presented. In comparison to Western dance forms, the facial gestures of *Bharata Natyam* are both articulated and stylized in greater detail, and in prescribed, not spontaneous, ways. The dancer's face is not neutral or "neutral-elevated" as we see in ballet. Many of the hand and arm gestures are obviously mimetic, but we would wrongly conclude that all of them are. Another notable feature is that movements are often momentarily frozen into sculpturelike poses. Marceau says of Western performance, "A mime sculptures space while a dancer fills it" (cited in Royce 1977:51). In classical Indian dance the dancer fills space and sculpts her or his body.

Since *Bharata Natyam* is a veritable catalogue of Indian sculptural iconography, one ought to ask to what extent the postures were hyperboles and to what extent, actually reflective of bodily comportment in India. The layering of gestures is thick. Among its sources are Indian temple carvings, ordinary Indian interaction, codified *Bharata Natyam* gestures, and improvisations of the dancers themselves, including some that seem recognizable as American gestural accents or female mannerisms.

The narratives in the *Bharata Natyam* performance we have seen were erotic, a quality Western audiences resist treating as religious. Besides being danced, *Bharata Natyam* performances are also told. Dancers become narrators telling stories of passion and love. In telling them, they play the roles of characters, for example, courtesans and deities. Though the dance, story, and drama are erotic, I doubt that on first viewing, our Westernized eyes actually perceived them as such, no matter how we conceived them. What was done with pelvis, breasts, buttocks, eyes, and thighs was not immediately recognizable to us as erotic. To be sure, the audience immediately perceived the sensuousness of the dance, but in the generalized way tree bark or flower petals are sensuous. It is another step from the sensuous to the erotic, and yet another from the erotic to the sexual (a step not taken in *Bharata Natyam*). As soon as the Westernized mind knows one of the performances is about a courtesan, the Westernized eye expects provocative, sexual gestures. But identifying courtesans and prostitutes, we learn from this performance, is ethnocentric. So the audience had to work to perceive the dance as religiously erotic rather than sensual only in the broad sense or sexual in the narrow sense. When we succeeded, perhaps we learned to imagine a courtesan as something other than degraded, the object of contempt, pity, or lust.

Western religions tend to segregate eroticism from spirituality. The exceptions are in mystical and romantic tributaries to mainline traditions.[124] As if to compensate, popular sentimentality makes a quasi-religion of passion and elevates gender display to iconic status only to exploit it commercially. The result is anything but spiritual or erotic. The efforts of spiritually minded choreographer-dancers such as Martha Graham and liturgical dance societies have chipped away at the wall that traps dance in aestheticism and identifies religion with private piety or public morality. But the Western eye is rooted in genre distinctions that are themselves classification grids in a cosmology and thus not likely to be overturned by a performance.

The language of *Bharata Natyam* is predominately gestural, not textual. There are texts, but texts alone are considered inadequate instruction; one must study with a teacher. The gestures themselves are highly formulaic and stylized. Seen formally, they appear ritualistic to Westerners, but "translated" into dialogue, some of the stories sound quite secular and dramatic.

Perhaps all gestures have meaning, but not in the same way. Some of them are codified, named, taught, and recognized; others are not. *Bharata Natyam* is full of the former sort. The codified ones in the dances were used less to tell than to illustrate or evoke a narrative based on a story about divinely inspired love. However, the dances included far more than the sum of its narratively inspired gestures.

The pantomimic vocabulary of *Bharata Natyam* is not a language in the strict sense. It is doubtful that anyone could actually use it to tell new stories to those who are not already familiar with them by other means. Western dance and drama have dropped many of the elements of gestural language from their vocabulary. Western artists have largely abolished the allegorical, nounlike postures and gestures that used to characterize elocution manuals and the stage. Such gestural vocabularies we associate with slapstick, melodrama, or the sign language of the deaf. Consequently, we have to do perceptual and attitudinal work not to see the *rasas* (mood stylizations) of classical Indian dance as stereotyped; archetype and stereotype seem to appear in the same image.

In cross-cultural situations, what gestures evoke from an audience may be dissonantly related to the intentions of performers. Gestural dissonance can be the occasion for various responses: concluding someone is ill or possessed, evoking fascination, or entering into intercultural conflict and misunderstanding. On some occasions it educates or even inspires.

In most respects this audience is like the ones that attend any aesthetic or cultural function in the West. However, we did not have to pay admission, and we are expected to reflect on what we have witnessed. Though audience members hardly function as a congregation, we are in limited ways a community. The conventional way a Western audience symbolizes its recognition that a performance is sacred is silence, nonapplause. Occasions such as this one are anomalous. We are not a religious community. Yet the semi-religiously motivated performance has been set in the midst of cultural-educational activities, so by definition we are not watching only to enjoy. From the point of view of those who subsidized the performances, they should have educated us. From the point of view of the dancers, they should have also inspired us. Whether or not the intentions of either dancers or audience are religious, the social definition of the situation is not, unless we want to claim that the study of religion is itself religious. For most audience members this performance was an object of study or aesthetic contemplation rather than a medium of sacred participation. Audience members have repeatedly remarked on the beauty of the gestures. This sort of comment is what observers sometimes offer when they like a performance but do not know what else to say. Beauty is a value-conferring notion, one that, historically speaking, refers to form as the object of that evaluation.

The actions of *Bharata Natyam* both frame and are framed. They are framed by being stylized, set on a stage, put in a specific time slot, and so on. They frame by constructing, at least momentarily, a worldview, a lens through which other things can be perceived. In comparison to modern Western dance or to classical Western liturgies the *Bharata Natyam* performances are quite plot-oriented, a feature North Americans associate with drama. However, most of the stories they tell are set in mythic time, a feature typical of ritual. Emphasis is upon theatrical rehearsal and spiritual preparation equally, but since small shrines were erected on stage, and performers made offerings to their teachers and patron divinities, some Western audience members might want to define the event as a rite. Most, however, probably frame the actions as drama or dance.

Much more could be said about this specific performance or about classical Indian dance in general, but my aim has been simply to engage in some brief reflections that indicate possible directions for the study of ritual and theater. A theater critic might have assessed the energy and precision of the dancer and, at least implicitly, compared her work to other *Bharata Natyam* performances, or, if daring, to classical ballet or modern jazz dance. Such a critic might have recommended one of the performers or performances above the others. A historian of religion, on the other hand, might have told us more about their rich textual and contextual allusions and, if predisposed to flirt with anthropology, compared it to pan-tribal pow-wow dances at the turn of the century. Both sorts of insight could lead us beyond, or deeper into, the impressionistic way most of us are bound to respond to classical Indian dance in North America.

I am hesitant to draw any general, scholarly conclusions on the basis of observing a few *Bharata Natyam* performances, but I would venture the following tentative theses for further reflection:

1. All performances include ritualistic and dramatic— confirmatory and conflictual—framing, though they do so in greatly varying degrees. The work of ritual criticism is to attend to and describe all the forms of action no matter how they are labeled. Only

subsequently ought one worry about the problem of relating various genres of action such as dramatic and ritualistic.

2. A performance should not be described as religious simply because a performer intends it so. Nor is it artistic because an audience determines to see it as such. The meaning of a performance, insofar as it resides in texts or in actors' intentions, can be drastically modified, if not inverted, by its meaning as a social event. A rite's intentions (in the formalistic, Aristotelian sense) may be in marked conflict with the intention of both performers and observers. The weight of social and spatial contexts may override intentions (in both the psychological and the formalistic senses of the word). Ritual criticism requires attention to the dissonance between intentions and functions.

3. Dissonance of intentions does not always imply that a performance has failed, since ritual regularly exploits such dissonance. In postmodern North America dissonance is increasingly being regarded as an achievement.

4. Performance in the Western world is commonly treated as a commodity with attendant dynamics of objectification, marketing, display, and research. No theory of ritual ought to denigrate this social fact as a substitute for interpreting it. The ritual critic must attend to basic social facts of enactment—in this case, at least gender and ethnicity.

5. North American audiences are typically split between those who "see" and those who "feel" a performance. Other cultures may "move" (kinesthetically) one or "hear" one. Cultures seem to have a tacit hierarchy in their way of valuing and ignoring sensory input (see Ong 1962:chaps. 2,5). An important factor in intercultural events is the difference between varying modes of sensorium organization. Ritual criticism must not presuppose that one sensory mode is more essential than another.

6. In the study of performative genres there is sometimes a hermeneutical circle operative not only between performers and viewers or performers and scenarios but also between artistic genres. This fact is humorously illustrated by a dialogue between King Vajra and the sage Markandeya.

> King Vajra requests the sage to accept him as his disciple and teach him the art of icon-making, so he may worship the deities in the proper forms. The sage replies that one cannot understand the principles of image-making without a knowledge of painting. The king wishes for instruction in this art and is told that unless he is accomplished as a dancer, he cannot grasp even the

rudiments of painting. The king requests that he be taught dancing, whereupon the sage replies that, without a keen sense of
rhythm or a knowledge of instrumental music, proficiency in
dance is impossible. Once again the king requests that he be
taught these subjects; to which the sage replies that a master of
vocal music is necessary before one can be proficient in instrumental music [from the *Vishnudharmottara Purana*, cited in
Vatsyayan 1968:2].

The king, we are told, learns them all. One is left suspecting that,
upon finishing, he will be advised by the sage that he must now
master the art of self-knowledge and observation. Whether this is so
or not, one conclusion seems clear: in India one art must be seen in
terms of another, and therefore, in North America seeing dance only
as dance is the surest way to alter its meaning fundamentally. The
ritual critic must attend to connections between media and their
modulations as they cross cultural boundaries.

A REFLEXIVE CRITIQUE

This excursion into classical Indian dance constitutes neither an ethnographic field study nor a fully developed work of ritual criticism. The
reason for including it is to ground these concluding, summary comments
in the same way that the opening chapter was tied to the Indigenous
Peoples' Theatre Celebration. Perhaps this example suggests well enough
how criticism can proceed only if it uncovers the implicit definition(s) of
the situation. Typically, such situations are multiply framed with implicitly
conflicting definitions. For the North American Indian-trained dancers the
performance was efficacious ritual; for the audience, it was entertainment,
education, and culture. But having recognized the differing definitions of
the situation, we have only begun the work of criticism. Much is missing
from the account.

In good ritual criticism one should describe fully, evocatively, contextually, and the descriptions should concentrate on action—movement, posture, and gesture. One needs to note positions and the structure of space as
well as the objects or persons that occupy it; likewise, timing and rhythm.
Further, the observer should document what precedes and follows the rite
proper, because preparation and reintegration are often ritualized. If repeated observation is possible, descriptions can take note of flaws, hitches, and
other infelicities.

Since criticism is a judgment-laden activity, adequate description must
precede it. Criticism is always present in any scholarly account, including

what appears to be sheer description. The ritual critic cannot hide behind such descriptions and phenomenologies. Descriptions, like performances, are implicit critiques. As Tyson (1975:35) puts it, "Modes of presentation are signals of evaluation." Criticism is inescapable, though one can minimize, disguise, or try to subdue it. There is no possibility of fully disengaging normative and critical intentions from descriptive ones, although both anthropologists and religiologists regularly try.

Knowing well that descriptions themselves are rife with covert criticism, many of us are nevertheless unwilling to give up the attempt to suspend judgment temporarily and thus separate, momentarily, description and criticism. Suspension of judgment, however, is an insufficient, though necessary, procedure.

Though I have been critical of hiding behind descriptions, especially when they function as covert theology, there is no substitute for an adequate, well-contextualized description of a rite as the basis for criticism.[125]

In retrospect, descriptions of *Bharata Natyam* in the preceding account seem both too brief, too generalized, and insufficiently contextualized both historically and sociologically. In some places I conflate more than one performance, thus my descriptions of the postural and gestural style of *Bharata Natyam* lack specificity. Much is missing: colors of costume, light intensity, sound quality, the smell of incense, quotations from dancers and audience. The work of generalizing begins too soon, and the philosophical preoccupations sometimes attenuate descriptive attentiveness.

Since my remarks were scheduled to follow the performance, it seemed unnecessary to describe what we had just seen; the need for description usually presupposes lack of familiarity. However, my comments soon reveal that we do, in fact, see "different" performances even when we see "the same" performance. So description can also be useful among those too familiar with a rite.

It is essential to articulate multiple points of view, infer the worldviews implied by them, and maintain the plurality of voices that embody them. Ritual criticism involves the identification of conflicts between at least two standpoints, often, but not necessarily, those known as insider / outsider, participant / observer, or emic / etic points of view. These are not always held by different persons. An insider can both participate and observe, just as an outsider can both observe and participate. So noticing and documenting simultaneously held attitudes, for example, awe and boredom or detachment and involvement, is important. Too often we assume that one mood alone dominates or that moods must follow one another serially or coexist harmoniously.

Points of view and purposes are often—perhaps, usually—plural and dissonant, so this plurality should be made explicit and treated as an object of criticism. This amounts to saying that ritual criticism, as a matter of principle, involves reflexivity. Criticism of a rite, particularly if it is someone else's, is warranted only if it eventuates in self-criticism as well.[126]

My account notices the multiplicity of viewpoints and the plurality of voices, but it fails to present them or infer their worldview. As we say of bad fiction, it *tells* us but does not *show* us. The reader has to take my word for it. Even though I might have been quizzed by participants and audience, their queries do not make it into my account. Even when I am, in fact, answering their questions, those questions are not presented as part of the account.

Good criticism locates the sources of indigenous criticism and accounts for them. Ritual criticism in postmodern North America seems to assume a highly reflexive event-orientation. Whether or not such an orientation is found elsewhere, some sort of ritual criticism is probably an aspect of ritual practice and study in every culture, including decidedly local ritual traditions found in societies more circumscribed than our own. Criticism is implicit in any performance. Thus a scholarly ritual critic, refusing the assumption that rites themselves are precritical, should formulate participants' criticism explicitly. Criticism is not only of rites but by rites. Practices, like theories, imply value judgments. Ritualists are seldom uncritical about their rites, although their criticism may be implicit rather than explicit, or they may select the audiences before whom critiques are aired. And participants have their own ways of explaining the explainers, by mime for example.

Participant, or indigenous, criticism can take a variety of forms: the social and religious critique implied by an actor's or a group's continuing practice; the ongoing criticism within a group or tradition that enables it to select this and reject that; and public criticism by observers of performances. Comments by a ritual critic are valid only insofar as they take account of the ways participants themselves evaluate their own activities.

My account of *Bharata Natyam* does not sufficiently distinguish or adequately develop the various axes along which criticism might move: between the dancer and her teacher, between audience and dancer, between audience and respondents, between respondents and dancer, between audience factions. Both on-stage and after-performance politics are opaque in the account. In addition, more sustained biographical interviewing probably would have uncovered other polarities generative of self-criticism, for example, between the dancer's North American and her Indian qualities, or between her desire to innovate and her desire to transmit a tradition, and so on.

A critic should make explicit the grounds of scholarly criticism. Criticism is always from a point of view and for a purpose, both of which should be specified. But often an explicitly stated purpose, such as the testing of a theory, is not the only purpose—maybe not even the real, which is to say dominant, purpose. Interpreters of rites are just as liable to have unrecognized agendas as participants are to have unrecognized functions for their rites. Consequently, one purpose for studying rites may be to discover one's own judgments and values. Whether or not this is a stated purpose, it is often a side-effect.

Ritual criticism needs to specify what it is against or what it is avoiding. When early anthropologists followed in the wake of missionaries, they were determined not to impose clothes and values. Like early anthropologists who defined themselves as not-missionaries, the first generation of religiologists defined themselves polemically as not-theologians. Not theologians, we have not wanted to be imitation anthropologists either.

A reader can smell these agendas behind the scenes of my account. In addition I wanted to avoid engaging in theater criticism calculated to inform culture consumers. But a reader has to infer these motives. Further, my account, like many that issue from religious studies, is theory-shy. It would probably be better if it were not. I can only hope this exercise moves one step closer to the formulation of ritual theory.

Theories and explanations imply values and criticisms, which can only be hidden but not escaped. Like it or not, theories and explanations are often experienced by participants as critiques. If we scholars can argue that rites function differently from ritualists' intentions, we should recognize that our theories often function differently from our intentions.

Explanation is a kind of criticism. Just as description and prescription are inevitably tangled, so are explanation, appreciation, and criticism. Functionalist and psychological interpretations of rites are often experienced by ritualists as critiques whether or not they are so intended.

Like theories and explanations, assumptions about the genre of a performance (e.g., that it is a "ritual drama," that it is a "rite of passage," etc.) imply principles of criticism: rites of passage should transform and weddings should wed. Even though genre definitions may be empirically derived, they often function as norms and determinants of scholarly expectation.

My treatment of genre, whether correct or not, is overt and played off conflicting specifications of genre. Genre and definition are tightly interwoven considerations, and they form, covertly or overtly, the basis of any evaluative conclusions that a ritual critic may tender.

Criticism should take the form of mutual consultation. Ordinarily, the right to engage in ritual criticism should be granted as well as earned. Because it is partly ethical in nature, this will probably be my most controversial proposition. By arguing that ritual criticism is not a right, I am emphasizing its interpersonal, intercultural nature. But this is not enough. In most situations the ritual critic should be granted the right to criticize by participants. I say "most" because in situations of ritual abuse, waiting for permission can itself become an ethically questionable act. Criticism may serve scholarship in the end, but in the beginning it must serve participants and performers. The practice and criticism of ritual are systemically interrelated tasks and their circularity is potentially infinite. In less metaphysical and more practical terms this means that the task of criticism is never finished. There is no such thing as the criticism that ends all criticism.

James Dittes (1977) has presented a strong argument for locating the reality of an event *between* an observer and a performer—which is to say, not *in* a dancer, tradition, script, or observer. In "The Investigator as an Instrument of Investigation," he illustrates ways of avoiding both an "inflated" approach (in which an observer substitutes himself or herself for the data) and an "incongruent" one (in which the observer's reactions are suppressed). He illustrates how to cultivate an "instrumental" method in which the observer's involvement is actually a critical tool, not merely an introductory, pre-investigative nuisance. His approach forces us to examine not just the formal structures of a performance but audience response as well, and a scholar is merely a particular sort of audience member. We must study performative events, not just the movements of the dance itself, and respondents are sometimes part of such events, both in Asia and in the West.

In my account of *Bharata Natyam* the parameters of consultation are barely perceptible; the reader has to guess the extent to which the response was consensual and the extent to which it was an individualistic tour de force. That I was invited and did not merely barge in is clear enough, but to work as valid ritual criticism my account should say much more about behind-the-scenes interaction.

It is tempting to concentrate critical attention only on actors, but critics must specify the audiences and reflect on the ways they shape the tenor of the various performances—religious, artistic, scholarly. Actual audiences and anticipated audiences often differ. When they do, the results can be quite revealing. This discrepancy is probably more the rule than the exception. Another rule implied by frequent practice is the segregation of audiences. For example, I recently heard an ethnologist say that he did not care what the people he studied thought about his book; he was writing it for other scholars. One, of course, cannot write for everybody, but if the "object" of study is not also among the audiences of the study, serious violations are possible. There is nothing wrong with scholars talking to other scholars, but an important loop in the critical process is missed if participants cannot criticize the results of a study about themselves.

My response takes account of certain features of the audience, for example, that it is educated, Western, and so forth, and the rhetoric of the presentation is attuned to the interests of such an audience. But it says nothing about the dancer's image of the audience both before and after performance. To what extent did it determine or influence her selection of dances? To what extent did it condition her attitude?

Anytime a response has to follow a performance immediately, it is inevitably pressured to serve as applause, as appreciation. Perhaps respondents can also provide further information, say, about the history of the art form. But probably only a scholar would feel obligated to try to turn postperformance response into theorizing or, if a theater critic, into criticism. My account lacks the edge required if the anticipated audience is the readership of a scholarly book, hence the necessity to examine its rhetoric.

Genres of criticism, like genres of performance, have different effects and so do assumptions about the ultimate destination of criticism. Knowing that participants will be present at one's interpretation of their performance makes a difference in what is said about them. Sometimes the effect is to censor; sometimes it is to make them more honest.

The hosts who posed the initial question—which was something like, "What could you as a ritual studies scholar contribute to our understanding of *Bharata Natyam*?"—were not the only ones to whom I addressed my response. For example, the dancer on this occasion was, in fact, quite eager for informed critique, but her response did not make it into my presentation, an unfortunate omission.[127]

Ritual criticism ought to be written reflexively. At its best, ritual criticism is self-critical. Scholars studying ritual have generally avoided systematic or overt criticism for a variety of reasons, among them a desire to avoid self-righteous, religiously inspired judgmentalism. Religiologists have tried to avoid religiocentrism, making judgments about one religious tradition from the point of view of a privileged other tradition. This view has often been buttressed by a rhetoric requiring authors to be missing, or more accurately, transparent but in full control. I am not suggesting that scholarly writing should lapse into autobiography or become self-pre-occupied, but it should be self-aware; an author should be sufficiently visible that readers have some idea how to compensate for inherent biases.

No doubt there is a danger that in ritual studies rites and ritualists can become displaced by ritologists bent on understanding what they are doing. So perhaps the call for reflexivity is only a necessary transition phase. But the notion of reflexivity, the capacity for performed self-observation, has recently become important in some anthropological approaches to ritual (see Ruby 1982), and it ought not be dismissed as mere academic narcissism. Significantly, anthropologists are locating reflexivity in ritual performance, not in scholarly observation. If this claim is at all true, it suggests that reflexivity, though it may in some instances be a disease, is probably both widespread and normal.

Reflexivity is at the center of my account. Attention is on the interaction of Western expectations and an Asian dance form. But it is not systematic in its exploration of the means and extent of performative self-consciousness. Consider the questions that are not entertained: Do *Bharata Natyam* dancers train with mirrors? How self-conscious was this dancer? How does she gain perspective on herself? By asking others? By imagining how she looks? What exists for the sake of what in this event? Does the dance give rise to reflection, both hers and ours? Or does reflection require the dance as illustration?

Reflexivity need not be personal or excruciatingly autobiographical, so similar questions can be raised about Western audiences. We desperately need an audience (or congregation) criticism that parallels reader criticism in the study of literature, because, just as authors alone do not make meanings, neither do ritualists.

Obviously, I am now in deep and murky waters, which I would have avoided if I could, but I have argued that criticism is inescapable. It can be rejected as altogether out of place and thus carried on clandestinely; left only to scholars as an arcane activity or only to practitioners as an esoteric one; regarded as antithetical to both traditional and experimental rites; or experienced as an exercise in racist, sexist, or ethnocentric judgmentalism. But it cannot be escaped, so it must be questioned.

A NEW IMAGE OF RITUAL

In the end, what does ritual criticism amount to? How is one to summarize the gains made by these case studies and essays? What do they suggest about ritual and about criticism that we did not already know? If no new theory and no new model eventuates, what is left? A new image. For many readers ritual, as it has been portrayed here, seems to have a surprising breadth despite the confinement of our case studies to North America. The reasons for the surprise are widespread assumptions that limit ritual to certain types such as liturgies or specific qualities such as repetitiveness. Here ritual appears with sprawling, not so clearly articulated, boundaries. And it bleeds into ordinary behavior, ethics, drama, and politics. In addition, criticism seems to have much less authority than we are used to attributing to it. It is no longer the work of professionals alone, and it asks as many questions as it makes pronouncements about authenticity. Criticism too bleeds—into interpretation, description, and mutual consultation.

At the end of this study, ritual and criticism look more akin to one another. Like ritual, criticism has its patterns and repetitions. And ritual has its edge, its ways of judging, of saying Yea and Nay. Thus it begins to resemble criticism. Whereas we began with an image of the two as some young mismatched couple, now I risk making them a pair of senior citizens who have lived together for so long they begin to look like.

But do not be misled. They still know how fight. Ritual and criticism, if I have been successful, appear in public as a pair. But they cling to their tensions and differences. Just because dancing no longer seems to preclude thinking is no reason to assume that most of us will not find it easier to do our dancing and thinking in different times and different places. As ritualists, our hunger for criticism will always be tempered by our desire to be seen as we wish to see ourselves. Even critics chafe at criticism if it is telling. So even though the desire for perspective on our performances may be great, the protective barriers that block our vision are thick.

Notes

1. The language is Ruel Tyson's (personal communication). I am deeply indebted to him for his reflections on case/theory relations.

2. As I use the terms, "ritual studies" and "ritology" are synonymous.

3. "Religiologist" is a neologism. It is only slightly less horrible than the various circumlocutions: "religious studies scholar" or "student of religion." No matter how lacking in euphony the term "religiologist" may be, it is time we named practitioners in the field of religious studies properly. When the word "anthropologist" was coined, it too grated on the ear. I use the term "religionist" to refer to religious persons.

4. Unlike Rabuzzi I would not call housework a cultic ritual. Rather, it is a process that one sees metaphorically as ritual.

5. Bruce Lincoln (1977) proposes another candidate for consideration as ritual: scholarly footnoting.

6. Other definitions that readers might find worth pondering are the following:

(a) Ritual is "a means of performing the way things ought to be in such a way that this ritualized perfection is recollected in the ordinary, uncontrolled, course of things" (Jonathan Z. Smith 1980:124–125).

(b) Ritual consists of "those carefully rehearsed symbolic motions and gestures through which we regularly go, in which we articulate the felt shape and rhythm of our own humanity and of reality as we experience it, and by means of which we negotiate the terms or conditions for our presence among and our participation in the plurality of realities through which our humanity makes its passage" (Roland Delattre 1978:282).

(c) Ritual is "a culturally constructed system of symbolic communication. It is constituted of patterned and ordered sequences of words and acts, often expressed in multiple media, whose content and arrangement are characterized in varying degree by formality (conventionality), stereotypy (rigidity), condensation (fusion), and redundancy (repetition)" (Stanley Tambiah 1979:119).

7. A fuller critique can be found in Grimes 1989b.

8. In his attack on the utility of the idea of ritual, Jack Goody (1977:33) says that in the Greek city-state only participation, not belief, was required.

9. Among scholars a rather widespread view of ritual is that it consists of components analogous to atoms or building blocks. These components are symbols. They are what give ritual its power; they are said to "condense" or "contain" that power.

These are linked together into "systems" (a cybernetic metaphor) or "structures" (an architectural metaphor). One might imagine these symbolic components strung together like pearls or "woven" together like a spider web. In practice some interpreters of ritual seem to imply that a rite can be exhaustively analyzed, factored into its parts, with nothing left over. Others seem to imply that rites consist "mainly" of symbols but have other ingredients too; the remainder is not specified. A few scholars, notably Sperber (1975) and Staal (1979), question whether rites are composed of symbols at all.

10. Kenneth Burke (1966) has argued eloquently and convincingly for the creative power of the negative.

11. No doubt, making things overt is a problem when working with esoteric traditions. In such instances ritual criticism is iconoclastic.

12. Using ritual as a hermeneutical key to such an extent that it becomes an ideology leads to what we might call "ritualism." One might compare ritualism with dramatism, the use of theatrical metaphors for imagining social interaction. The Spanish playwright Calderon, as well as Shakespeare, regarded all the world as a stage. Erving Goffman treats the daily "presentation of self" as if it were a performance in which human beings are like actors wearing masks. Extended in such a manner, ritualism would be the treatment of the world-as-enactment rather than, say, the world-as-language. World-as-language and world-as-drama are two historically significant "anagogical" symbols, that is, symbols for the whole of things.

13. See, e.g., Richard F. Hardin's "'Ritual' in Recent Criticism: The Elusive Sense of Community" (1983).

14. In ordinary usage the word "performance" means something like play-acting, not believing the role one is temporarily putting on, or it means simply whatever goes on in theaters. By contrast, in theater circles the opposite of performance is either drama (understood as the playwright's text) or rehearsal (one phase of the preparation that precedes the public performance). Whether one speaks of performance historically or theoretically, it is not altogether obvious what one is talking about. Much depends on what a given usage is against, thus on what is *not* performance.

In the broadest usage performance is simply a synonym for action—the implied opposite being motion. Performance, then, refers to any activity characterized by intentionality or communication. For some theorists, only human beings perform; for others, animals do as well. Any social action, including walking down the street or sitting in a chair, is a performance in the sense that it communicates meaning and proceeds on the basis of motives.

For many, this definition of the term is too broad, and performance is used more specifically to designate the opposite of ritual. Typically, those who prefer this usage further link performance with the social institution we know as theater and ritual with religious institutions. In this way performance is associated with entertainment and ritual with efficacy. This polarized, if not dualistic, way of separating theatrical performance from ritual enactment serves well the interests of a secularizing Protestant culture. It establishes a clear boundary that enables us to separate religion from the leisure industry just as we supposedly separate it from the state. It also serves universities well, because it enables them to distinguish who belongs in the drama or performance-studies department and who belongs in religious studies.

But there is a third, more recent trend toward conceiving performance in a way that enables us to speak of "ritual performance" without engaging in self-contradiction. Here, performance has the connotation of process or transformation as opposed to structure or stasis. In this case performance is thought to effect, not merely confirm, status. Further, a performance does not merely mime, repeat, or reflect social structures, but it actually challenges, perhaps even undermines, them.

15. Perhaps a better, though not as widespread, way of naming the transition is that of Ruel Tyson (personal communication), who calls this the postcolonial era.

16. If postmodernism succeeds in permeating North America, highly verbal, strongly narrative cultural forms such as liturgies and modern mystery plays, discussed in chapters 2 and 4 respectively, risk being mismatched to the people's fundamental sensibility.

17. In the history of Christianity renewed preoccupation with the Holy Spirit (Hassan's symbol for postmodernism) has typically been accompanied by disinterest in ritual, not a craving for it. The rites that most radically combine a predilection for the Spirit (which "listeth where it will") with a need for ritual are possession rites. We do well to ask who in postmodern ritual situations is being possessed by whom or by what? In possession—and I do not equate possession with demonic possession—a striking combination of theater and religion transpires. Possession rites are, we might say, "absolute performance"—performance so complete that participants may not even remember the roles they played after the event concludes.

18. In one of the most trenchant studies of "the other," Tzvetan Todorov's *The Conquest of America* (1984) exposes the subtle as well as the blatant ways in which sympathy toward other traditions becomes a way of conquering and assimilating them. He suggests that in our society of self-fashioned exiles, the dialogue of cultures ceases: ". . . It is replaced by eclecticism and comparatism [*sic*], by the capacity to love everything a little, of flaccidly sympathizing with each option without ever embracing any" (251). He contends that we try either to obliterate the strangeness of the other or to heighten and romanticize it.

19. On celebration-botching and other sorts of ritual violations and failures, see chapter 9.

20. The Corpus Christi Center for Liturgy (Phoenix, AZ); Georgetown Center for Liturgy, Spirituality and the Arts (Washington, DC); Loyola Pastoral Institute (New York City); and Notre Dame Center for Pastoral Liturgy (Notre Dame, IN).

21. Each critic was to approach the text from the point of view of an assigned discipline or topic: (1) sociology, (2) ritual, (3) grace, (4) Christology, (5) ecclesiology, (6) symbol, (7) liturgical history, and (8) liturgical theology.

22. Lack of continuous pagination in *LR* makes precise references difficult. In one respect this is a petty point, hardly worth mentioning, especially since organizers were eager to get the document to evaluators. But since so much time and energy is obviously invested in these 820 pages, one has to ask what the tacit message is. Sacred books typically have not only page numbers but chapter and verse designations, suggesting that the details are important. The tacit message here seems to be that only the big picture is important. Lack of pagination says, This is raw data, it has not yet been cooked into conclusions. Data organized in this way tend to evoke impressionistic ("Liturgy in the United States seems to be . . .") or idiosyncratic responses ("I found it really interesting that . . .").

23. Since *LR* does not give names of respondents, they are identified here by parish and place.

24. In view of the liturgical reforms of Vatican II it would be a mistake to emphasize uniformity, since this is precisely one of the features of the Mass that has changed. As a worshiper from Sacred Heart in Richmond, VA, puts it, ". . . We're a congregational church. Now I can't go to Germany and have the same Mass that I have in Richmond. When I was a student and I was in Germany, it was the same Latin Mass, and I was not lost in German. I would be lost now. And I now feel I'm very much a member of the Cathedral Parish. I feel less a member of other Catholic churches when I occasionally go to them, even in this city, so that, although I feel akin in terms of faith and in terms of social outreach, which seems to me to be new and part of Vatican II, we're not so universally Catholic as we are congregational" (*LR* VIII:238–39).

25. Roy Rappaport (1979:175) is one of the few social scientists to offer a non-theological definition of liturgy. He says, "I take ritual to be a form or structure, defining it as the performance of more or less invariant sequences of formal acts and utterances not encoded

by the performers . . . . Since to perform a liturgical order . . . is to *conform* to it, authority or directive is *intrinsic* to liturgical order" (192). ". . . By performing a liturgical order the performer accepts, and indicates to himself and to others that he accepts, whatever is encoded in the canons of the liturgical order in which he is participating" (193).

26. Aidan Kavanagh (1982b:10–11) and Jacob Needleman (1980:24–25) cite favorably Metropolitan Anthony Bloom's remark that liturgy ought to avoid emotion, i.e., enthusiasm, for the sake of openness and vulnerability.

27. One notices that an altar boy has gone to sleep (*LR* VIII:2, Christ the King). Another notices congestion in Tom's throat (*LR* VIII:5, Holy Redeemer). And another notices a reader's projection (*LR* VIII:23, Holy Rosary). And so on.

28. The quality of the interviews varies, of course. Two brief, contrasting examples illustrate how. A parishioner at St. Gregory the Great is repeatedly asked questions that are normative rather than descriptive questions, e.g., "What to you is a good homily?" And generalized, not specific questions: "How do [not "did"] you see the Psalm? What is [not "was"] your experience of the Psalm?" (*LR* VIII:261).

In contrast is the approach of the person who interviewed the "more active" parishioner at St. Augustine's, Washington (*LR* VIII:40ff.). He or she prompts the interviewee to recall specific details: ". . . What were they [the worshipers] doing when they were watching the reader? Can you describe some of the people's faces or how they were attending to the person who was reading" (49)? This interviewer has interviewees draw out implications and inquires about today, not all time: "What did that [the procession with bread and wine] do for you today?"

29 The quotation marks are theirs. Although such marks indicate a recognition that the working / not working dichotomy may not be appropriate for evaluating liturgy, most of the leaders interviewed do not reject it. An exception is the Bellarmine Chapel interview summary, which concludes, "And, the 'work / not work' format on [the] questionnaire didn't 'work'" (*LR* IX:259).

30. Other terms are "reader criticism" and "audience criticism." One liturgiologist, John Melloh (1987:155), has recently suggested applying reception criticism to liturgy.

31. If one were to do a thorough reception-critical study of LR, we would have to inquire, not only into the reception of liturgies but the reception of the document. Who are its anticipated and implied audiences? Rhetoric is always rhetoric for someone. We regularly segregate our audiences; the story we give to one person is not the account we give another. If, for example, the people being interviewed suspected that outsiders and higher-ups were to be the ultimate readership for their remarks, they would be wary of washing dirty laundry in public. They would want to evoke respect and sympathy. If those who constructed the instrument anticipated that scholars outside the fold might read their work, they might couch their questions in sociologically respectable terms; they would want to be seen as open and objective. And to complete the hermeneutical circle, if I anticipate that liturgists will read what I write here I shall feel obligated to exercise care not to alienate them.

32. Perhaps one reason for the clarity of this interview was that it was *not* with a group but with a single individual (a presider-preacher at St. Augustine's in Washington, DC). In the group interviews, which were coded "Q" or "I" for "questioner / interviewer," and "A" or "P" for "answerer / parishioner," it was impossible to distinguish discrete persons, because there were no indicators such as "A1," "A2," etc. For a reader the result is the emergence of an amorphous, many-headed "ritual leader." However, I do not think this stylistic device is the only reason for the difference between this interview and the others.

33. My original critique of the study stopped here, because it seemed presumptuous to

assess the rites themselves, since I had not observed them or collected the field data. Upon receiving the critique several weeks prior to the conference, the organizers pleaded with me to focus my address more directly on the new liturgy itself. I finally agreed despite my reservations. The actual address began with a summary of the critique above and concluded with the following reflections and speculations on the liturgy. The change in tone illustrates how the audience of criticism determines its style and content.

34. Photographs were sent to critics—to help us visualize the liturgical environments, I assume. Most of these depicted unanimated church buildings. Fifty-five out of the sixty-four photos (86%) were person-free, suggesting, unintentionally no doubt, that objects and buildings tell us more about liturgy than peoples' bodies and faces do.

35. There are a few exceptions. For instance, one respondent complains about "a person who has been directing the ministers for years" (*LR* IX:190), who changes agreed-upon plans, and is difficult for women to deal with. But the interviewer simply ignores the complaint instead of probing to find out what principles inform the difficulties.

36. Doing so would only contribute further to the complaint that Vatican II reforms were the result of an imposition by scholars (see Dinges 1987).

37. Some of the best examples of this kind of writing about ritual can be found in *Diversities of Gifts: Field Studies in Southern Religion* (Tyson et al. 1988).

38. On the issue of creating tradition, see Roy Wagner's *The Invention of Culture* (1981), and *Writing Culture: The Poetics and Politics of Ethnography* by James Clifford and George Marcus (1986).

39. For a concise summary, see Alan L. Miller's article "Power" (1987).

40. "White" people are, of course, no more white than "red" people are red. The colors are symbolic rather than literal.

As a White man I have no choice but to exercise power. I and others like me must decide where to put our money, "weight," and other tokens of power. White people seldom write or speak deliberately as Whites, just as men seldom write as men but, rather, as supposed generic human beings. In contexts where power is being negotiated across ethnic, gender, or class lines, one ought not presume to speak generically as a human being. White male colleagues advise me that speaking either as a man or as a White is a step toward a debilitating paralysis, a kind of permanent *mea culpa* stance, which will leave us, like the millipede, worrying about our own feet and thus unable to move. I am not convinced. Even if they are correct about the self-consciousness involved, it is does not necessarily lead to paralysis.

41. Originally known as AID.

42. Unfortunately, using answers to these questions to make decisions about whether or not to excavate is almost impossible, since excavation is usually required to answer them.

43. Many of these issues are presented or debated in *The Point* (Wilfrid Laurier University 1988).

44. This term means "being so centered in one's own religious tradition as to be unable to understand that of another." Thus it parallels "ethnocentrism."

45. In a recent video by Philip L. Walker called "Science or Sacrilege" (reviewed by Merbs 1985), a religiologist was asked to respond to the issue. Another religiologist, Robert Michaelsen (1980:109), in his analysis of the American Indian Religious Freedom Act, urged colleagues in religious studies to become actively involved in cross-cultural and comparative studies of "the phenomenology of sacralization, desacralization, and resacralization of land forms and particular sites."

46. Excavation, cataloging, and analysis of human remains are not just "procedures," they are "practices," the acting out of sacredly held and defended cultural values. As practices

they are power-laden, and the rhetorical ploy of claiming neutrality is a power play despite claims that this was not the intention of White scientists.

47. Since I am neither an archaeologist nor an Indian, I have little to lose in this debate, which means my opinion is either valuable because it is comparatively non-partisan or useless because it costs me nothing—neither my research nor my ancestors.

48. Anthropologists' codes of ethics and behavior in the field qualify as religious according to numerous definitions. Among them are these: "A religion is a system of symbols which acts to establish powerful, pervasive, and long-lasting moods and motivations in men by formulating conceptions of a general order of existence and clothing these conceptions with such an aura of factuality that the moods and motivations seem uniquely realistic" (Geertz 1973:90). "Religion is a synthesis of thought, emotion and behavior expressing man's attitude towards his environment and towards his existence within it" (Gaster 1951:374).

49. Note that I do not use this term to mean teachers in humanities divisions of universities but subscribers to humanistic codes of ethics.

50. Whether or not one agrees that professional codes are quasi-religious documents should not deter scholars from recognizing that many codes governing research on humans require that, if there is any conflict between the aims of research and the welfare of the people being studied, the latter, not the former, should take precedence.

51. See Fabian (1973) for a discussion of the folklorization of death.

52. See Grolnick and Lengyel (1978) on burial symbols as "transitional objects."

53. In discussions about excavation and reburial one finds several types of attitudes toward the dead: (1) remains-as-data, the object constituted by scientism. As Gerald Schaus (Wilfrid Laurier University 1988:11) put it, "Dead is dead . . . . When Living beings die their bodies are inanimate objects"; (2) remains-as-dead-person, that is, one with human rights that exceed the imperatives of research; (3) remains-as-sacred-memory, the conventional religious view; (4) remains-as-sacred-ancestor, a Native view: remains are more-than-person, they constitute the seat or home of spirit.

54. Laird Christie (Wilfrid Laurier University 1988:15) suggested that scholars, by "exploitatively commodifying and purveying for our own interests those cultural patterns we study," engage in morally questionable behavior. Of this I have no doubt, but our recognition of the widespread ambiguities of scholarly research does not obviate our responsibility for dealing with the specific issue at hand.

55. Lawrence Toombs, an archaeologist colleague, suggests that such humor and iconoclasm may be our culture's nervous way of recognizing the presence of the sacred.

56. J. V. Wright (Wilfrid Laurier University 1988:12) made a compromise suggestion, namely, that remains be placed in a standardized container that would be deposited in a regional provincial mausoleum.

57. I have deliberately omitted the names of all participants in order to respect their anonymity. My speaking in the first-person-plural does not mean either that I speak for everyone or that we were always unanimous.

58. Totems possessing such power, though perhaps silent, are hardly mute. Some would say that owning such totems is a symbolic expression of the dominant culture's power to purchase, display, and thus control supposedly dependent cultures. And they would contend that returning icons to their tribal contexts is the only possible way of changing or compensating that balance of power.

59. This phrase is repeated in the "Vision Statement" (Canadian Museum of Civilization 1987) and was heard repeatedly among CMC staff, hence my inference of its importance.

60. Catherine Bell (1988:8–9) follows Pierre Bordieu in regarding ritual knowledge as

unself-conscious, as "embedded in the instincts of the social body." Obviously, juxtaposing realities would precipitate self-consciousness and disrupt the supposedly instinctual qualities of such ritual. So one must either question Bordieu's and Bell's depiction of ritual knowledge or worry about the iconoclastic effects on Native cultures.

61. The University of British Columbia Museum has created a class of non-catalogued objects called "touchables" to try to deal with the problems of accessibility and usability.

62. I have no objection, of course, to using actors and actor-training when the context is theater as such. But animating visitors in a museum is not the same kind of activity as performing before an audience.

63. Possible criteria might include: the accessibility of the rites elsewhere, the "fit" of those rites with the educational aims of the institution, indigenous or participant authorization to perform them, and practical time and space considerations.

64. Catherine Albanese, who responded to this paper at the "Ritual and Power Conference," perceived the ambiguities and iconoclasm inherent in my own version of this glass-breaking. She described my position as the "least worst" among the alternatives.

65. Let the reader beware. Charts themselves are symbolic devices, mappings of sacred precincts, signals of a professorial worldview. They are bound to convey a sense of order often lacking in whatever is being charted.

66. "Space-related." The term is Hall's (1966;1973).

67. So powerful was the hypothesis-testing motive that it was given formal statement in the program:

> Our hypothesis concerning the method of production, therefore, is that the sequence was performed in the round outside one of the parish churches, possibly in Wakefield. The production, however, was shared by the parishes in the district. It is also possible that some of the local religious houses sponsored episodes.
>
> In our production each university or local group is intended to represent a parish contributing to a large single performance, in a town in the West Riding of Yorkshire, in 1475.
>
> We hope to determine if this method of production will work dramatically and secondly to assess whether or not the sequence is sufficiently unified to be accepted as a cycle.

68. It was interesting to note that those who had insights into the political and social context of the Towneley text were nervous about the presence of an "anthropologist," whom they took to be making similar observations about their production. The study of performance is clearly no less political than the production of it.

69. The boast is inaccurate because such a production has, in fact, been mounted in England. However, this is an interesting bit of festival lore that warrants further sociological and historical analysis than can be provided here.

70. See the discussion of rites and ritualization in chapter 1.

71. One must not put too much weight on genre tags, however. People who attend the sacred rites of the Pueblos in New Mexico, e.g., refer to them as "dances." Some Native people have taken up this usage as well. Doing so does not automatically make them less ritualistic or less sacred.

72. The distinctions among celebration, liturgy, decorum, etc. are worked out in more detail in my *Beginnings in Ritual Studies* (1982:chap. 3).

73. I use the term "counterculture" rather than "new age" in order to emphasize the oppositional nature of the movement. Its search for alternatives opposes mainline culture and yet is deeply dependent on it.

74. See *Rituals in Families and Family Therapy* (Imber-Black et al. 1988), a good combination of scholarly and popular approaches.

75. In *Getting Saved from the Sixties*, Steven Tipton (1982:237) discusses the centrality of direct experience for alternative religions in America. Experience is a central value not just to the people Tipton studied but to Tipton's own theory of religion. Religion, he suggests, is a "circle of reciprocally reinforcing links." Rites, he says, "induce experiences. Experiences prove teachings. Teachings interpret experiences." Note that he does not say that rites *are* experiences; rather, they induce them. For Tipton experience is a central, indisputable, human fact, but ritual is treated more as a cause of experience than as a type of experience.

76. There are others who claim to be carrying out Black Elk's vision, e.g., Eagleman, who is introduced as "a Sioux who has done the Sun Dance many times."

77. The phenomenon of Whites having recourse to ancient sacred sites in order to empower or validate their rites has become increasingly popular. Witness, for instance, the Harmonic Convergence celebration in the ruins of Casa Rinconada, a great kiva in Chaco Culture National Historical Park, New Mexico.

78. One wonders what will happen now that the Polish Theatre Lab has been shut down under government pressure and Grotowski has moved to California.

79. Fox has recently been silenced by the Roman Catholic Church. Among other things, he is supposed to contemplate his support of witches and pagans.

80. Any comments I might make would fall into the third category and would be valid only insofar as they took account of the ways participants themselves evaluated their own activities.

81. In a symposium on authenticity held in 1985 at the American Anthropological Association, Broner attacked the whole notion of ritual criticism as patriarchal—a debate we have yet to finish.

82. The classic work in the field is Mircea Eliade's *Shamanism: Archaic Techniques of Ecstasy* (1964); a recent, popular anthology is Joan Halifax's *Shamanic Voices: A Survey of Visionary Narratives* (1979).

83. There has been considerable discussion about ritual authenticity. Because part of it was paid for and presumably staged, Frits Staal and Robert Gardner's film *Altar of Fire* is but one example that has precipitated debate about what sorts of rites are authentic and what sorts are not. Richard Schechner (1985:chap. 2), in his attack on the staging of the rite, implies that rites have always been borrowed and reinvented. In his discussion of "the restoration of behavior," it seems that "tourist rites" (e.g., Voodoo performed in Port-au-Prince nightclubs) are no less authentic than any other. Perhaps only a latent "Protestant aesthetic" makes us worry about overt and deliberate use of theatrical techniques in ritual performance. Richard Handler (1984) insists that our raising the question of authenticity at all is an ethnocentric act. So what are we to do? We are trapped in the ethical conundrums of our own culture. On the one hand, if we ignore, say, the rites of Native shamanism, we are smug and ill-liberal. On the other, if we go searching for them, we are indulging in nostalgia and engaging in cultural imperialism. If we borrow the symbols and rites of others, we deceive ourselves into some elaborately rationalized version of cross-cultural slumming (cf. Burke 1978:28 on "bi-culturalism" in early modern Europe). But if we do not, our own ritual traditions atrophy.

84. Those who knew Turner have no difficulty imagining either the look on his face or his rhythms of torso as he did so. To those who would peek through the cracks of his scholarly writings for a glimpse of the man himself, this article is more transparent than some others. For this very reason, however, it is likely to be ignored once grief stops tempting his students to hunt for traces of his biography.

85. After Turner's death, his wife Edith directed a performance of an Ndembu marriage-initiation rite before an audience of the American Anthropological Association. She also returned to Africa, having been away for thirty-one years, and recently wrote about herself as a "qualified healer" and the Ndembu as "enthusiasts for performance" (1986:12–13; cf. 1987).

86. Cipolla (1973) uses Polanyi's theory of "tacit knowing" in a way that is different from my usage. Whereas I use the word "tacit" to refer to nascent ritualizing—actions not yet recognized as a distinct ceremony, celebration, or liturgy—Cipolla uses it to refer to non-normative parts of the Mass. For him, ceremony is tacit in relation to specifically liturgical elements. Ceremony consists of all parts of the Mass subsidiary to the focal or normative ones. The terminological snarl is typical of those that make communication between liturgiology and anthropology so difficult. A similar one arises if one compares a liturgiologist's definition of liturgy with that of an anthropologist such as Roÿ Rappaport (1979).

87. D. W. Winnicott (1958) was criticized much in the same way for overextending the idea of transition objects to include all transition phenomena. See, e.g., Flew (1978).

88. Turner's characterization of flow is borrowed from Csikszentmihaly (1975).

89. This judgment is based on my fieldwork in 1980 with Grotowski.

90. However, under the influence of anthropology, liturgiologists have recently made acculturation an important theme.

91. A more theoretically oriented course is sometimes taught after this one; at other times it is preceded by such a course. After both, students who want to do further research can do fieldwork on ritual.

92. Sociologists Hesser and Weigert (1980) have proposed a statistical, non-normative framework for comparing liturgical styles. The framework encompasses both formal and functional factors—"actional, interactional, and symbolic levels," as they put it (215). Lardner (1979) has proposed some liturgical criteria. But the split between social-scientific and liturgical interpretation is still immensely problematic. Mary Collins (1975), John McKenna (1976), Urban T. Holmes (1973, 1977a, 1977b), and Aidan Kavanagh (1982a, 1982b) are among those who have most successfully addressed the issue from the point of view of theology or liturgics.

93. Ruel Tyson's phrase (personal correspondence).

94. The most useful expositions of the role of metaphor in the construction of world-views are those of Gerhart and Russell (1984) and Lakoff and Johnson (1980).

95. On the notion of metaphoric predication, see various works by James Fernandez, especially "The Mission of Metaphor in Expressive Culture" (1974).

96. One of the most fruitful theories for relating ritual to the human body, particularly the brain, is that of biogenetic structuralism (see, e.g., d'Aquili et al.)

97. On institutions as symbols of death, see May (1976).

98. Contempt for magic is typical of dominant North American cultures. The same is not true of many other cultures.

99. Pastoral psychology often follows the lead of popular, secular psychology. Consequently, with the shift in popular psychology toward more hands-on, less talk-oriented therapy, one can probably expect the trend to show up in pastoral psychology.

100. A method that resembles this suggestion can be found in Wepner's (1973) discussion of orientation therapy.

101. Even though the community mental health movement challenges some of the fundamental assumptions and values of hospitals, it is not without its own dangers. One's health is not *necessarily* in better hands when those hands belong to "the people." On the

fringe of the movement is countercultural healing. A tide of interest in such healing is swelling in contemporary North America, and it goes far beyond hospitals and community health organizations. For example, in Santa Fe, NM, a small city of 85,000 inhabitants, *Who's Who in the Healing Arts* (von Erffa 1986) is published. It lists 228 alternative healing modes, not including the usual medical and psychiatric specializations. Among them are Rolfers, sclerologists, shamanic counselors, rebalancers, pyramid therapists, flower-essence therapists, homeopaths, flotationists, dowsers, dreamworkers, and etheric body healers.

This proliferation has been spawned in part by the narrowness of vision and procedure in modern Western hospitals. There are, of course, other reasons: the never-ending search for jobs during a time of high unemployment, the influence of indigenous and Asian cultures, changing paradigms in the sciences, and the psychologically preoccupied "habits of the heart" (Bellah et al. 1986) peculiar to the American people.

Whatever the causes, one who is ill immediately faces a critical question: How do I decide between hospital and "other," and if I decide on other, which other? And having undergone treatment, how do I know whether it has worked? How do I judge the results?

Counterculture healers are greatly interested in ritual, and its practitioners would probably agree with much of what I have said in assessing hospitals. These healers have no difficulty understanding the importance of space, objects, symbols, and the like. But often one has to be as wary of them as of hospitals.

Although some elements in this movement are "counter" to mainline values, many are not. The movement, if that is the proper label for it, uses many of the same advertising techniques, playing off the same hopes and fears, as do mainline commercial advertisers.

102. More general evidence is available in the writings of Schechner (1980, 1981a, 1981b), Morgan (1977), Babcock (1978), and Turner (1979a), so I shall not re-argue the case already made by anthropologists for the presence of reflexive consciousness in ritual.

103. Turner refers to them as "star groupers." Fortunately, he drops the term in subsequent writings.

104. In view of the claims for narrative discussed in the previous chapter, it is easy to see why the time-conscious Turner might choose narrative as a primary vehicle for ensuring that theories remain rooted in historically conceived time.

105. For an interdisciplinary bibliography of scholarly works on ritual, see Grimes, *Research in Ritual Studies* (1985). For a brief survey of ritual studies, see Grimes, "Ritual Studies" in the *Encyclopedia of Religion* (1987).

106. One might want to examine other models and motives for evaluating cultural action. For example, Howard Richards in *The Evaluation of Cultural Action* (1985) attempts to reflect philosophically on the problem of evaluating programs in Latin America. Not only does he face the problem of how to integrate ethical concerns with those of productivity, he approaches the problem with considerable philosophical sophistication concerning the epistemology of cross-cultural evaluation.

107. Theologian and performance critic Tom Driver (1970) has said that theology is to religion what literary criticism is to literature. Literature, like religion, is a primary process upon which secondary, analytical processes depend.

108. Nevertheless, I have written about the ritual dimensions of literary works (see Grimes 1989a). For a discussion of the relations between literature and ritual, see Hardin (1983).

109. Schechner further distinguishes "transformation" from "transportation" (1981a: 91). In Euro-American acting traditions, actors are transported, which is to say, "carried away" by their roles but "returned" to themselves. Their performances do not effect a change

of status. They reenter ordinary life at the same point they left it. In contrast, rites of passage effect a transformation of social state: a dead person becomes an ancestor, a man and a woman become "one flesh." However, transportation is not identical with theater, nor transformation with ritual. Possession rites can transport and certain kinds of theater, that of Grotowski for instance, can transform.

110. For a good discussion of the tacit religious and ethical dimensions of anthropology, see Mark Kline Taylor's *Beyond Explanation: Religious Dimensions in Cultural Anthropology* (1986).

111. Recall the anthropologist mentioned in chapter 3 who worried that self-criticism and self-consciousness would immobilize researchers.

112. Catholic theologians reflecting these social-scientific interests are mentioned in chapter 2. Protestant theologians include Theodore W. Jennings, Jr., and Tom F. Driver. Driver has a forthcoming book on ritual and human transformation, which is deeply marked by ethnographic interests.

113. The works of James Fernandez (e.g., 1974, 1982, 1986) will soon have to be added to this list.

114. Many liturgical theologians learned their methods from biblical critics. Just as the Bible was made approachable by scholarly methods, so the liturgy is being relativized by historical and literary critical scholarship.

115. For a Protestant perception of the political ramifications of prayer and worship, see Theodore W. Jennings, Jr., *Life as Worship: Prayer and Praise in Jesus' Name* (1982a: chap.3).

116. Theology and the social sciences both have their ways of putting judgments into force; each is normative in a different way. Social-scientific explanation exercises normative power by looking for latent social functions beneath the avowed intentions of those who enact the rites. As Talal Asad (1986:161) suggests, the attribution of implicit meanings to alien practices without the acknowledgment of the practitioners is a "theological" exercise.

117. Another volume relevant to the interface between theology and anthropology is John H. Morgan's *Understanding Religion and Culture: Anthropological Perspectives* (1979). See also Urban T. Holmes, "What Has Manchester to Do with Jerusalem?" (1977b). Manchester is his symbol for the home of British social anthropology; Jerusalem, the home of three major religions.

118. For a fuller treatment of enculturation and liturgy see Chupungco (1982).

119. See, e.g., the *Journal of Ritual Studies* 2(2), 1988. The entire issue is devoted to fieldwork and religion.

120. Tyson's richest descriptive work is in *Diversities of Gifts: Field Studies in Southern Religion* (1988).

121. For Tyson criticism is virtually synonymous with interpretation. For me it is not; criticism is only one kind of interpretation. To be more specific, it is interpretation *in the service of practice*. It is that phase of intercultural hermeneutics in which judgments are exercised and conflicting definitions of the situation made overt. Thus it may evoke conflict and controversy.

122. The following account is based on three performances as follows: (1) *Bharata Natyam* and a subsequent workshop with audience members by Maureen Sanderson (Madhurika) during Wilfrid Laurier University's Festival of Play in 1977; (2) "Images of the Feminine in Indian Dance" by Roxanne Kamayani Gupta and subsequent formal discussion by those attending a meeting of the Eastern International Region of the American Academy of Religion meeting at Syracuse University in 1983. For study purposes I had access to video

tapes of a previous performance; (3) *Odissi* style dance by Menaka Thakkar and Guru Kellucharan Mahapatra at the Victoria Memorial Museum in Ottawa, Canada, 1987, followed by informal discussion with performance theorist and theatre director Richard Schechner.

123. The very fact that church stages are typically in basements tells us a great deal about the place of drama in Christianity.

124. Denis de Rougemont (1963:7–8) remarks, "We find no single Christian equivalent . . . of the *Kama Sutras*, of the *Tantras*, of so many other treatises on eroticism in the *Vedas* and the *Upanishads*, relating the sexual to the divine; still less, of the famous sculptures on the facades of the great Hindu temples, illustrating in the most precise manner the unions of the gods and their wives . . . . Confronted with [the] endocrine crisis [of puberty], Christianity is content with extremely severe moral counsel and vague or hygienic advice."

125. One problem with descriptions outside ethnographic circles, where the need for such is assumed, is that publishers and editors tend to view description as "journalistic," therefore not scholarly. Chapter 4, in its original publication, was cut in half for this reason.

126. Like description, reflexivity runs into problems with editors, some of whom consider the latter inappropriate because of its first-person references and rhetoric.

127. On another occasion response was met with indifference; on yet another, it would have been defined as out-of-bounds.

Sources Cited

Abbott, Walter M., ed. 1966. *The Documents of Vatican II*. Translated by Joseph Gallagher. New York: Guild, America, and Association.

Ackerman, Robert. 1975. Frazer on Myth and Ritual. *Journal of the History of Ideas* 36:115–134.

Ackroyd, Peter. 1984. *T. S. Eliot: A Life*. New York: Simon & Schuster.

American Indians against Desecration [AIAD]. 1984. A Resolution on the Protection, Avoidance, and Treatment of Ancestral Remains and Sacred Objects. Vermillion, SD. Photocopy.

Ames, Michael M., and Claudia Haagen. 1988. A New Native Peoples [*sic*] History for Museums. *Native Studies Review* 4(1–2):119–127.

Apuleius, Lucius. 1962. *The Golden Ass*. Translated by Jack Lindsay. Bloomington: Indiana University Press.

Aries, Philip. 1981. *The Hour of Our Death*. Translated by Helen Weaver. New York: Knopf.

Asad, Talal, ed. 1973. *Anthropology and the Colonial Encounter*. New York: Humanities Press.

Austin, J. L. 1962. *How to Do Things with Words*. New York: Oxford University Press.

Babcock, Barbara A., ed. 1978. *The Reversible World: Symbolic Inversion in Art and Society*. Ithaca, NY: Cornell University Press.

———. 1980. Reflexivity: Definitions and Discriminations. *Semiotica* 30(1–2):1–14.

Bachelard, Gaston. 1950. *La Dialectique de la durée*. Paris: P.U.F.

Barthes, Roland. 1984. Jeunes Chercheurs. In *Le Bruissement de la langue*. Paris: Le Seuil.

Bateson, Gregory. 1972. *Steps to an Ecology of Mind*. New York: Chandler.

Bell, Catherine. 1988. The Ritual Body Re-examined: The Social Dynamics of Ritual Power. Paper presented at the Workshop on Ritual and Power, University of California, Santa Barbara, May 21–22. Photocopy.

Bellah, Robert, et al. 1986. *Habits of the Heart: Individualism and Commitment in American Life*. New York: Harper & Row.

Benamou, Michel, and Charles Caramello. 1977. *Performance in Postmodern Culture*. Theories of Contemporary Culture, vol. 1. Madison, WI: Center for Twentieth Century.

Black, Max. 1962. *Models and Metaphors: Studies in Language and Philosophy*. Ithaca, NY: Cornell University Press.

Booth, Gotthard. 1979. *The Cancer Epidemic: Shadow of the Conquest of Nature*. New York: Edwin Mellen.

Booth, Wayne. 1979. *Critical Understanding: The Powers and Limits of Pluralism*. Chicago: University of Chicago Press.

Bourdieu, Pierre. 1977. *Outline of a Theory of Practice*. Translated by Richard Nice. Cambridge, Eng.: Cambridge University Press.

Bruner, Edward M., ed. 1984. *Text, Play and Story: The Construction and Reconstruction of*

246

Self and Society. Proceedings of the American Ethnological Society, 1983. N.p.: Stewart Plattner.

Burke, Kenneth. 1966. *Language as Symbolic Action: Essays on Life, Literature, and Method*. Berkeley: University of California Press.

————. 1969. *A Grammar of Motives*. Berkeley: University of California Press.

Burke, Peter. 1978. *Popular Culture in Early Modern Europe*. New York: Harper & Row.

Burkert, Walter. 1966. Greek Tragedy and Sacrificial Ritual. *Greek, Roman and Byzantine Studies* 7:87–121.

————. 1972. *Homo Necans: Interpretationen Altgreischischer Opferriten und Mythen*. Berlin, Germany: Walter de Gruyer.

Burns, Elizabeth. 1972. *Theatricality: A Study of Convention in the Theatre and in Social Life*. New York: Harper & Row.

Canadian Museum of Civilization [CMC]. 1987. Vision Statement: Canadian Museum of Civilization. Ottawa, Canada: N.p. Photocopy.

Cannizzo, Jeanne. 1983. The Shit Devil: Pretense and Politics among West African Urban Children. In *The Celebration of Society: Perspectives on Contemporary Cultural Performance*, edited by Frank E. Manning. London, Canada: Congress of Social & Humanistic Studies.

Capps, Donald, et al. 1977. *Encounter with Erikson: Historical Interpretation and Religious Biography*. Missoula, MT: Scholars Press.

Carrier, Hervé. 1985. Understanding Culture: The Ultimate Challenge of the World-church. In *The Church and Culture since Vatican II: The Experience of North and Latin America*, edited by Joseph Gremillion. Notre Dame, IN: University of Notre Dame Press.

Chapman, Robert, et al., eds. 1981. *The Archaeology of Death*. Cambridge, Eng.: Cambridge University Press.

Chupungco, Anscar. 1982. *Cultural Adaptation of the Liturgy*. New York: Paulist.

Cipolla, Richard G. 1973. Ceremonial and the Tacit Dimension. *Worship* 47(7):398–404.

Clifford, James, and George E. Marcus, eds. 1986. *Writing Culture: The Poetics and Politics of Ethnography*. A School of American Research Advanced Seminar. Berkeley: University of California Press.

Collins, Mary. 1975. Liturgical Methodology and the Cultural Evolution of Worship in the United States. *Worship* 49(2):85–102.

————. 1987. *Worship: Renewal to Practice*. Washington, DC: Pastoral.

Coult, Tony, and Baz Kershaw, eds. 1983. *Engineers of the Imagination*. London: Methuen.

Crites, Stephen. 1971. The Narrative Quality of Experience. *Journal of the American Academy of Religion* 39(3):291–311.

Crossan, John Dominic. 1975. *The Dark Interval: Towards a Theology of Story*. Niles, IL: Argus.

Csikszentmihalyi, Mihaly. 1975. *Beyond Boredom and Anxiety*. San Francisco: Jossey-Bass.

d'Aquili, Eugene, et al. 1979. *The Spectrum of Ritual: A Biogenetic Structural Analysis*. New York: Columbia University Press.

De Rougemont, Denis. 1963. *Love Declared*. Translated by Richard Howard. New York: Pantheon.

Delattre, Roland. 1978. Ritual Resourcefulness and Cultural Pluralism. *Soundings* 61(3): 281–301.

Deren, Maya. 1970. *Divine Horsemen: Voodoo Gods of Haiti*. New York: Chelsea House.

Dinges, William D. 1987. Ritual Conflict as Social Conflict: Liturgical Reform in the Roman Catholic Church. *Sociological Analysis* 48(2):138–158.

Dittes, James E. 1977. The Investigator as an Instrument of Investigation: Some Exploratory Observations on the Compleat Researcher. In *Encounter with Erikson: Historical Interpretation and Religious Biography*, edited by Donald Capps et al. Atlanta: Scholars Press.

Dixon, John, Jr. 1979. *The Physiology of Faith: A Theory of Theological Relativity*. New York: Harper & Row.

————. 1983. Art as the Making of the World: Outline of Method in the Criticism of Religion and Art. *Journal of the American Academy of Religion* 51(1):15–36.

Dossey, Larry. 1982. *Space, Time, and Medicine*. Boulder, CO: Shambala.

Doty, William G. 1986. *Mythography: The Study of Myths and Rituals*. University, AL: University of Alabama Press.

Douglas, Mary. 1973. *Natural Symbols: Explorations in Cosmology*. New York: Random House.

————, and Aaron Wildavsky. 1982. *Risk and Culture: An Essay on the Selection of Technical and Environmental Dangers*. Berkeley: University of California Press.

Driver, Tom F. 1970. The Study of Religion and Literature: Siblings in the Academic House. In *The Study of Religion in Colleges and Universities*, edited by Paul Ramsey and John F. Wilson. Princeton: Princeton University Press.

Dunne, John S. 1973. *Time and Myth*. Notre Dame: University of Notre Dame Press.

Editors. 1987. Editorial Notice. *Worship* 61(1):80ff.

Eisenberg, Leon, and Arthur Kleinman, eds. 1981. *The Relevance of Social Science for Medicine*. Dordrecht, Holland: Reidel.

Eliade, Mircea. 1957. *The Sacred and the Profane*. New York: Harper & Row.

————. 1964. *Shamanism: Archaic Techniques of Ecstasy*. Translated by Willard R. Trask. Princeton, NJ: Princeton University Press.

Eliot, T. S. 1963. *Murder in the Cathedral*. New York: Harcourt, Brace, and World. First Published 1935.

Fabian, Johannes. 1973. How Others Die—Reflections on the Anthropology of Death. In *Death in American Experience*, edited by A. Mack. New York: Schocken.

Fenn, Richard K. 1982. *Liturgies and Trials: The Secularization of Religious Language*. New York: Pilgrim.

Fernandez, James W. 1974. The Mission of Metaphor in Expressive Culture. *Current Anthropology* 15:119–145.

————. 1982. *Bwiti: An Ethnography of the Religious Imagination in Africa*. Princeton, NJ: Princeton University Press.

————. 1986. The Argument of Images and the Experience of Returning to the Whole. In *The Anthropology of Experience*, edited by Victor W. Turner and Edward M. Bruner. Urbana: University of Illinois Press.

Finnegan, Ruth. 1969. How to Do Things with Words: Performative Utterances among the Limba of Sierra Leone. *Man* (N.S.) 4:537–552.

Fish, Stanley E. 1972. *Self-Consuming Artifacts: The Experience of Seventeenth-Century Literature*. Berkeley: University of California Press.

Flew, Anthony. 1978. Transitional Objects and Transitional Phenomena: Comments and Interpretations. In *Between Reality and Fantasy*, edited by Simon A. Grolnick and Leonard Barkin. New York: Jason Aronson.

Foster, George, and Barbara Anderson. 1978. *Medical Anthropology*. New York: John Wiley,

Foster, Steven, and Meredith Little. 1987. The Vision Quest: Passing from Childhood to Adulthood. In *Betwixt & Between: Patterns of Masculine and Feminine Initiation*, edited by Louise Carus Mahdi et al. LaSalle, IL: Open Court.

Foucault, Michel. 1973. *The Birth of the Clinic: An Archaeology of the Human Sciences.* New York: Pantheon.

Fowler, James, et al. 1980. *Trajectories in Faith: Five Life Stories.* Nashville: Abingdon.

Frei, Hans. 1974. *The Eclipse of Biblical Narrative: A Study in Eighteenth and Nineteenth Century Hermeneutics.* New Haven: Yale University Press.

Friedrich, Rainer. 1983. Drama and Ritual. In *Drama and Religion*, edited by James Redmond. Themes in Drama. Cambridge, Eng.: Cambridge University Press.

Frye, Northrop. 1968. *Anatomy of Criticism.* New York: Atheneum.

———. 1982. *The Great Code: The Bible and Literature.* Toronto: Academic.

Gaster, Theodor. 1951. "Errors of Method in the Study of Religion." In *Freedom and Reason: Studies in Philosophy and Jewish Culture*, edited by Salon Baron et al. New York: Conference on Jewish Relations.

Geertz, Clifford. 1973. *The Interpretation of Cultures.* New York: Basic Books.

———. 1980. Blurred Genres. *The American Scholar* 49:165–179.

———. 1988. *Works and Lives: The Anthropologist as Author.* Stanford, CA: Stanford University Press.

Georgetown Center for Liturgy, Spirituality and the Arts. 1988. Liturgical Renewal, 1963–1988: A Study of English-speaking Parishes in the United States. Photocopy

Gerhart, Mary, and Allan M. Russell. 1984. *The Metaphoric Process: The Creation of Scientific and Religious Understanding.* Fort Worth: Texas Christian University Press.

Gill, Sam D. 1977. Hopi Kchina Cult Initiation: The Shocking Beginning of the Hopi's Religious Life. *Journal of the American Academy of Religion*, Supplement 45(2):447–514.

Girard, René. 1972. *Violence and the Sacred.* Translated by Patrick Gregory. Baltimore: Johns Hopkins University Press.

Goethals, Gregor T. 1981. *The TV Ritual: Worship at the Video Altar.* Boston: Beacon.

Goffman, Erving. 1967. *Interaction Ritual: Essays on Face-to-Face Behavior.* Garden City, NY: Doubleday.

———. 1974. *Frame Analysis: An Essay on the Organization of Experience.* New York: Harper & Row.

Goldberg, Michael. 1982. *Theology and Narrative: A Critical Introduction.* Nashville: Abingdon.

Good, Byron, and Mary-Jo Delvecchio. 1981. The Meaning of Symptoms: A Cultural Hermeneutic Model for Clinical Practice. In *The Relevance of Social Science for Medicine*, edited by Leon Eisenberg and Arthur Kleinman. Dordrecht, Holland: Reidel.

Goody, Jack. 1977. Against "Ritual:" Loosely Structured Thoughts on a Loosely Defined Topic. In *Secular Ritual*, edited by Sally Falk Moore and Barbara Myerhoff. Amsterdam: Van Gorcum.

Grimes, Ronald L. 1982a. *Beginnings in Ritual Studies.* Washington, DC: University Press of America.

———. 1982b. Defining Nascent Ritual, *Journal of the American Academy of Religion* 50(4):539–555.

———. 1985. *Research in Ritual Studies.* Metuchen, NJ: Scarecrow Press and the American Theological Library Association.

———. 1987. Ritual Studies. *The Encyclopedia of Religion*, 12:422–425, edited by Mircea Eliade. New York: Macmillan.

———. 1989. "Bound to Baptize: Ritualization in Flannery O'Connor's *The Violent Bear It Away*." *Religion and Literature* 21(1):9–26.

———. 1990. "Victor Turner's Definition, Theory, and Sense of Ritual." In *Between*

Literature and Anthropology, edited by Kathleen M. Ashley. Bloomington: Indiana University Press (forthcoming).

Grolnick, Simon A., and Alfonz Lengyel. 1978. Etruscan Burial Symbols and the Transitional Process. In *Between Reality and Fantasy: Transitional Objects and Phenomena*. New York: Jason Aronson.

Grotowski, Jerzy. 1968. *Towards a Poor Theatre*. New York: Simon & Schuster.

Gunn, Giles. 1987. *The Culture of Criticism and the Criticism of Culture*. New York: Oxford University Press.

Halifax, Joan, ed. 1979. *Shamanic Voices: A Survey of Visionary Narratives*. New York: Dutton.

Hall, Edward T. 1966. *The Hidden Dimension*. Garden City, NY: Doubleday.

————. 1973. *The Silent Language*. Garden City, NY: Doubleday.

Halprin, Anna. 1989. Planetary Dance. *The Drama Review* 33(2):51–66.

Hammil, Jan, and Larry J. Zimmerman. 1983. Reburial of Human Skeletal Remains: Perspectives from Lakota Spiritual Men and Elders. Rapid City, SD: American Indians against Desecration and the University of South Dakota Archaeology Laboratory. Photocopy.

Handler, Richard. 1984. On Authenticity. Paper presented to the annual meeting of the American Anthropological Association, Denver, CO.

Hardin, Richard F. 1983. "Ritual" in Recent Criticism: The Elusive Sense of Community." *PMLA* 98(5):846–862.

Harner, Michael. 1980. *Way of the Shaman: A Guide to Power and Healing*. New York: Harper & Row.

Harrison, Jane. 1927. *Epilegomena to the Study of Greek Religion and Themis: A Study of the Social Origins of Greek Religion*. New Hyde Park: University Books.

Harwood, Alan, ed. 1981. *Ethnicity and Medical Care*. Cambridge, MA: Harvard University Press.

Hassan, Ihab. 1971. *The Dismemberment of Orpheus: Toward a Postmodern Literature*. Madison: University of Wisconsin Press.

Hauerwas, Stanley. 1973. The Self as Story: Religion and Morality from the Agent's Perception. *Journal of Religious Ethics* 1(1): 73–85.

————. 1976. Story and Theology. *Religion in Life* 45:339–350.

————. 1977. *Truthfulness and Tragedy*. Notre Dame, IN: University of Notre Dame Press.

————. 1981. *A Community of Character: Toward a Constructive Christian Social Ethic*. Notre Dame, IN: University of Notre Dame Press.

Hesser, Garry, and Andrew J. Weigert. 1980. Comparative Dimensions of Liturgy: A Conceptual Framework and Feasibility Application, *Sociological Analysis* 41(3):215–229.

Hillman, James. 1972. *The Myth of Analysis*. New York: Harper & Row.

————. 1975. The Fiction of Case History: A Round. In *Religion and Story*, edited by James B. Wiggins. New York: Harper & Row.

Hine, Virginia H. 1981. Self-Generated Ritual: Trend or Fad? *Worship* 55(1):404–419.

Holmes, Urban T. 1973. Liminality and Liturgy. *Worship* 47(7):386–399.

————. 1977a. Ritual and the Social Drama. *Worship* 51:197–213.

————. 1977b. What Has Manchester to Do with Jerusalem? *Anglican Theological Review* 59(1):79–97.

Horrobin, David F. n.d. *Medical Hubris: A Reply to Ivan Illich*. Montreal: Eden.

Hutcheon, Linda. 1980. *Narcissistic Narrative: The Metafictional Paradox*. Waterloo, Canada: Wilfrid Laurier University Press.

Illich, Ivan. 1975. *Medical Nemesis: The Expropriation of Health*. London: Calder & Boyars.

Imber-Black, Evan, et al. 1988. *Rituals in Families and Family Therapy*. New York: Norton.
James, William C. 1981. The Canoe Trip as Religious Quest. *Studies in Religion* 10(2):151–166.
Jennings, Theodore W., Jr. 1982a. *Life as Worship: Prayer and Praise in Jesus' Name*. Grand Rapids, MI: Eerdmans.
———. 1982b. On Ritual Knowledge. *History of Religions* 62(2):111–127.
John Paul II, Pope. 1985. Man's Entire Humanity Is Expressed in Culture. In *The Church and Culture since Vatican II: The Experience of North and Latin America*, edited by Joseph Gremillion. Notre Dame, IN: University of Notre Dame Press.
Kapferer, Bruce. 1986. Performance and the Structuring of Meaning. In *The Anthropology of Experience*, edited by Victor W. Turner and Edward M. Bruner. Urbana: University of Illinois Press.
Kavanagh, Aidan 1978. *The Shape of Baptism: The Rites of Christian Initiation*. New York: Pueblo.
———. 1982a. *Elements of Rite: A Handbook of Liturgical Style*. New York: Pueblo.
———. 1982b. Liturgy and Ecclesial Consciousness: A Dialectic of Change. *Studia Liturgica* 15(1):2–17.
Kearney, Michael. 1984. *World View*. Novato, CA: Chandler & Sharp.
Keen, Sam. 1970. *To a Dancing God*. New York: Harper & Row.
———, and Anne Valley Fox. 1973. *How to Tell Your Story: A Guide to Who You Are and Who You Can Be*. New York: Signet.
Kidd, Ross. 1984. Reclaiming Culture: Indigenous Performers Take Back Their Show. *The Canadian Journal of Native Studies* 4(1):105–120.
Kirby, E. T. 1974. The Shamanistic Origins of Popular Entertainments. *The Drama Review* 18(1):5–15.
Kirk, G. S. 1970. *Myth: Its Meaning and Functions in Ancient and Other Cultures*. Berkeley: University of California Press.
Kleinman, Arthur. 1980. *Patients and Healers in the Context of Culture*. Berkeley: University of California Press.
Kliever, Lonnie D. 1977. Story and Space: The Forgotten Dimension. *Journal of the American Academy of Religion*, Supplement 45(2):529–563.
———. 1981. Fictive Religion: Rhetoric and Play. *Journal of the American Academy of Religion* 49(4):658–669.
Kluckhohn, Clyde. 1965. Myths and Rituals: A General Theory. In *Reader in Comparative Religion: An Anthropological Approach*, edited by William A. Lessa and Evon Z. Vogt. 3rd ed. New York: Harper & Row.
Koser, Constantine. 1966. Liturgical Piety and Pious Exercises. In *The Liturgy of Vatican II*, vol. 1, edited by William Barúna. English edition edited by Jovian Lang. Chicago: Franciscan Herald.
Lakoff, George, and Mark Johnson. 1980. *Metaphors We Live By*. Chicago: University of Chicago Press.
Lardner, Gerald V. 1979. Evaluative Criteria and the Liturgy, *Worship* 53:357–370.
Leacock, Seth and Ruth. 1975. *Spirits of the Deep: A Study of an Afro-Brazilian Cult*. Garden City, NY: Anchor.
Lears, Jackson. 1981. *No Place of Grace: Antimodernism and the Transformation of American Culture, 1880–1920*. New York: Pantheon.
LaVey, Anton. 1969. *Satanic Bible*. New York: Avon.
Lentricchia, Frank. 1980. *After the New Criticism*. Chicago: University of Chicago Press.

Lévi-Strauss, Claude. 1967. *Structural Anthropology*. Translated by Claire Jacobson and Brooke G. Schoepf. Garden City, NY: Doubleday.

Layton, Robert, ed. 1989. *Conflict in the Archaeology of Living Traditions*. London: Unwin Hyman.

Lincoln, Bruce. 1977. Two Notes on Modern Rituals. *Journal of the American Academy of Religion* 45(2):147–160.

Lindbeck, George E. 1977. Erikson's *Young Man Luther*. In *Encounter with Erikson: Historical Interpretatioin and Religious Biography*, edited by Donald Capps et al. Missoula, MT: Scholars Press.

Lopresti, James, director of the North American Forum on the Catechumenate. 1988 (May 6). Letter to author.

Luckmann, Thomas. 1967. *The Invisible Religion: The Transformation of Symbols in Industrial Society*. New York: Macmillan.

McClendon, James William, Jr. 1974. *Biography as Theology: How Life Stories Can Remake Today's Theology*. Nashville: Abingdon.

MacDonald, George F. 1987a. Epcot Centre in Museological Perspective. Paper presented at the Canadian Museum Association, Winnipeg. Photocopy.

———. 1987b. Facing the Competition: Museums in the Marketplace. Paper presented at the Canadian Museum Association, Winnipeg. Photocopy.

McGimsey, Charles R., III, and Hester A. Davis. 1977. Archeology and Native Americans. In *The Management of Archeological Resources: The Arlie House Report*. Washington, DC: Society for American Archeology.

McKenna, John H. 1976. Ritual Activity. *Worship* 50:347–352.

McLuhan, T. C. 1971. *Touch the Earth: A Self-Portrait of Indian Existence*. New York: Outerbirdge & Dienstfrey.

Mahdi, Louise Carus, et al. 1987. *Betwixt & Between: Patterns of Masculine and Feminine Imitation*. La Salle, IL: Open Court.

Marcus, George E., and Michael M. J. Fischer. 1986. *Anthropology as Cultural Critique: An Experimental Moment in the Human Sciences*. Chicago: University of Chicago Press.

Martin, Bernice. 1979. The Sacralization of Disorder: Symbolism in Rock Music. *Sociological Analysis* 40(2):87–124.

May, William F. 1976. Institutions as Symbols of Death. *Journal of the American Academy of Religion* 44:211–223.

Merbs, Charles F. 1985. Review of *Science or Sacrilege* by Philip L. Walker. *American Anthropologist* 87:490–491.

Merod, Jim. 1987. *The Political Responsibility of the Critic*. Ithaca, NY: Cornell University Press.

Michaelsen, Robert S. 1980. The Significance of the American Indian Religious Freedom Act of 1978. *Journal of the American Academy of Religion* 52:93–115.

Miller, Alan L. 1987. Power. In *The Encyclopedia of Religion*, vol. 11, edited by Mircea Eliade. New York: Macmillan.

Morgan, John H., ed. 1979. *Understanding Religion and Culture: Anthropological and Theological Perspectives*. Washington, DC: University Press of America.

Morgan, Sophia S. 1977. On Rituals and Reflection. Paper prepared for the Wenner-Gren Foundation for Anthropological Research, Burg Wartenstein Symposium, No. 76. Photocopy.

Myerhoff, Barbara. 1978. *Number Our Days*. New York: Simon & Schuster.

Myerhoff, Barbara, and Deena Metzger. 1980. The Journal as Activity and Genre: Or Listening to the Silent Laughter of Mozart. *Semiotica* 30(1–3):97–114.

Neale, Robert. 1969. *In Praise of Play: Towards a Psychology of Religion*. New York: Harper & Row.

Needham, Rodney. 1967. Percussion and Transition. *Man* (N.S.) 2:606–614.

Needleman, Jacob. 1985. *Lost Christianity*. New York: Harper & Row.

Neumann, Erich. 1973. *The Child: Structure and Dynamics of the Nascent Personality*. New York: Putnam.

Nietzsche, Friedrich. 1956. *Thus Spake Zarathustra*. New York: Viking.

Norbeck, Edward. 1967. African Rituals of Conflict. In *Gods and Rituals: Readings in Religious Beliefs and Practices*, edited by John Middleton. Garden City, NY: Natural History Press.

Novak, Michael. 1971. *Ascent of the Mountain, Flight of the Dove: An Invitation to Religious Studies*. New York: Harper & Row.

O'Connor, Flannery. 1962. *Wise Blood*. New York: Signet.

Ong, Walter J. 1962. *The Barbarian within and Other Fugitive Essays and Studies*. New York: Macmillan.

———. 1967. *The Presence of the Word: Some Prolegomena for Cultural and Religious History*. New Haven: Yale University Press.

Opler, Morris E. 1969. *Apache Odyssey: A Journey between Two Worlds*. New York: Holt, Rinehart & Winston.

Palmer, Richard. 1977. Toward a Postmodern Hermeneutics of Performance. In *Performance in Postmodern Culture*, edited by Michel Benamou and Charles Caramello. Madison, WI: Coda.

Pfifferling, John Henry. 1981. A Cultural Prescription for Medicocentrism. In *The Relevance of Social Science for Medicine*, edited by Leon Eisenberg and Arthur Kleinman. Dordrecht, Holland: Reidel.

Polhemus, Ted, ed. 1978. *Social Aspects of the Human Body*. Middlesex, Eng.: Penguin.

Polkinghorne, Donald E. 1988. *Narrative Knowing and the Human Sciences*. Albany, NY: State University of New York Press.

Prosser, Elanor. 1961. *Drama and Religion in the English Mystery Plays*. Stanford: Stanford University Press.

Rabuzzi, Kathryn A. 1982. *The Sacred and the Feminine: Toward a Theology of Housework*. New York: Harper & Row.

Ramsey, Paul. 1979. Liturgy and Ethics. *Journal of Religious Ethics* 7:139–171.

Rappaport, Roy. 1971. Ritual, Sanctity, and Cybernetics. *American Anthropologist* 73(1):59–76.

———. 1979. *Ecology, Meaning, and Religion*. Richmond, CA: North Atlantic.

———. 1980. Concluding Comments on Ritual and Reflexivity. *Semiotica* 30(1–2):181–193.

Ray, Benjamin. 1973. "Performative Utterances" in African Rituals. *History of Religions* 13(1):16–35.

Reynolds, Frank E., and Donald Capps, eds. 1976. *The Biographical Process: Studies in the History and Psychology of Religion*. The Hague: Mouton.

Richards, Howard. 1985. *The Evaluation of Cultural Action*. London: Macmillan.

Ricoeur, Paul. 1967. *The Symbolism of Evil*. Translated by Emerson Buchanan. New York: Harper & Row.

————. 1973. The Model of the Text: Meaningful Action Considered as a Text. *New Literary History* 5(1):91–117.

————. 1980. Narrative Time. *Critical Inquiry* 7(4):169–190.

Roberts, William O., Jr. 1982. *Initiation into Adulthood: An Ancient Rite of Passage in Contemporary Form*. New York: Pilgrim.

Rosaldo, Renato. 1976. The Story of Tukbaw: "They Listen as He Orates." In *The Biographical Process*, edited by Frank Reynolds and Donald Capps. The Hague: Mouton.

Royce, Anya Peterson. 1977. *The Anthropology of Dance*. Bloomington, IN: Indiana University Press.

Rubenstein, Richard. 1966. *After Auschwitz: Radical Theology and Contemporary Judaism*. Indianapolis: Bobbs-Merrill.

————. 1974. *Power Struggle: A Confessional Autobiography*. New York: Scribners.

Ruby, Jay, ed. 1982. *A Crack in the Mirror: Reflexive Perspectives in Anthropology*. Philadelphia: University of Pennsylvania Press.

Sacks, Oliver. 1984. The Lost Mariner. *New York Review of Books* 31(2):14–19.

Savage, Howard G. 1977. Meeting of Representatives of Indian Groups and Archaeologists of Ontario. *Arch Notes*, October-November, 34–36.

Scarf, Maggie. 1980. Images that Heal: A Doubtful Idea Whose Time Has Come. *Psychology Today* 14(4):32–46.

Schechner, Richard. 1977. *Essays on Performance Theory, 1970–1976*. New York: Drama Book Specialists.

————. 1980. The End of Humanism. *Performing Arts Journal* 4(1–2):9–22.

————. 1981a. Performers and Spectators Transported and Transformed. *The Kenyon Review*, N.S., 3(4):83–113.

————. 1981b. Restoration of Behavior. *Studies in Visual Communication* 7(3):1–45.

————. 1985. *Between Theater and Anthropology*. Philadelphia: University of Pennsylvania Press.

————. 1986. Magnitudes of Performance. In *The Anthropology of Experience*, edited by Victor W. Turner and Edward M. Bruner. Urbana: University of Illinois Press.

————, interviewer. 1989. Anna Halprin: A Life in Ritual. *The Drama Review* 33(2):67–73.

Searle, John. 1969. *Speech Acts: An Essay in the Philosophy of Language*. Cambridge, Eng.: Cambridge University Press.

————. 1979. *Expression and Meaning: Studies in the Theory of Speech-acts*. Cambridge: Cambridge University Press.

Searle, Mark. 1981. The Pedagogical Function of Liturgy. *Worship* 55(4):332–359.

Siebers, Tobin. 1988. *The Ethics of Criticism*. Ithaca, NY: Cornell University Press.

Siirala, Aarne. 1981. *The Voice of Illness: A Study in Therapy and Prophecy*, 2nd ed. New York: Edwin Mellen.

Simonton, Carl. 1975. Belief Systems and Management of the Emotional Aspects of Malignancy. *Journal of Transpersonal Psychology* 7:29–47.

Smith, Grover. 1956. *T. S. Eliot's Poetry and Plays: A Study in Sources and Meaning*. Chicago: University of Chicago Press.

Smith, Jonathan Z. 1978. The Bare Facts of Ritual. *History of Religions* 20(1–2):112–127.

————. 1987. *To Take Place: Toward a Theory in Ritual*. Chicago: University of Chicago Press.

Social Sciences and Humanities Research Council of Canada [SSHRC]. 1983. Ethical Guidelines for Research on Human Subjects. Ottawa: SSHRC.

Sontag, Susan. 1977. *Illness as Metaphor*. New York: Farrar, Straus, & Giroux.

Sperber, Dan. 1975. *Rethinking Symbolism*. Translated by Alice L. Morton. Cambridge Studies in Social Anthropology. Edited by Jack Goody. Cambridge, Eng.: Cambridge University Press.

Spretnak, Charlene, ed. 1982. *The Politics of Feminine Spirituality: Essays on the Rise of Spiritualist Power within the Feminist Movement*. Garden City, NY: Doubleday.

Staal, Frits. 1979. The Meaninglessness of Ritual. *Numen* 26:2–22.

———. 1986. The Sound of Religion. *Numen* 33(1):33–64, 185–224.

Stahl, Abaraham. 1979. Ritualistic Reading among Oriental Jews. *Anthropological Quarterly* 52(2):115–120.

Starhawk (Miriam Simos). 1979. *The Spiral Dance: A Rebirth of the Ancient Religion of the Great Goddess*. New York: Harper & Row.

Szasz, Thomas. 1975. *Ceremonial Chemistry: The Ritual Persecution of Drugs, Addicts, and Pushers*. Garden City, NY: Doubleday.

Tambiah, Stanley J. 1968. The Magical Power of Words. *Man* (N.S.) 3:175–208.

———. 1979. A Performative Approach to Ritual. *Proceedings of the British Academy* 65:113–169

Taylor, Mark Kline. 1986. *Beyond Explanation: Religious Dimensions in Cultural Anthropology*. Macon, GA: Mercer University Press.

Tillich, Paul. 1960. The Religious Symbol. In *Symbolism in Religion and Literature*, edited by Rollo May. New York: Braziller.

Tipton, Steven M. 1982. *Getting Saved from the Sixties*. Berkeley: University of California Press.

Todorov, Tzvetan. 1984. *The Conquest of America. The Question of the Other*. Translated by Richard Howard. New York: Harper & Row.

Turnbull, Colin, and Nathan Garner. 1979. *Anthropology, Drama and the Human Experience*. Washington, DC: George Washington University, Division of Experimental Programs.

Turner, Edith. 1986. Philip Kabwita, Ghost Doctor: The Ndembu in 1985. *The Drama Review* 30(4):12–35.

———. 1987. *The Spirit and the Drum: A Memoir of Africa*. Tucson, AZ: University of Arizona Press.

Turner, Victor. 1967. *The Forest of Symbols: Aspects of Ndembu Ritual*. Ithaca, NY: Cornell University Press.

———. 1969. *The Ritual Process*. Chicago: Aldine.

———. 1971. "An Anthropological Approach to the Icelandic Saga." In *The Translation of Culture: Essays to E. E. Evans-Pritchard*, edited by T. O. Beidelman. London: Tavistock.

———. 1974a. *Dramas, Fields and Metaphors: Symbolic Action in Human Society*. Ithaca: Cornell University Press.

———. 1974b. Liminal to Liminoid in Play, Flow, and Ritual: An Essay in Comparative Symbology. *Rice University Studies* 60(3):53–92.

———. 1976. Ritual, Tribal and Catholic. *Worship* 50(6):504–526.

———. 1979a. Dramatic Ritual/Ritual Drama: Performative and Reflexive Anthropology. *The Kenyon Review*, N.S., 1(3):80–93.

———. 1979b. *Process, Pilgrimage and Performance: A Study in Comparative Symbology*. New Delhi: Concept Publishing.

———. 1980. Social Dramas and Stories about Them. *Critical Inquiry* 7(4):141–168.

———. 1982. *From Ritual to Theatre: The Human Seriousness of Play*. New York: Performing Arts Journal.

————. 1985. Liminality, Kabbalah, and the Media. *Religion* 15:205–217.

————. 1986a. Dewey, Dilthey, and Drama: An Essay in the Anthropology of Experience. In *The Anthropology of Experience*, edited by Victor W. Turner and Edward M. Bruner. Urbana: University of Illinois Press.

————. 1986b. *On the Edge of the Bush: Anthropology as Experience*. Edited by Edith L. B. Turner. Tucson, AZ: University of Arizona Press.

————, and Edith Turner. 1978. *Image and Pilgrimage in Christian Culture*. New York: Columbia University Press.

————. 1982. Performing Ethnography. *The Drama Review* 26(2):33–50.

————, and Edward M. Bruner, eds. 1986. *The Anthropology of Experience*. Urbana: University of Illinois Press.

Twaddle, Andrew C. 1981a. Sickness and the Sickness Career: Some Implications. In *The Relevance of Social Science for Medicine*, edited by Leon Eisenberg and Arthur Kleinman. Dordrecht, Holland: Reidel.

————. 1981b. *Sickness Behavior and the Sick Role*. Boston: Schenkman-Hall.

Tyson, Ruel W., Jr. 1975. Program Notes on the Practical Criticism of Religious Action. Working paper for the Systematic Study of Meaningful Forms, a Consultation of the American Academy of Religion. Photocopy.

———— et al., eds. 1988. *Diversities of Gifts: Field Studies in Southern Religion*. Urbana: University of Illinois Press.

Vaihinger, H. 1935. *The Philosophy of 'As If': A System of the Theoretical, Practical and Religious Fictions of Mankind*. Translated by C. K. Ogden. London: Routledge.

Vaillant, George C. 1962. *Aztecs of Mexico*. Revised by Suzannah B. Vaillant. Baltimore: Penguin.

van der Leeuw, Gerardus. 1963. *Religion in Essence and Manifestation*, 2 vols. Translated by J. E. Turner. New York: Harper & Row.

van Gennep, Arnold. 1960. *The Rites of Passage*. Translated by Monika B. Vizedom and Gabrielle L. Caffee. Chicago: University of Chicago Press.

von Erffa, Julie. *Who's Who in the Healing Arts: Optimum Choices for Wellbeing*. Santa Fe, NM: Julie von Erffa.

Vatsyayan, Kapila. 1968. *Classical Indian Dance in Literature and the Arts*. New Delhi: Sangeet Natak Akademi.

Vogt, V. Ogden. 1951. *Cult and Culture: A Study of Religion and American Culture*. New York: Macmillan.

Wagner, Roy. 1981. *The Invention of Culture*. Revised and expanded edition. Chicago: University of Chicago Press.

Wakeman, Mary K. n.d. Alternatives to Autobiography as Modes of Discovering Human Selfhood. Paper presented at the American Academy of Religion, Women in Religion Section. Photocopy.

Wallace, Anthony F. C. 1970. *Culture and Personality*. 2nd ed. New York: Random House.

Weber, Max. 1922. *The Sociology of Religion*. Translated by Ephraim Fischoff. Boston: Beacon.

Wepner, Franklyn. 1973. The Theory and Practice of Orientation Therapy. *The Drama Review* 17(3):81–101.

White, Hugh C. 1979. A Theory of the Surface Structure of the Biblical Narrative. *Union Seminary Quarterly Review* 34(3):159–173.

Wiesel, Elie. 1966. *The Gates of the Forest*. Translated by Frances Frenaye. New York: Holt, Rinehart & Winston.

Wilfrid Laurier University. 1988. *The Point: Newsletter of the Wilfrid Laurier University Archaeological Society* 4(4):3–20.

Winnicott, D. W. 1958. Transitional Objects and Transitional Phenomena. In his *Collected Papers: Through Pediatrics to Psychoanalysis*. New York: Basic Books.

Winquist, Charles E. 1978. *Homecoming: Interpretation, Transformation and Individuation*. Missoula, MT: Scholars Press.

————. 1983. Theology, Deconstruction, and Ritual Process. *Zygon* 18(3):295–309.

Woolf, Virginia. 1936. *Three Guineas*. New York: Harcourt, Brace & World.

INDEX